The Trouble I've Seen

Also by Paul Good

THE AMERICAN SERFS: *A Report on Poverty in the Rural South*

ONCE TO EVERY MAN

CAIRO: *Racism at Floodtide*

CYCLE TO NOWHERE: *A U.S. Civil Rights Commission Report on Alabama*

THE TROUBLE I'VE SEEN

White Journalist / Black Movement

Paul Good

HOWARD UNIVERSITY PRESS
WASHINGTON, D. C.
1975

Printed in the United States of America

Library of Congress Cataloging in Publication Data

Good, Paul.
    The trouble I've seen; white journalist/Black movement
    1. Negroes—Civil rights. 2. United States—Race question. I. Title.
E185.615.G66   322.4'4'0973   74-10923
ISBN 0-88258-020-5

Grateful acknowledgments are made to the following:

Joan Daves for permission to reprint excerpts from the speeches of the Rev. Martin Luther King, Jr., copyright ©1967 by Martin Luther King, Jr.

Harcourt Brace Jovanovich, Inc., for permission to reprint excerpts from **Seven Storey Mountain** by Thomas Merton.

The Nation for permission to reprint excerpts from "Bossism, Race and Dr. King" by Paul Good.

New South for permission to reprint excerpts from "The Meredith March" by Paul Good.

The Washington Post for permission to reprint "It Was Worth the Boy's Dying" by Paul Good.

For my wife, Ruth, who worked and sacrificed so that this book and others could be written.

CONTENTS

The Trouble I've Seen

The Lead

INTRODUCTION

A book whose time has come is a fortunate piece of creation. The book can speak with moral or artistic authority to an audience persuaded by events of the moment to listen to what the book has to say. But a book whose time has come and gone usually is left talking to itself upon publication. I hope that *The Trouble I've Seen* escapes that fate although its prime time was a decade ago, its subject the 1964 Civil Rights Movement in the South.

To begin with, *The Trouble I've Seen* is a first-hand account of happenings in the Movement during that tumultuous and pivotal year of 1964 when a certain style of racial protest and civil rights strategy reached its crest. After that year, the Movement would never be the same. So many emotionally stirring and politically significant events were crammed into that year—Dr. King's Saint Augustine campaign that helped to pass the 1964 Civil Rights Act; the Mississippi summer with its Freedom Houses and the murders of Chaney, Schwerner, and Goodman; black churches stirred to fervor by the Movement, then put to the torch or dynamited by Klansmen or their cohorts; the formation of the Mississippi Freedom Democratic Party in Jackson and its betrayal by the national Democratic Party on the Boardwalk in Atlantic City. The list seems as long as those marches by day and night on Southern streets and highways that merge in my mind into a vision of marching as an end in itself. The illusion stood that by simply walking forward one could really get some place.

Beyond describing these events as I saw them, the book describes me, a white writer no longer young, who was learning about black and

3

white American realities. Thirty-five was a little late in the game to be getting down to basics and much, but not all, of the blame for the delay can be laid to my own character. My American experience convinces me that most of us—particularly, but not exclusively, in my generation—spend a disproportionate amount of our adult time trying to undo what the past has done to us. We waste days, even years, trying to unlearn lessons of racial arrogance or inferiority programmed into us by our schools and social tribes. We try to replace those bitter lessons with a mature comprehension of what this country and its people (ourselves) are really about. We waste so much time and energy undoing our ignorance that, before we know it, the opportunity to use our lives productively—to perfect whatever skills and sensibilities we have for both the personal and common good—has passed. We remain unrealized individuals, debilitated by our inner contradictions and ambiguities.

Probably that amorphous institution we call "the system" plans our lives this way. That both education and the prevailing "conventional wisdom" combine to limit our knowledge of the true state of things, thereby obscuring our view of social injustice and blunting our instinct to change what is unjust, is a suspiciously happy accident.

For whatever combination of reasons, I did not know very much about race when I started 1964 as a television correspondent and Atlanta news bureau chief for the American Broadcasting Company. In the middle of the year, ABC and I severed connections; the rest of the year was devoted to free-lance writing for newspapers like *The Washington Post* and magazines like *The Nation*. All of my writing experience provided invaluable on-the-job training on the subject of racism, Americanism, and journalism. By year's end I knew a good deal more than when I had started.

With all this personal and professional background for the events of 1964 to be set against, a question still hangs: How does one justify the present publication of a book whose time admittedly has come and gone?

I think that there are three reasons. First, the work is a contribution, however small, to the historical record of those days that otherwise might have gotten lost in the shuffle of American journalism. Historians don't chase after phenomena like the Movement. Decades after the event, traditional historians cull what they conceive to be the truth from contemporary accounts. I've read too many contemporary accounts to trust a history based on their assessments. However questionable some of my concepts or opinions might be, *Trouble* provides

an accurate record of 1964. Sometimes that record describes an evil
man named Lester Maddox careening on a bicycle while trying to
rally segregationists in front of his Pickrick Restaurant in Atlanta.
Sometimes this record tells the story of how the first black political
television program in the history of Mississippi managed to get on the
air (and at what eventual cost to this writer). But sublime or ridiculous,
my book hews close to the truth of things.

The second reason for this book's existence could come under the
heading of "Lest We Forget." *Trouble* is a reminder of how things were
racially in the South ten very short years ago. The media are currently
telling us that all is well in the South. We are supposed to believe that
in one decade—not even time enough for a generational changing of
the guard—the racist wolf is ready to lie down with the now-rambunc-
tious, once-victimized lamb. Well. At a time when major leaders of
both political parties are paying court to Alabama Governor George
Wallace and, by extension, to all the regressive ideals he epitomizes,
we do well to remember that the New South was the Old South just
ten years ago. I think my book helps us to remember.

Finally, *The Trouble I've Seen,* along with its epilogue bringing my
journalistic experiences up to date, examines the performance of the
national news media when race is the subject. I know at least as much
about this performance as any white writer in the country. Over the
last decade, I've covered race for radio and television, and for newspapers and magazines. I've written commercial books, studies for such
groups as the National Sharecroppers Fund, and book-length monographs
for the United States Commission on Civil Rights. Credentials, of
course, prove nothing; what is written provides the ultimate measure.
What is written in this book is not in debt to hearsay or any manner of
the second-hand. All of the material, on the mark or awry, is based on
personal experiences with a cross-section of those editorial minds who
decide what the black and white American public will or will not be
told about the ongoing story of race in America.

I wish I could say at this point that the book you will read on 1964 was
a uniformly expert, well-written whole. It wasn't, isn't. The beginning, in particular, contains passages that on rereading make me
wince for their social or political naïveté and wrongheadedness, their
literary awkwardness. At their most elemental level, these deficiencies include use of the word "colored." Even though black had not
yet been declared beautiful in 1964, "colored" was and always had been
a demeaning racial description, suggesting something that children do
with crayons to figures in a coloring book. The word did not bother me

then; nor did a phrase like "amoral ghetto animals," written by a man who knew nothing of the ghetto or what constituted amorality inside the ghetto experience. I overpraised white men like *Atlanta Constitution* editor Ralph McGill, who had courageously championed racial justice in the forties and fifties *on his terms,* but could not handle the sixties when black men and women insisted on championing racial justice *on their own terms.* I also overpraised black men like the Reverend Wyatt Tee Walker, who seemed heroic during an Atlanta sit-in but soon abandoned the hard struggle to become a Harlem acolyte of Governor Nelson Rockefeller.

I could recall other judgmental errors but the perceptive reader will find them soon enough. The temptation is to cut out, smooth over, and rearrange to conform to the perspective the ensuing ten years has created. But once such a process is begun, first in a single sentence, then in a paragraph or page, where does it end? An ill-phrased description is reworked to make for easier reading. Next, an idea that today seems dated or unconvincing is spruced up. Pretty soon you have something that the reader can no longer be certain is vintage '64; the book is strengthened or diluted but the essence is gone. In an introduction to an edition of *Brave New World* brought out twenty years after the original, Aldous Huxley conceded defects that he was not correcting.

". . . in order to correct them," he wrote, "I should have to rewrite the book—and in the process of rewriting, as an older, other person, I should probably get rid not only of some of the faults of the story, but also of such merits as it originally possessed."

The volume contains one exception. A footnote has been added in the chapter "Summertime" to explain more fully my departure from ABC. Since the subject of journalistic mores receives considerable attention in the epilogue, the reader deserves more information about this earlier incident with the insights into media mentality.

DATELINE:
SELMA, ALABAMA

Selma, Ala., March 21.—It was like a Fourth of July picnic and a pilgrimage, a protest and an exultation. It was like nothing Selma had ever seen before or dreamed of.

One 82-year-old black man marching at the head of the line perhaps knew better what it was like than anyone else. For him, it was loss and gain to the roots of his soul.

Cager Lee was the grandfather of Jimmie Lee Jackson, the twenty-six-year-old Negro from nearby Marion who died nearly a month ago after being shot by an Alabama state trooper, following a protest demonstration.

Marion Negroes had urged a march to Montgomery to protest his death and today it became a reality.

"Yes, it was worth the boy's dyin'," said Lee as he walked in the front line with the Reverend Dr. Martin Luther King, Jr. "He was my daughter's onliest son but she understands. She's takin' it good.

"And he was a sweet boy. Not pushy, not rowdy. He took me to church every Sunday, worked hard. But he had to die for somethin'. And thank God it was for this."

Behind him stretched the column, black and white, pennants fluttering, winding down Broad Street, the main thoroughfare of Selma. A record shop blared "Bye, Bye, Blackbird" over a public address system. And cars carrying white boys went by bearing slogans like "Open Season on Niggers—Cheap Ammo Here" and "Too Bad, Reeb." But Lee seemed not to notice.

"There was but one white man said he was sorry about Jimmie Lee,"

7

he said. "He sent me the biggest box of groceries—rice, coffee, sugar, flour. And he called me and said, 'I'm so sorry. I don't know what to do.' But no other white man said a word. And I lived and worked in Perry County every day of my life."

The marchers crossed the Edmund Pettus Bridge over the muddy Alabama River. A federalized National Guardsman walked through weeds along the bank below, looking for trouble that never came. At the end of the bridge, where Negroes were routed by state troopers and possemen two Sundays ago, stretched the commercial clutter familiar to the approaches of many American towns: a hamburger stand, gas station and roadside market.

". . . This is the place where the state troopers whipped us," Hosea Williams, aide to Dr. King, was crying out. "The savage beasts beat us on this spot."

Lee—his thin black cheeks sucked in by age, his eyes reflecting a mind in full command—paid as little attention to that as he had to "Bye, Bye, Blackbird."

"I wanted to leave here but I waited to raise my seven children and then it was too late," he said. "But now I just want what is mine. In all those years that passed by, I was used as a boy. Never treated as a man. But I ain't mad at white people. No. You have to believe it. I ain't got no evil or spite whatever."

Down the line from him on the other side of Dr. King was an aged New York rabbi with bushy white hair and billowing white beard bright in the sun.

Behind them was a blind man tapping with a cane . . . a one-legged man walking on crutches . . . beatniks and patrician ministers. And James Forman, field secretary of the Student Nonviolent Coordinating Committee giving an interview in French to the Canadian Broadcasting Company on U. S. Route 80 in Alabama.

"How could you ever think a day like this would come?" asked Lee to himself as much as to a reporter. "My father was sold from Bedford, Virginia, into slavery down here. I used to sit up nights till early in the morning to hear him tell of it. He'd tell how they sold slaves like they sold horses and mules. Have a man roll up his shirtsleeves and pants and told: 'Put on your Sunday walk.' So they could see the muscles, you know.

"He was Leftage . . . that was the name of his master in Virginia. But he was sold to a Lee down here. That's where he got his name and I got mine."

And that's where Jimmie Lee Jackson got the middle name he

carried to the grave. And that was the beginning of what today's march was all about.

The Washington Post, March 22, 1965

Author's Note:
I wrote this article a few months after 1964 ended and the Selma-to-Montgomery march began. It is included so that the sacrifice of Jimmie Lee Jackson is recorded and remembered.

AS WELL AS
IT IS...

It was a brilliant Sunday morning in Mexico City on September 15, 1963. The sky was blue and filled with sunlight which showered on the glass facade of the bank building across the circle from the United Press International (UPI) office. The office was on the tenth floor and was a shaky perch during Mexico City earth tremors, which the tourist-minded government would deny were happening even while plaster dropped around your ears. But on this Sunday morning all was solid and beautiful. The bank was tall and curved in the shallowest of crescents along Paseo de la Reforma, and the sunlight polished its black glass, reflecting the street which had been swept and watered and still was clean of traffic. I looked down on the plane trees stretching like a full green bush along Reforma and into Chapultepec Park and Maximilian's Castle, thinking of the pleasant moment and the pleasant day ahead, the slow sun-filled Sunday with my wife and son, the bulls and novilleros in the late afternoon, and after the bulls in the cool dusk outside the plaza, hot corn with chili powder and probably tequila in the loud mariachi bar across the street.

It was not a hard life for a television correspondent. Or for anybody. On Sundays like that one, I would go into the UPI office down the hall from mine to check the teletype machines and see if anything was going on in Latin America that I should know about. Not that my employer, the American Broadcasting Company (ABC), cared very much. For eighteen months I had been covering Mexico, Central America, the Caribbean and some of South America. In that time I had learned that neither ABC nor the American public really gave much of a damn about what happened in Latin America—unless Fidel Castro was actively connected with it, and sometimes not even then. I didn't agree that 200 million people were disregardable, particularly when they were so close and we regularly viewed with alarm developments in minor African and Asian countries oceans and cultures away.

I turned from the window toward the slowly chattering Latin American machine. The lone Sunday worker, a Mexican boy on hand to watch for catastrophes, was engrossed in a sport newspaper filled with pictures of *fútbol* stars and big-hipped Mexican girls' overflowing bikinis. Latin America, said the machine, was calm. But the world wire was unusually busy. At first I did not trust my translation because the Spanish words under the Birmingham, Alabama, dateline told a story that was hard to believe. I went over it again, word for word, and it was so. Someone had exploded a bomb in a Negro church and four young girls were killed. I tore off the copy and sat down with it by the window. I suppose all decent men and women who read that story anywhere in the world filled with the same emotions—a grab of pity at the heart for young innocents slaughtered, grief in the mind for the parents, and quick hate in the blood for those who did it. Any child's death wounds a parent who hears of it because it is a reminder of *his* child's mortality. So my son Sean and the four Negro girls fused, and that beautiful Sunday morning lay streaked outside the window. Later, I would turn against those tears as a cheap coin of indignation, an easy self-absolution for my sins of indifference over the years at what America was doing to Negroes. And to itself.

I don't admire professional American apologists overseas who promiscuously knock their country in the belief it endears them to the natives. Such people usually arouse suspicion and a faint contempt among those natives. But now the fact of my nationality impelled me to say something to the Mexican boy, to apologize.

"*¡Que espantoso!*" I said. "How frightful. Have you read of this thing that happened in the South of my country?"

Smiling, he looked up from his soccer-and-sex reverie.

"The Negro girls who were killed," I said.

"Yes, yes," he said, losing the smile and shaking his head. "What a bad thing."

"It's the work of the ignorant," I said.

He nodded and sighed. I had the strong impression he wanted to forego any discussion and get back to the paper, but out of politeness was indulging my interest.

"The Negroes in your country," he said, "they're very bad, true?"

"No, no," I replied. "But there are white men who hate them without cause, men of prejudice, *fanaticos.*"

"Ah, yes," he said. "*Fanaticos.*"

He shook his head again, but his fingers felt to turn the page. I left him, the apology unspoken. He did not understand or care, and to persist would have been to indulge my conscience at the expense of his lazy Sunday. Did I care or try to understand when the one-inch newspaper story told me that a thousand Indians or Chinese died of flood or cholera? No. Too bad but too remote, and we turn the page to the next diversion. But walking down the hall, I felt that this happening was part of me in a way that few things had ever been, the guilt of it in me and the death, too.

I went into my office and thought about it, trying to put aside emotion and assess what I felt. All that year I had been periodically outraged by what was happening in the South—the murder of Medgar Evers, firehoses in Birmingham, the insults to Negro children as they went to schools and to adults at lunch counters. But beyond the outrage there was nothing except a vague belief in equal rights that sometimes sputtered into emotional life and then idled. I was very American in this reaction; as a people we have a child's attention span, seizing on a new cause or fad one day, tossing it aside the next.

I had been acquainted with a handful of Negroes in my life and mostly in my youth. My early home was Sheepshead Bay in Brooklyn where I was locked in the narrowness of bourgeois Irish Catholic environment, taught "to hate the Negro and despise the Jew." How and when do glimmers of enlightenment reach us? Maybe the first one came on the cold December day when I was six and a bunch of us on our block surrounded a raggedy Negro kid on his way home from school through our section to "Niggertown" over by the Long Island Railroad tracks. Someone had been swiping Christmas bulbs from the front lawn decorations and the "nigger" was an obvious suspect. We made him cry, I remember, but we let him alone after he blubbered:

"I wouldn't steal no light. We ain't got no tree home to put 'em on anyway."

How terrible! A boy at Christmas without a tree. I think—but am not certain—we wound up giving him some pennies. The first lesson of the good white heart: pity and generosity. Other lessons followed which had a humanizing effect on the conventional prejudice surrounding me but left the prejudice intact. My father had a golf driving range and employed colored men to pick up the balls. They worked for virtually nothing and although he had qualms about what he paid them and tried sporadically to be fair, he lacked the moral staying power to establish a truly just relation. Some golfers found pleasure in aiming at the men as they worked, and one loyal worker named Willie Jameson was hit a number of times in the eyes, suffering acute loss of vision. He was an Uncle Remus—now it would be Uncle Tom—type, fawning over me, the young master, coming around at Christmastime for handouts. Finally when the business failed, he drifted off somewhere half-blind. By prep school, I could write a mawkish essay about him, ending with something about my being the happiest boy in the world if I could only see Old Willie's smiling face once more.

But prep school brought realities, Negro boys who became friends, although exotic ones. There was a Christmas vacation in New York and a trip to an ice-skating rink and one of them who is now a lawyer was not allowed in. Conscience pricks, and what began at six as pity grows to something better, but still is incomplete. Army service brought two years in North Carolina and a glimpse of the Southern white mind, but the Negro remained more a question of conscience than a human being with dimensions. I remember one day a colored driver brought me home from the post and had to wait while I picked up something. My wife invited him inside for coffee and on the way back to camp he told me that was the first time a white woman had ever treated him like a decent man. Again, the emotion turned inward, a warming about the heart at our goodness and understanding. In those early days of marriage, preoccupation with Ruth and my own self blurred the world around. It seemed enough to feel and let the thinking wait. After service, as a reporter in New York, I began to see the Northern face of prejudice more clearly, in Harlem and on Madison Avenue and up and down every street of my youth and manhood. But I comprehended only the surface. One night in Brooklyn Heights at the home of a writer who was a former Communist, an agitated and slightly drunk Negro friend of his kept shouting:

"I wants to be free!"

"There's no denying discrimination," I said, "and we all despise it. But you're free. I mean, you can say anything you like any place you want to."

Later that night at home, we laughed over him, a typical example, we thought, of the shrill Communist-shaped colored product.

"I wants to be free," I mimicked. "I wants to be free."

Awareness of my immaturity and ignorance grew slowly. From age twenty-five to thirty-five I gradually saw that the "Negro" situation was becoming, not just *a* human and political problem that America must solve, but *the* problem running deep into the country's guts. I began to consider myself an uncompromising liberal. And still I stayed outside the problem except for those conversational encounters in which I flaunted my precious beliefs and ego. With the Birmingham deaths there was something new to talk about, to denounce over drinks at the correspondents' club.

"The dirty sons of bitches," I would say.

"I mean, to kill a helpless kid," someone else would say. "All right, you hate Martin Luther King, you shoot him, that's wrong. But what kind of a gutless . . ."

"That's what we've produced," I would say. "And we're trying to peddle democracy to these people down here."

"It's a farce," he would say.

"A tragic farce," I would say.

And we would drink tragically, strong men capable of deep indignation. Because this imagining became insupportable as I sat in that office, an alternative was necessary. What evolved was the knowledge that I should go home, that I should be in my country at this time, to participate by presence—if by nothing else—in the crisis. I did not want to lose by default the chance to be part of an historic struggle. I think some ancient pull of earth calls people home to their country's crises, something less sophisticated than nationalism or patriotism. That Sunday it became suddenly absurd, even contemptible, that I should be preoccupied with the Alliance for Progress and the fate of Guatemala and the trials of Romulo Betancourt, when Martin Luther King remained an unknown quantity to me—even though (I felt) the fate of America was tied to him and to his movement and to the four girls in Birmingham.

My wife agreed and from that Sunday things began to turn. Everything worked out as if ordained. I let it be known to the New York assignment editor that I could fly quickly into Southern cities if they were shorthanded on big racial stories. I wrote to John Madigan, ABC news director. I told him that ABC was wasting money on a bureau it did not use and that I thought would never use because no one in the States cared about Latin America. I told him I was wasting my time and would like to cover the racial story. Fortunately, ABC on virtually the same day had independently arrived at the conclusion that its Mexico bureau was expendable. How the corporate mind moved and finally decided that I should be reassigned to open a new ABC bureau in Atlanta, Georgia, which would cover the South, is one of those coincidental strokes of good fortune that add interest to life.

So on November 20, I arrived in Atlanta to survey the area for the company and, for myself, to catch up with history. An "historian" drove me from the airport, a bulbous-nosed, elderly Georgia cabdriver who stopped at an orange warning light and reported his version of the times: "If I run that light I'd get a ticket. But a nigger wouldn't. They're afraid to give a nigger a ticket aroun' here. They give a white man one though. You didn't know the goddamn niggers ran Atlanta, did you? Yeah, they do."

In the next few days, I would get used to "niggers" as a conversational topic—sometimes seemingly the only conversational topic in the South. I would meet a convivial man at the bar of the Dinkler Plaza Hotel and he would tell me what a fine city Atlanta was and how pleasant the city would be for my family. He himself lived in Rome, Georgia, where he had a small factory and that also was a fine town.

"Course you know we got this nigger problem, that's the crux of it. Northerners don't understand it the way we do down here. You know why they're called shines, don't you? It's because those big, black, greasy niggers have oil in them that makes them shine. That's the reason and you can't trust them. Any of them."

I was shocked to hear that seemingly educated and mannerly man lapse into talk that I would expect from a millhand, like a sudden snigger and gutter joke from a priest. Do black Negroes sweat and glisten, shine? Yes, they sometimes do. But why was this on the top of his head, the first thing to be said on the subject, when there were so many aspects of importance that needed talking about? I would find that this kind of preoccupation with the physical side of Negroes—"nigger" smell, sex prowess, brain capacity, cleanliness, hair quality—was everywhere, an unhealthy and universal absorption in his body that hinted at psychological and sexual obsessiveness. I don't stress this atmosphere now to abuse the South or to prejudice this account from the beginning, but to present the environment that surrounded me from the first. I came to the South fresh from a year and a half in an environment generally free from such obsessions. I was a native son with alien eyes who would have to learn a lot, fast, to know what he was seeing and reporting to others.

Conversations with other whites, some active in groups promoting civil rights, indicated that Atlanta was moving along a reasonable road toward enlightened race relations. Atlanta liked to call itself "The City Too Busy to Hate," and was aggressively conscious of its progressive "image." The city was booming industrially and no one wanted to see the money stop coming in. Two years before, a very successful businessman named Ivan Allen had been elected mayor against virulent segregationist opposition and in the interim the city had formed biracial committees, had ended public segregation, instituted good police racial policies and had earned praise from President John Kennedy. And, of course, it had the *Atlanta Constitution* and the liberal voice of Ralph McGill, who years before had spoken out for equality when the word was only whispered and whose voice had not faltered. However, what the city thought of itself and what people thought of it did not mean very much unless I knew what Negroes thought of it. My first appointment was with James Forman, field secretary of the Student Nonviolent Coordinating Committee (SNCC). I had been told that SNCC was the militant young arm of the Negro movement in the South and it seemed a logical place to begin hearing the other side of the story. The date of the appointment was November 22.

Sometime after noon, I got to the office—a cluttered second-floor walkup in a nondescript building in the colored section of Atlanta. It would be a prototype of such offices throughout the South, a confusion of integration posters, disorderly stacks of mimeographed releases, and milling young workers. I felt no other movement in American history was so dependent on youth with all its idealism, callowness, courage, conceit, and indomitable energy. Future social historians may conclude that the significance of the Movement, in addition to the racial changes it brought, was that it saw American youth finally come of age, to think and act after generations of mental lollipop-sucking.

But I had little time to scrutinize these black and white zealots, and I never got to talk to James Forman. Everyone seemed strangely distracted when I arrived, and then I heard a radio announcing that President Kennedy had been assassinated. A call to New York and I was ordered to Dallas. A Negro cabdriver carried me to my hotel from the SNCC office and to him, as to so many Americans during those stunning hours, the assassination was seen as an act of right-wing hate. I cannot quote much of what he said but I do remember how calm his voice was as he expounded his outrage, and I wondered whether a Negro's lifelong exposure to physical and emotional assaults gave him a tolerance for the drastic, what was cataclysmic to me only inevitable to him.

"Those people who would do a thing like that, they sick," he said. "The same way you get these people here in Atlanta. Shit, a Russian can get served in a restaurant here. Some yellow Communist Chinese man or a Cuban can get served. But a black man what's an American can't. Now that's not right, it's just not right."

Nothing was right that day or in the days immediately ahead. I chased the haunted face of Lee Harvey Oswald with a microphone down a jail-house corridor and the next day waited for him to arrive at the county courthouse while Jack Ruby was killing him a few blocks away. Death poisoned the air, physical death and spiritual death. Dallas, the whole country, seemed to me to be involved in dying, love and hope forgotten, thug-faced hate relentlessly pulling triggers, shooting up hearts and souls. Our emotions then made things seem worse than they were. But it was bad enough. And still is.

I returned to Atlanta the day before Thanksgiving and finished the survey. A flight would get me home to Mexico City for Thanksgiving dinner. But I learned that Dr. King was going to preach at the Ebene-zer Baptist Church where he shared the pulpit with his father. Given a chance to see the man for the first time, I stayed over. That Thursday in Atlanta was grim in all ways. A dirty grey sky, damp cold, flags lank against poles in mourning. Grey and silent. The veteran pacifist A. J. Muste led an oddly assorted group of bedraggled peace marchers into the church before the service began, their worn air contrasting to the Negro congregation that seemed middle-class, well-dressed, and on this day more comfortably American than these white people who had started out across the country somewhere intent on walking to Guantá-namo Bay in Cuba. I remember a preacher giving them a kindly intro-duction as people of good will, but the fact that there was water be-tween the marchers and Guantánamo nagged at him, and he finally smiled hugely and told the congregation:

"They say they're gonna *walk* over to Cuba, but how they're goin' to do *that* I *don't* know."

Dr. King, when I first saw him, seemed Oriental, a face from a Japa-nese print, light-skinned and broad with ovoid eyes that sometimes looked in and other times out, but were always part of a self-contained expression so set that it was masklike. Beside him was the Reverend Ralph Abernathy, who along with Dr. King had forged the Civil Rights Movement in the South. Beginning in Montgomery, Alabama, and continuing through a series of jail cells they shared, King and Abernathy made a legend in the Movement. I had read much about Dr. King's ability to move crowds, whether it was a country church congregation or the tens of thousands who marched on Washington, with his speech. I was anxious to hear him and curious how he would meet the challenge of a Thanksgiving theme on that dismal day. I was attending a Negro service for the first time and it was also the first time in a long time I had attended any service. The hymns raised old ghosts of youth and the dark faces were new creatures in a time just beginning for me.

The first ten minutes of his sermon were a disappointment. His locution seemed affected, words overpronounced and the thoughts banal. He began by describing the first Thanksgiving, referring to "our forefathers," then quickly adding, "the forefathers of this nation." Jesus, I thought, are we going to bog down in black and white distinctions here? I discovered that however middle-class that congregation, the church retained the old Southern Negro custom of responding verbally to the preacher, calling out words of encouragement or affirmation, singing out phrases, muttering and grunting as the spirit moved.

"I know," said Dr. King; "there are those asking today, is there anything for which to be thankful? (Uh-huh) The cynics are probably standing up with an emphatic 'No.' I guess it is a legitimate question to be raised because of the events of last week. (All right now) Our whole nation was stunned into somber confusion at the vicious, tragic, untimely and dastardly murdering of our President. (Oh, yes) We watched the great thirty-fifth President of this nation go down like a great cedar. (Umm-mmh) And so we are confused, bewildered, grief-stricken. (True) And clouds of sorrow are floating in our mental skies—the deep tides of despair are all but rising to flood proportions." (Amen)

Amen, I thought. Can this be the mover of mountains? "Clouds of sorrow floating in our mental skies". . ."tides of despair". . ."great cedar." Newspapers had been using "great cedar" for days to refer to Kennedy and I wondered if Dr. King were appropriating the noble phrase as his own. He went on to quote Carlyle ("It seems that God sits in his heaven and does nothing"), Shakespeare ("Life is a tale told by an idiot, full of sound and fury, signifying nothing"), Isaiah ("Verily Thou art a God that hideth thyself")—to which Rev. Abernathy growled, "Aw, come on now"—and Jesus Christ ("My God, My God, why hast Thou forsaken Me?"). I had the apprehension that Dr. King might be that type of educated Negro I had read about, the man who struts quotations before the undereducated, flaunts an empty erudition—a hollow man in a hollow time. The words had no light in them, no warmth for listeners who, if they felt as I did, were chilled down to the soul's marrow.

And then, Dr. King went into the Bible for his theme, to the Book of Kings and the prophet Elijah. It was a tale about a barren woman made fruitful through faith. But Dr. King was interested in it only for the form of a question the prophet asked the woman years later: "Is it well?" Dr. King asked the question that Thanksgiving Day and answered, "No, it is not too well. But thank God it is as well as it is."

Now he was ready to preach. He drifted a little from the Berlin crisis to the Cuban crisis to South Vietnam as he asked how "well" it was. I felt no one in that church then had mind or heart for those places. The only place that existed was our America, our black and white America that was trying to learn through death what it was in life.

"Preach, Mart," Rev. Abernathy called out, and Dr. King began.

"Is it well on the human relations horizon in the United States of America?" he said. "Oh, no (No, sir) indeed it's midnight in human relations. (Yes) If you don't believe it's midnight, go with me if you will (Mmh) to Jackson, Mississippi. (Ohhh) Watch a misguided, brutal, demented mind shoot to the ground a courageous Medgar Evers. (Mmm) If you don't believe it's midnight, go with me if you will, to Birmingham, Alabama (Yeahh) and watch some psychopathic case (Mmm, yes) drop a bomb at the Church of God on Sunday morning when little children are in Sunday School. (Right) Watch the lives of four unoffending, beautiful innocent girls be taken away. (Mmmm) If you don't believe it's midnight, think of the fact that way back in 1776 (Preach, preach, preach) the Founding Fathers of our nation wrote All men are created equal (That's right) and endowed by their Creator with certain inalienable rights. (Yeah) That among these are life, liberty and the pursuit of happiness. (All right) Yet in 1963 in a nation founded on the principle that all men are created equal (Uh-huh) men are still arguing over the question of whether the color of a man's skin determines the content of his character. (Right) It's midnight . . . How are things on the human relations horizon? (Well) Things are not too well there. The Negro is still dominated politically (Preach), exploited economically (Preach on), segregated and humiliated. The Negro is still a thing to be used rather than a person to be respected. (All right now) No, things are not too well (Well?), but this morning I want to thank God (Preach, preach) that it is as well as it is. I want to thank God this morning (Yes, sir) that changes have taken place. (Mm) Our foreparents were brought here as slaves way back in 1619. (Umm-hh) And let nobody fool you, they try to romanticize slavery with all the magnolia trees and what have you. (Laughter) Slavery was a low, dirty, evil thing. (Yes) Men and women chained to ships like beasts. It is a terrible thing to uproot someone from their family, land and culture. (True) They knew the rawhide whip of the overseer . . . sizzling heat . . . long rows of cotton. . . . (Preach on) They had their songs to give them consolation because they knew how dark it was. One moment they would sing 'Nobody Knows the Trouble I've Seen' (Ummm) because it was dark. (Yes) Sometimes they had to work in their bare feet and that's why they started singing, 'I Got Shoes, You Got Shoes, All of God's Chillun Got Shoes.' (Mm-mmmmh) When I get to heaven gwine put on my shoes (Huh), I'm just gonna walk all *over* God's heaven. (Preach, Martin) 'Cause they knew they had no shoes. (Preach) They knew that darkness surrounded their lives. (Yes) It looked like we were confined to slavery for the years and the centuries. (Uh-huh) But evil can't survive forever. (No) Thank God, it is as well as it is."

These words on paper can only suggest the cadences that Dr. King was building, his voice deliberate and outraged as the crimes of Birmingham and Jackson were recounted, then gathering emotional momentum with remembrance of slavery. I was surprised to hear slavery, a dead historical issue for me, introduced. But the grandparents of many of the congregation had been slaves, possibly the parents of a few. Dr. King was touching a racial remembrance, speaking of known things among them in a way that no white man could speak because his American existence did not start in 1619, because his children could not have been in the Birmingham church. So, this bond between speaker and listeners made any white person in the audience an eavesdropper on a family discussion. But the eavesdropper was also part of it, the condemnation bitter in him as well as the hope, the irresistible swell of hope that Dr. King next began creating, making that church bloom inside when the country outside seemed shrivelling. . . .

"We've broken loose from the Egypt of slavery. (Yes, sir) We've moved through the wilderness of separate but equal and now we stand at the promised land of integration. (Amen) I'm here to tell you this morning that we're gonna get in. (Yes) They have been some sent over to spy the land and they are worried. (Laughter) They're telling us there are giants in the land (Yeah) . . . saying that we can't make it in. (No) There *are* giants in the land. (True) Giants of vested interests . . . giants of old political dynasties . . . giants of economic power structure. (Preach) But thank God, Caliph and Joshua have come back with a minority report. (All right) They are saying we *can* possess the land. (True) Thank God, it is as well as it is. (Come on now) Atlanta is a better city today than it was three years ago. (Umm-hh) We can go places now we couldn't go one year ago. (True) We have jobs that we didn't have five months ago. (True) Thank God, it is as well as it is. (Preach on) We're sitting in places we couldn't sit six months ago. . . . We are going places (Preach, preach, preach) we couldn't go months and years ago. (Yes) Thank God, it is as well as it is. (Preach on) God has brought us a long, long way. (Preach now) We've been to the mountain tops and able to see the promised land. (Yeah) We can say, God of our weary years, (Ummm) God of our silent tears, Thou who hast brought us thus far on the way (Yes), Thou who hast by Thy might led us into Thy light, (Well)

Keep us forever in the path, we pray (Preach), Lest our feet stray from the places, our God, where we met Thee (God), Lest our hearts drunk with the wine of the world we forget Thee, Shadowed beneath Thy hand may we forever stand, True to our God, True to our native land. (Yes, yes) Thank God, it is as well as it is."

The poetry was from the Negro National Anthem by James Weldon Johnson. I suspect that many of the strongest Negro voices today would not sing along, would scorn it as Uncle Tom loyalty to a country that had debased its citizens and to a God that had permitted it. That could be another sermon. I write of this sermon and I can see the church stirring in the closing moments, people hearing what they needed to know if the day were to have meaning and a life to have hope, preacher and congregation now one in a testament to faith that ran like grace in the blood.

"Though there are trials and tribulations ahead, thank God, it is as well as it is. (Yes, Lord) Even though America has a long, long way to go before she realizes her dream, thank God, it is as well as it is. (Preach now) Even though we have met the storms of disappointment (Yes) and the jostling winds of hatred are still blowing and the mighty torrents of false accusations are still pouring on us, thank God, it is as well as it is. (All right) Even though we do not know what tomorrow will bring, (Preach, preach) thank God, it is as well as it is. Even though we know not what the future holds, we know who holds the future. (Yes, yes) Thank God, it is as well as it is. (Go ahead) Even though we are burdened down with the agonies of life (Yes, sir), even though we can't understand, even though we cry out my God, my God, why?—thank God, it is as well as it is. This morning it is well with my soul, that is what we can cry on this Thanksgiving morning."

The pilgrim mood these words inspired remained with me long after the service, and far away in Mexico City, watching wood-panelled manger scenes take shape along Reforma, they made me certain that I was going where I belonged. It was the time to go. After 1964, the South and the rest of the country would never be the same. And though the year hung for only a moment in our history, the agonies and glories of 1964 were long ago locked in the national seed. This book is concerned with how America was revealed to me in that year of bitter bloom. The revelation was sometimes episodic, sometimes patterned and always laced together by my involvement. The involvement and my reflections at first are basic and naive. I think that they develop with experience. At the close of the book, a different American is writing than the one who began it. By the end of 1964, many Americans had been altered. The introduction of my personal relationship to employers and to black and white participants in our drama seemed necessary to understand my point of view because the point of view conditions every observation and affects the "truth" of what is observed. The troubles I've seen derive from us all. And in finding out what happened in the South to *us* during 1964, we find out things about ourselves who live in the storm of conflict called America.

Winter

THE SIGN
IN THE WINDOW

It was a raw Sunday in January and the frost was on the peach trees when I saw the six Klansmen, wind billowing their white satin robes, conical hoods upright, faces uncovered, coming down Forsyth Street in the heart of Atlanta. They were young and old, fat and lean, but their faces were set in a uniform hardness, eyes clear or rheumy, staring straight ahead. They seemed an apparition from the past, out of joint with the street where undistinguished old buildings merged haphazardly with new ones, and with the well-dressed strollers. I felt as if a band of World War I doughboys in their puttees, round steel helmets, and hobnailed boots had suddenly swung down the sidewalk. Some spectators smiled in their confusion. The Klansmen did seem the ultimate absurdity in our male mentality that produces groups that run around in fezzes and fraternal orders with their ritualistic mumbo jumbo. One stout Klansman from the rear looked like a corpulent beadle waddling in his cassock. And yet, there was something else, a cross between Halloween spookiness and vestiges of the old dread those ghostly trappings had once inspired. To complete the anomaly, these Knights of the Invisible Empire were not carrying guns or bullwhips but picket signs.

"Don't Trade Here!" said the neat, professional lettering. "Owners of this business surrendered to RACE MIXERS."

They passed a hotel that had just desegregated its facilities and headed down the street where other pickets were parading. Negro youngsters and a few whites marched in front of Leb's Restaurant, an Atlanta landmark, and their picket signs said: "Segregation Must Go" and "Make Atlanta an Open City."

25

The restaurant, with big plate glass windows, occupied a busy corner at Forsyth and Luckie Streets. The patrons were looking out with some apprehension while little thin waitresses directed hateful glares at the pickets. Leb's, a glorified cafeteria that serves ketchup in plastic squeeze bottles and seats customers in leatherette booths, was a favorite spot for Atlanta's middle class. Charles Lebedin, the owner, was a Jewish immigrant who steadfastly refused to desegregate. His religion plus the prominence of his place made him a special target. Many persons believed there was a necessary correlation between a Jew and liberality, or between a Jewish restaurateur and good kosher food. I do not think either conclusion should apply to Charlie Lebedin.

The Klansmen crossed the windy street and headed for the restaurant. There were police in the area but they made no move to interfere. My cameraman positioned himself to record the action when the two groups met and I switched on the portable tape recorder. The strollers stopped and watched. The entire street seemed to freeze with anticipation and random phrases that might go into a radio report went through my head . . . "the city of Scarlett O'Hara" . . . "a specter from *The Birth of a Nation.*" The tension ended suddenly with laughter and cries from the Negroes.

"Boo, boo, boo, KKK!" shouted the restaurant pickets.

"KKK must go!"

"Who does your sheets, Mr. Bogeyman?"

The Klansmen ignored the jibes and marched stolidly past the black and white line. At a certain point, they executed a Sad Sack imitation of an about-face and came back up the sidewalk. Their deportment was exemplary. The young integrationists seemed bent on taunting them into violence.

Inside, one customer seated near a window began waving and when he had attracted the attention of newsmen, held up a sign he had just penciled.

"If you was white," it read, "you could eat here, too."

"He can eat," said one young Negro girl, "but he doesn't know the difference between 'was' and 'were.' "

On a corner across the street, a tall husky man was pointed out as the Grand Dragon of the Georgia Ku Klux Klan. He wore a well-fitting business suit and his rather handsome face was topped with a crew cut. He was Calvin Craig, a thirty-five-year-old bulldozer operator, who proved a ready conversationalist.

"We don't intend no violence," he said. "You see how that bunch is carryin' on. Well, we don't do that. We just march peacefully."

He continued in an even voice to explain that the Klan did not hate the Nigra but was only bent on safeguarding white rights.

"We don't go where we're not wanted," he said. "so why do they go where they're not wanted?"

"That's right," said a white man beside him. "Actin' like a bunch of damn monkeys."

I asked him if he personally would object to a Negro eating next to him in a restaurant. He paused and smiled. The little crowd around us pressed in to hear.

"They'd have to tie me to the chair," he said.

The listeners appreciated that. Craig readily gave me his phone number for future use, and I left him feeling somehow cheated of a portion of Americana. Grand Dragons had crew cuts and urbanely gave their phone numbers to reporters. *The Birth of a Nation* be damned. But it still was the city of Scarlett O'Hara and there must be distinguished old Southern gentlemen, snowy hair and faces imbued with both fire and melancholy, who could, with ringing rhetoric of the old school, articulate their feelings before the new blasts of protest which might take all that had not gone with that great wind. Somebody said that Lester Maddox was on the scene. I had heard of him. Two years before he had run unsuccessfully for mayor of Atlanta but obtained a sizable vote. He was the owner of a popular cafeteria called the Pickrick, where heaping portions of Southern fried chicken and segregation were served to his followers.

I found Maddox shivering in a doorway out of the wind. He was a narrow-shouldered man wearing rimless spectacles, skin mottled red and grey with cold, and his strikingly dome-shaped head was aggressively bald. The words jumping out in a nervous staccato; he was pleased to record an interview in a high-pitched Southern accent.

"Do I think all people are equal?" he said, repeating my question. "No, sir, I do not. I think that when we teach people to eat successfully, to sleep successfully, to educate successfully, economic conditions that they've got to be together that we're teaching them that they're not equal."

The tape recorder is a severe judge of rhetoric.

"These people demonstrating today," he continued, "are saying that the white people have something we don't have and instead of doing it on our own we're not going to take it away from them. And back in the Bible when we talk about the talents, we used to give to the man who would do something with his talents, and take away from the fellow that wouldn't. Today we turn that around. We take away from the fellow who will do something and give it to the skunk."

Before that hectic afternoon in the middle of Atlanta was out, I would witness more strange sights and sounds. A group of integration pickets broke off from Leb's and descended on a Chinese restaurant. In their midst was a Chinese student. He was barred along with them and stood outside chanting:

"We want egg rolls, we demand our egg rolls."

As a nose-freezing twilight fell, reports came in of trouble a few blocks away at a hamburger shop called the Krystal with its white metal front, steamy window, spatula scraping grease off a grill. The big capital K in its sign coincidentally symbolized the theme because inside about ten KKK men were staging a kind of sit-in—maybe the first in the Klan's history.

Young Negroes had been roaming about downtown, sitting in segregated establishments, but the Klansmen had beaten them to Krystal's. Now they were reluctant to leave, either from fear or determination to show that two could play the game.

"Go tell it on the mountain," sang the Negroes pressing about the window. "Tell every hill and dale. Go tell it on the mountain, to let my people go."

James Forman was there, wearing his "uniform" of blue bib overalls adopted by SNCC to demonstrate solidarity with poor rural Southern Negroes. It was my first chance to meet him since our November appointment had been broken by the Kennedy assassination. His big head, high bushy hair, and small but compelling dark eyes marked him out among the demonstrators. His age, too. They were mostly kids in their teens and he was as old as I.

"We're just demonstrating to show what kind of a city this really is," he said. "Atlanta has built up an image for being a great desegregated city and it's not. Now you have these Klansmen sitting in there with all their regalia and we want to have a hamburger, too. They seem to be afraid to come out but we're here peacefully."

He broke off and shouted to the kids:

"What do we want?"

"Freedom!"

"When do we want it?"

"Now!"

"Where do we want it?"

"Here! Freedom! Freedom! Freedom!"

The police arrived and the Klansmen left, looking sheepish before the jeering youngsters. The lights went out in Krystal's and with a few more shouts, the demonstrators departed. I was left chilblained, my mind numb from impressions and my voice husky from interviewing and making reports. The reports had followed a pattern: A dash into a phone booth with some tape of Craig, Maddox, or the demonstrators, a few introductory and closing words thrown around the tape, and all of it delivered into a phone for New York recording within forty seconds. Forty seconds was the arbitrary ABC limit on network radio news reports, unless the material concerned the Second Coming of Christ. With introductory scene-setting and a signoff, it was not much time to give the significance of a story, even if I had known it. And, of course, I didn't. I went home wondering what the hell the Grand Dragon and the pickets and Atlanta were really all about.

The city was supposed to be the racial bellwether of the South, basking in a progressive image. Forman had mentioned this "image" and the word would come to be both cant and key to understanding Southern reality. Whites and blacks used it continually in discussing the racial situation, but the meaning depended on whose mouth said it. To compound the confusion, it meant different things to different Negro factions. These interpretations became apparent at a mass meeting which clearly sketched out patterns of conflict I would encounter over and over again throughout the South.

It was a so-called summit meeting of the various Atlanta Negro groups loosely organized to press for desegregation—NAACP, Dr. King's Southern Christian Leadership Conference, SNCC, the Urban League, church groups. They met in Allen Temple, a Baptist auditorium, which was a surprise in itself. I suppose I had expected something poor and run-down. But the room was new and handsome, walls of dusty-rose brick, ribbed to a vaulting white ceiling by graceful wooden arches. Down below, the eternal battle between young and old, conservative and militant was being waged with hoary-headed patriarchs striving without much success to restrain the pressing younger generations.

Interracial meetings, centered on desegregation of schools and public accommodations and the hiring of Negroes by the public and private sectors, had been going on for months with city hall. Strong sentiment was growing to leave the conference table and take to the streets in earnest. Bitter wrangling began over which reports took precedence in the considerations, and what had begun as an orderly, parliamentary meeting dissolved into sporadic uproar.

"Every meetin' seems to end the same way," cried one indignant middle-aged lady. "But every time it's just another report. I want to know *who* appointed *who* to do *what*."

There was great applause.

"Seems like," she continued, "they bring a plan here and if we don't accept it, they won't let us talk."

Greater applause. "They" seemed to refer to an elderly faction whose most conspicuous members were A. T. Walden, a lawyer and veteran spokesman for the Atlanta Negro community, and the Reverend Martin Luther King, Sr., whose successful and illustrious ministerial career was now all but eclipsed by his internationally famous son. The older faction favored a report which would have permitted further discussions with the city, more time, more time. But "more time" was the old song of the white man, and the majority were demanding adoption of a battle plan by SCLC's Wyatt Tee Walker to include massive demonstrations and economic boycott. A voice vote seemed to defeat the milder motion but the chair, representing the old guard, ruled it had carried. There was bedlam. Angry men rose shaking fists, gavels rapped, youngsters began singing:

Oh-oh Freedom
Oh-oh Freedom
Oh-*oh* Freedom over me,
And before I'd be a slave
I'd be buried in my grave
And go home to my Lord and be free.

Although he was parliamentarian for the meeting, Rev. King, a portly man leaning heavily on a stout cane, came to the rostrum without waiting to be recognized. With his strong, broad face and iron-gray hair, he seemed a symbol of aged dignity and authority. His famous son was not there and in fact took no part in the Atlanta protests.

"The way you're all acting," he said into the microphone, "I don't want to help you but I will."

But his help was not wanted. The chair, sensing rebellion, gently eased the microphone away. Times had changed in a twinkling, his son had helped change them, and old authority—black or white—was expendable.

A man who said he represented many neighborhood organizations popped up to say to Rev. King and the old order in general:

"My people are beginning to doubt your leadership abilities."

"We're the ones going to have to implement *any* plan," shouted a boy wearing a moth-eaten goatee. "You won't be out in the streets but we will."

Motions, resolutions, and points of order flew around like confetti. A matronly Negro woman in a flowered straw hat smiled apologetically at a white reporter. What is happening is not us, the smile seemed to say, we are orderly and dignified.

"Can't we behave with good manners and have some decorum?" cried a pretty young woman.

"Bless that young lady," growled a gray-haired man.

"How can anyone make a triple motion?" Rev. King was demanding in the middle of a mild tug-of-war for the microphone. "He made the second and third motions before the first was disposed of. It's unconstitutional."

A wave of derisive laughter poured over him.

A man with a mocking manner and sardonic smile took the floor, identifying himself as a dentist named Roy Bell. He began urging immediate action.

The venerable lawyer Walden, often honored by Atlanta's white community, tried to squelch him.

"Dr. Bell, sit down," he commanded. "If I had it within my power, I'd exclude you from this meeting."

"I know you would," Dr. Bell replied, remaining on his feet.

Dr. Sam Williams, a professor from Atlanta's Negro Morehouse College, with a bemused look warned the assembly:

"There are reporters here and you'll read tomorrow: 'Negro community split down the middle.'"

Rev. King tried for the floor again and was hooted down by youngsters. His aplomb shattered and he screamed at them:

"I am not going to be part of a split in the Negro community. But I *am* going home now."

And out stomped the father of the most notable Negro leader in the country. No one had asked him to stay. The rout of age was completed when Walden, his face weary and frustrated, his bald head glistening, said to the crowd:

"If I die sooner than I ought to, it will be because Negroes killed me—not white people."

The meeting ended in a ragged drifting away, with no announced agreement, but the determination of certain individuals and groups to begin protest action was plain. It had been a messy performance. I remember thinking that if that behavior came from the cream of the crop of Atlanta's Negro leadership, not much could be expected of the masses.

In retrospect, these were the conclusions of a priggish white mind trying to superimpose bourgeois standards of reaction on a problem that defied bourgeois solutions. Underlying the conclusion was the hangover from childhood prejudice that persisted, dogging the rational intellect and the renovated heart: That's how Negroes are. I would come to see what passed for disorderly disagreement was more than just that; it was a symptom of the Negro's desperate need to break free of himself before he broke free from the white man.

For years in the South, a tyranny of black authority, mainly ministerial, had kept its place of material status by helping the white man to keep Negroes in their place. Certain very limited goals of progress might be set with white approval. But Christian patience, love, and understanding were given emphasis with the mighty sanction of God and the Bible backing them, for these were virtues that blunted independent thrusts that challenged the white man *or* the black hierarchy. That hierarchy developed powerful personal prerogatives and its first inclination was always to maintain them, not to sacrifice for the common good. This tyranny presented surface aspects of immense dignity and unchallengeable authority. Because it would not survive honest questioning, this order sought to stifle free debate which might reveal the vulnerability of that dignity and the ultimate source of that authority. The dignity, vulnerable because it did not derive from the people in a natural order of esteem for character and appreciation of achievement, was laid on like a flashy decoration. The source of authority was, of course, God's word—the white man.

That ministers should have sold out, consciously or subconsciously, should not be surprising, because this is a familiar aspect of human nature, white or black. Exploiters throughout history have used it to buy off with gold, advantage, prestige, those head men who might pose a threat to privilege once they exerted true leadership. One of the paradoxes of the Movement was how it was able to use this corrupted Christianity as its indispensable soul, recruiting a minority of able ministers to its side, convincing the faint-hearted, and overwhelming and bypassing the apostles of black-on-black supremacy. I witnessed a part of this process in Allen Temple.

If the militants were right in their clamor for action, this rightness implied that Atlanta was wrong. But the city, carrying a self-made banner reading "Best in the South," denied this, pointed to past racial accomplishments and counseled a little more patience. Here lay the heart of Atlanta's dilemma and, I think, the American dilemma as it was confronted by Negro demands: the assumption by the perpetrators of injustice that they were competent to set the rules and timetable of redress.

All kinds of white men with all kinds of motives were handling

Atlanta's racial problem: Callous men motivated solely by economic self-interest who did not want to see the city suffer financially from being turned into a battleground. Men who liked noble sentiments about Negro advance so long as they deferred action while satisfying white conscience and calming colored impatience. Politicians who believed that morality never won a primary but knew what did—a hand, black or white, pulling a lever. That hand had to be won by any means. There were racists and good Christians, hypocrites and the sincere. Atlanta had a newspaper with a conscience and a mayor who struggled, within his limitations, for racial harmony.

But all were white and because they were white, they could be tolerant, to a degree that maddened Negroes, of the privations and indignities endured by a colored population. Of course this ability of white men to take an unhurried approach to racial equality (because they basically believed in racial superiority and could not contradict themselves, preferring to leave the contradicting to a later generation) was not limited to the South. Two great monuments to its Northern existence are Harlem and Chicago's South Side. The greatest monument is the collective white mind that denounces prejudice and racial violence but moans that Negroes are going too far when, in fact, they are barely moving at all. Atlanta Negroes were in motion, a tantalizingly slow motion.

Ten years after the Supreme Court school decision, only a thousand colored children were in integrated classes. All public facilities were desegregated. Yet, not a single Negro held an office job in Mayor Allen's well-run city hall, or served on the city council, or was found in any policy-making capacity.

After long negotiation, a handful of Negroes had moved into retail jobs in the city's major department stores. Still, downtown offices, suburban offices remained virtually all-white. Negro job-seekers who bought the morning *Constitution* could read a vigorously liberal column by Ralph McGill, then scan the want ads to have "white only" jab at them, column after agate column. Atlanta Negroes knew they could not buy houses in the good sections. They knew they *could* come to work each morning by the thousands to those sections, however, and after laboring as yardmen and domestics for four or five dollars a day and carfare, they could go home posthaste each night to the colored section. Naturally, the white man in Atlanta, throughout the South, and also in the North, was in no hurry to do anything that might "spoil" or eventually cut off this rich source of cheap labor kept docile by the unavailability of other jobs. Just as naturally, the Negro saw with awful clarity what the white man was doing. He saw through the pretense of

white declarations of good will for his race, the white posture of helpful-
ness and concern. He was supposed to be grateful for the hand-me-down
suit at Christmas, but not to question why he did not earn enough to buy
a new one. He was supposed to be delighted when the white man joshed
him, while he burned to be taken seriously. And when, as in recent years,
the Negro began to assert himself, most whites were truly confused,
felt duped, and became angry at what they considered gross ingratitude.
Despite centuries of intimate contact, the white man had never bothered
to observe the Negro as an individual and was congenitally blind in
this regard. This failure and its tragic consequences would become
clearer to me in the months ahead. But another quirk was obvious from
the start, buttressing the blindness to produce an almost impenetrable
wall to understanding. This was what W. J. Cash, in his classic *The
Mind of the South,* calls the Southerner's "habitual incapacity for
distinctions."

For example, during those days I met an Atlantan who had been my
section sergeant in the Army at Fort Bragg, North Carolina. He was
dealing in real estate, and although we had not liked each other much
before, we had a drink. Half-hearted talk about jolly old times that
never existed soon gave way to race. The subject was introduced by him
since I was determined to avoid it in social situations. He began by
attacking Martin Luther King and outside agitators for picking on a city
that was good to blacks. What did they want, anyway? I repeated,
without endorsing, the Negro complaints—schools, city hall, housing,
jobs.

"Now, okay, let's stop right there," he said, his voice fairly crackling
with friendly enthusiasm of the born salesman, which he was. "Paul,
lemme tell you. Martha and I had a young Nigra girl working for us
for six months and we treated her just fine. She was a smart girl, had been
going to school and all that. Why, you know, we even let her help our
children with their lessons."

He smiled, I suppose, at the incongruity of a white child learning
anything from a Negro.

"But we were real good to her. You just believe that. She wasn't
being exploited or anything like that. She didn't make much, we paid
her the going rate, but where else can a girl with no experience get
twenty-five dollars a week for easy work in pleasant surroundings? Well,
one day she just told my wife she didn't want to work for us any more.
Wouldn't say what was wrong. Just didn't want to work. When she
didn't show up the next day, I called her house, and asked her what
happened. 'Course, I know she was screwin' some young buck and maybe

she got knocked up. But she wouldn't tell me. Didn't want to work, that was all. But that's the way they are, Paul, and that's what we have to contend with."

I tried to move from the specific case, which might have contained just grievances on his part, to appraisal of the Negro complaints. But he either kept returning to the maid's ingratitude or to a similar story involving a friend of his, or else would say something like:

"Jobs? Listen, there's plenty of Nigras in this town have more money than you or I put together. There's Nigras driving great big Cadillacs all over Atlanta."

His mind, I'm convinced, could not make distinctions between limited personal experience and general realities, between what he felt to be true and what existed, between wealthy and poor Negroes. His tale of the maid revealed a mind conditioned to react to Negroes with paternalism and condescension. The girl was permitted to help his children with their studies. Thus labor was neatly turned into privilege. A probable reason for her leaving a job so pleasant that only an ingrate would quit had to involve her sexual habits because to flaw her character assured that her working conditions could not be questioned. And finally, "she" is transformed into "they"; the habitual incapacity for distinctions comes full turn.

If this ex-sergeant were an exception, I would be just as guilty in citing him as he was in using the maid to malign her entire race. But while many Southern minds have struggled toward rational attitudes, the majority have not taken the introspective pains needed for this reformation. Cash's "incapacity for distinctions" remains as endemic as the boll weevil.

My neighbor, a municipal judge and an amiable man, could dismiss the Movement as a money-making scheme for Dr. King and not feel impelled to probe beyond this judgment. Then there was the owner of a South Georgia peach orchard, a convivial gentleman filled with good stories and bourbon, of which he was a connoisseur. He had traveled North frequently on his business and was well acquainted with liberal attitudes. At first, he seemed to agree that equality was right and desirable, but the more he drank, the further he slipped into a point of view that was not so much hostile toward me and the North, but ironic. How could people up there having so much trouble with their Nigras have the audacity to think they understood the Nigra better than the Southern white man who had been dwelling with him in harmony for so many years? From this he launched into the cliché about the poor but happy Nigras who worked on his peach plantation, and finally, the inevitable exhibit of the Southern white man's generous good will. It was Old Sam or Old Bill, a Negro too broken to work any more. But he was permitted to live rent-free in a shack on the plantation. Welfare gave him enough to live on and he was apparently passing his days in black bliss when one night the shack caught fire.

"I looked out at it burning and I thought sure he was dead," he recalled. "I didn't even stop to put my shoes on but ran out barefoot. Ran out barefoot and it was December and cold. Well, when I saw him safe outside the shack, I could have cried. And he said, 'Mr. Carter, you'd better get some shoes on afore you catch your death of cold.'"

What chance did considerations of the effects of segregation on a Negro's psyche or the relation between inferior schooling and economic shiftlessness have to do against graphic proof of interracial humanitarianism—white, barefoot, hurrying across cold ground to save a colored man's life? I am ridiculing, yet mean no malice, because Mr. Carter does not see the incongruities in his attitude and feels only warm and noble. But Atlanta Negroes, long acquainted with Mr. Carter's mercifulness and the ex-sergeant's annoyance and the judge's suspicions, felt impelled to move against what they could not intellectually penetrate. And so the demonstrations, aimed at revealing an image without substance in Atlanta, began.

Public accommodations—rooms in a hotel or seats in a restaurant—had long been a target for the Movement because it is an area of extreme sensitivity. To a segregationist, the intimate rituals of eating and sleeping—at least public eating and sleeping—were contaminated if shared by Negroes. To a Negro, denial of access to such elemental needs as food or lodging because of his person were ultimate insults. The Civil Rights Bill pending in Congress would remedy this tradition. But Negro leaders who attended the Allen Temple meeting argued that if Atlanta really brimmed with good racial faith, it did not have to wait for a federal law opening public accommodations but could pass its own ordinance. Negroes throughout the South were looking for such acts of good faith, and if white men had responded during that winter, bitterness that brought much future grief might have been averted. About a dozen Atlanta hotels and restaurants did desegregate voluntarily even as the Negroes were debating each other at the summit meeting. One prominent holdout was—of all names—the Heart of Atlanta Motel.

I had a stereotype of a sit-in—pickets chanting outside a five-and-dime store, young Negroes bravely sitting at a counter while white people tried to knock them off and pour ketchup on them as equally brave television cameramen ground away. But because the setting was so genteel, the atmosphere so subdued, the experience so personal, the Heart of Atlanta sit-in, to me, laid bare in a deeper way the essence of humiliation suffered by the Negro. Harry Boyte, SCLC's white man, had alerted two other newsmen and myself that an attempt would be made to obtain service, but to keep it unobtrusive and dignified, no cameramen were wanted. Two groups of whites and blacks arrived, about fifteen in all, including ministers, officials of NAACP, SNCC, and others. One group went to the bar for a drink, the other to the motel's restaurant. The protesters were well dressed, quietly well mannered. The waitresses and barman, called upon to serve those they had never served and those they were under orders not to serve, seemed to me intimidated. The protesters were not the stinking "niggers" of *their* stereotype asking service but persons who, by dress and deportment, might even be a social notch above them. I don't suggest that they wanted to serve these Negroes. But I felt they *were* confused, which indicated conflict within minds grown to maturity in the conviction that there were no conflicts, there is only one side to race. The barman was so confused he stopped serving everybody—integrationist, newsman, and casual customer alike. Then he locked the glass door and would let no one in or out. This action smacked of kidnapping to the free press and Karl Fleming of *Newsweek* threatened to kick out the glass. I had brought my wife along for the experience and made an angry speech demanding a drink for her. On a moment's retrospection, I felt a posturer for injecting myself, out of personal indignation and showy display of principle, into a happening that meant spiritual life or death for the Negroes.

In the genteelly dreary motel dining room, when the people from another planet walked in, white patrons were consuming bland food and piped-in music. The Negroes stepped sedately over thick carpet like proper ladies and gentlemen and sat for meals they knew would not be served.

The Reverend John Morris, white executive director of the Episcopal Society for Cultural and Racial Unity, was among the sit-in group. So was SNCC's James Forman who—tiring of not being served at a Krystal hamburger joint—had decided not to be served in the Heart of Atlanta. The owner, Morton Rolleston, a lawyer destined to fix his name to a Supreme Court case rivaling in importance the Dred Scott decision, was summoned by employees and arrived in a state of high agitation. Within minutes he had ripped the wires from a phone booth for reasons best known to him, threatened Forman with a tear-gas pen, and called the police.

Atlanta police, at this juncture, were verging on a state of schizo-phrenia. On one side were the majority of segregationists insisting on summary arrest for demonstrators, who, on the other side, invited it. But above them were the protectors of Atlanta's image bent on smooth-ing things over and safeguarding the city's good name. No one was to be arrested unless it were absolutely necessary and, if at all possible, not even then. In years past, demonstrators galore had been arrested but publicity-shy owners had not prosecuted, and the demonstrators were released.

"We're just running a taxi service, that's all," complained Police Sergeant B. F. Marler, who was sent to the motel.

Marler and his superiors insisted on arrest warrants which entailed court appearances and all the dreary, time-consuming rigmarole of law. But Rolleston was adamant and began calling judges to get the war-rants. The integrationists sat before empty plates on shining white tablecloths, while the other diners ate, glancing now and then at the despoilers, and sometimes glaring. Rev. Morris, John Lewis, SNCC chairman, and some others tried to carry off the waiting moments with small talk. But the talk at the integration tables was constrained. No one, unless he is a masochist, likes to occupy a situation in which he is either unwanted or actively hated. This psychological aspect of demon-strations always seemed to me to be overlooked by the critics who saw all kinds of ego benefits accruing to the demonstrators. A demonstration might have been simply a night at the end of a day traveling on the road with your family, trooping in with your children, tired and hungry, and sitting down to be told you and your children were not permitted in this place.

After an hour, a police captain arrived with the warrants and went from table to table.

"You've been asked to leave the Heart of Atlanta Motel," he said, softly but in that cop tone that brooks no rebuttal. "Will you leave?"

"I came to eat," said a Negro.

"Well, you're not gonna eat here," said Rolleston.

"Then you're under arrest," said the captain. "I ask you to leave the Heart of Atlanta Motel," he told the next one, Rev. Morris.

"We came for a drink and something to eat," said Morris.

"We're not going to serve you food or drink," said Rolleston.

"Do you want to leave or do you want to go to jail?" inquired the captain.

"No, I'd rather have a drink and something to eat. I don't want to go to jail but . . ."

"Okay, you're under arrest."

As they left the dining room, the white patrons applauded their arrest with restrained clapping.

"I apologize to the rest of you for what's going on," Rolleston said.

The patrons nodded sympathetically. They understood. Outside, with cold rain falling as the police paddy wagon drew up, the scene was not so decorous. A couple of SNCC kids had slipped behind a steel drop-gate lowered by the motel when the trouble started and one girl, dodging a pot-bellied motel guard, had fallen to the ground, unhurt. She lay there, a light-skinned, honey-eyed little Negro teen-ager from Tarrytown, New York, named Judy Richardson, staring straight up like a catatonic doll. Outside the gate, a white woman wailed:

"Police brutality! Help! They're killing us! Police brutality!"

It was the first and last time I saw this woman, who may have been an alumna from some Union Square May Day parade. There were no mounted police or I'm sure we would have heard "Cossacks!" Sgt. Marler, a professional who subordinated his own Southern feelings to the job, disregarded the lady Bolshevik and tried to ask Miss Richardson if she wanted an ambulance. Miss Richardson continued staring silently with the almost frightening calm so many Negro youngsters in the front ranks of the Movement can muster during frenetic moments. An ambulance was called to be on the safe side. Rolleston was storming about, demanding that the young teen-ager be arrested and that *I* be arrested because I had been tape recording proceedings on his property without his permission. I suppose he had a point. While the paddy wagons were loaded with those who had been neither wined nor dined, I moved outside off the property. They were singing "We Shall Overcome" as they were courteously escorted into the wagon, and after the door was shut and the wagon rolled down the dark and rainy street, I could still hear the muffled refrain ". . . deep in my heart, I do believe, we shall overcome someday."

Divorced from any emotionalism, the Atlanta story seemed significant and important. First, it was news when the new year, the year of the Civil Rights Bill, began with racial turbulence in the city generally acknowledged to be the most racially progressive in the Deep South. But more important, Negroes were raising questions about the quality of Atlanta's image in a manner that addressed itself to the whole country. When one looked closely at Atlanta, one found little substance behind the image. But the same lack of substance applied to Philadelphia and New York, Boston and Los Angeles, to Everywhere, U.S.A. From what I saw on television and read in newspapers and magazines and heard in conversations, America had slipped back into its old lazy and muddled attitude on race. Birmingham police dogs had snapped the national conscience to life in the summer. The church bombings had sickened us. But there had been no real catharsis, only passing revulsion. Now we would be getting a Civil Rights Bill sometime in 1964. Oh, it might be delayed by a filibuster, but filibusters were sort of fun, a little political diversion. Remember *Mr. Smith Goes to Washington,* how Jimmy Stewart put the apple and thermos on his Senate desk as he began to speak? So seeing how things were going ahead and the Negro had the government on his side, why didn't he declare a moratorium on demonstrations before he alienated a lot of new-found friends by being pushy and impatient?

The Northerner preferred to bank on the Civil Rights Bill to solve everything. At the same time, he regarded the problem as basically a Southern one. This belief spared him the self-analysis which he was as incapable to perform as the Southerner was incapable of making distinctions. This adherence was more a national than a regional lack, I suppose, and the inevitable result of generations of national self-love, of underthinking and overevaluating our democracy.

Minds, individual or national, that do not put forth the effort to separate reality from myth grow lax in their ability to perform. I think this laxness produced the American people's child's span of attention I referred to earlier—an inability to focus on problems over long periods if these problems will not yield to quick and dramatic solutions. The headlong dynamism in Teddy Roosevelt's "Charge!" at San Juan Hill curses our Caribbean and South American relations to this day. Where the hill does not yield to the swift stroke, we lose interest. For example, this mentality may account for our long toleration of slums which have complex social and economic origins, and which we deal with by occasionally tearing down a block or two to build a housing project. This limitation may be the reason why we never have had a consistent foreign policy demanding long-range goals, dispassionate thinking, self-examination on a continuous basis, and perseverance.

Negro leaders, in Atlanta and elsewhere, understood the prevailing white frame of mind—if not all its ramifications. They were cynical about that frame of mind but at the same time saw they had to work with it, activate it, and force the realization on white America that any Civil Rights Act would only be the beginning, not the end, of the struggle for racial equality. The Civil Rights Act would also be the beginning of some hard thinking and meaningful, not token, action. All this interaction seemed significant to me, whether or not you favored the civil rights drive, and so I was not prepared for the reaction of the men who ran the television news shows in New York. They were not interested.

Excuses might be made for their lack of interest in Latin America, remote from the world stage, minor countries swinging little international weight. But here the essence of America was involved and yet, during conversations with editors and producers, I received the impression that they were weary of civil rights stories, they were in basic sympathy with the image Atlanta presented, and they did not want or need any analyses of current white-black attitudes or projections of how these attitudes could affect the course of the civil rights story in the days ahead. Their attitude was that blunt when you cleared away evasions and excuses.

"Let's wait till something really happens," they said. "This is the same old same."

I had become accustomed to this kind of obtuseness and irresponsibility in Latin America. If, as in Santo Domingo or Nicaragua, I got film or tape of gas grenades exploding or police shooting during riots, congratulatory cables usually followed. But if I attempted to explain quietly why the grenades had gone off, or where they might go off the next time because of what reasons, the cables would read:

"Let's hold the analysis for the time being."

The news department had been in the throes of reorganization for three years, and former White House Press Secretary James Hagerty had been recently eased out as vice president in charge of news, replaced by CBS executive Elmer Lower. Insecurity was widespread since a new broom must always sweep—clean or otherwise. Great pressure was on everyone at ABC because a news department without a tradition of excellence or even competence was supposed to be competing with CBS and NBC on an equal footing. I had fared well under the new administration, getting the bureau I wanted and a lush salary. The purpose of this apparent digression is not to attack men and an organization left behind but to make events understandable as they transpired. To a great extent the producers who did not want the Atlanta story were only reflecting the public they serviced. Since the producers were supposedly better informed than the man staring at his television set for his ration of news, they might have been expected sometimes to direct his attention to what was important. But unfortunately, most of the ABC news producers were like delicatessen clerks slicing salami when it came to apportioning the news shows—a quarter of a pound for Washington, three ounces for the rest of the country, four ounces for Africa.

They were slaves to wire service concepts of what was news instead of developing independent ideas on what was newsworthy.

If one hundred persons were killed in a plane crash, the morbid public taste to see the unvarying picture record of wreckage and weeping relatives must be satisfied because UPI was leading with it. A Paris-based commentator might pontificate on what was going through General De Gaulle's mind concerning NATO because newspapers that afternoon were front-paging NATO. A certain amount of this repetition is unavoidable if a news show is to keep the public's newspaper-oriented attention and fulfill *one* reportorial function. But I saw something else in the ABC producers, a reflection of their society and their own personalities. The feeling pervaded that speculation about the Congo or reports from a White House correspondent whose existence depended on not bruising his contacts were more vital to the American awareness than stripping down the civil rights question to its bone and marrow. If there were violence, fine. That concept we all can understand and get interested in.

The weekend of January 25 began to produce the kind of action New York wanted, but unfortunately they had no network news programs on that weekend. What a waste. It was a hectic show with the Negroes appearing at their worst and the city of Atlanta reacting like a fond and reasonable uncle who finally must take the switch to a devilish nephew who goes too far and breaks everyone's patience. Police had been bending over backward to avoid making arrests, as we have noted, and this action frustrated the demonstrators as well as the segregationists. Civil disobedience falls flat when the visible opposition, the physical defense, drops away and nothing is left to contend against except the amorphous system. Violence-prone reactionaries, psychologically needing an atmosphere of acceptance in which to carry out legally unacceptable behavior, were stymied by Southern police who seemed to be, of all things, "nigger" lovers.

The bizarre weekend began with the arrival of a group of members from the fourteen-nation United Nations Subcommission on the Prevention of Discrimination and the Protection of Minorities. They possibly could have been invited at a worse time, but no Atlantan could imagine when that might have been, except in 1864 when Sherman burned the city. Their host was Atlanta attorney Morris Abram, a subcommission member, who during the weekend wore the air of a man who had mistakenly invited a ladies' garden group to visit a bordello. SNCC pickets met the UN group at the airport, and the delegates, including members from the Soviet Union, saw placards reading:

"Atlanta's image is a fraud."

They went from this welcome to a meeting at the Riviera Motel which had a segregated bar. In a private room off the bar, *Constitution* publisher McGill allowed that "we have our idiots" without specifying whether he meant SNCC or the segregationists. He went on to tell the integrated group, a first in the motel's history:

"I would not disguise the fact that we deplore Mississippi and Alabama, and the lack of developments there. We don't want to hide anything. We want you to know that we are trying."

Bob Thompson, head of the Atlanta Urban League, followed with what I thought an unfortunate speech, the kind of declaration made by men who have lived under unnatural tensions all their lives and in a moment of release are carried too far by the momentum of long-bottled emotion:

"I'm sorry that Mayor Allen is not here," he said, "because I would say to him that as a member of the minority I still have the right to say to Mr. Allen, 'You may go to hell,' if he were to do something I don't like. I can still say to the President of the United States, 'You go to hell, I don't like what you are saying.' . . ."

I felt sorry for Thompson and sorrier still for State Senator Leroy Johnson, the first and only Negro legislator since Reconstruction. When all the delegates had adjourned to the bar, Senator Johnson stuck his head in, looked around and departed. An hour earlier, a Negro couple had been refused admittance.

Such were the incongruities in the city too busy to hate, the city that white America and ABC producers were anxious to believe in. But some representatives of black America were even more anxious to put Atlanta in a different perspective, and the next day roving bands of SNCC-inspired demonstrators roamed the city, testing establishments where locked doors and baleful stares met them. Since the raw nerve and strong legs of the young often were needed as much as mature convictions, part of the technique of the Movement was mobilizing youth to carry the ball in demonstrations. But letting kids loose indiscriminately is dangerous, particularly when they are supercharged from the same kind of repression that powered Thompson. Many of the groups were disorganized and undisciplined when they poured downtown. In Birmingham or Jackson, this would have been suicidal; Atlanta, however hypocritical, was civilized.

Roy Bell, the sardonic dentist of the summit meeting, was trying to build a militant reputation quickly and move into politics after Senator Johnson's seat. I watched him, like a Pied Piper, lead scurrying groups of children ten and twelve years old into a side entrance of the Holiday Inn. They raced through a basement laundry room up a back stairway into the lobby, dressed in the motley of childhood, sneakers and sweatshirts. They were out of place by virtue of age and dress in that motel and milled about avoiding white eyes, managing somehow to maintain a ragtail dignity. The motel tolerated their presence as Dr. Bell lectured an assistant manager about segregation. The assistant manager who was under instructions not to create an incident seemed not to give a damn one way or the other. Inertia finally triumphed and the Piper led his children away.

The day-long Saturday demonstrations, without arrests, had charged the Atlanta atmosphere. A very square sort of city, Atlanta abhors the unseemly, which could be anything from a homeowner mowing his lawn on a Sunday to a free thinker. That Sunday the horrors visited on the city included the comedian Dick Gregory, a man carrying deep anger around with him that so weighted his moony face I could not imagine his telling jokes under any circumstances. A hunch-shouldered white boy yelled to him outside Leb's:

"So you're a big deal. Maybe you make more in a month than I do in a year."

"I make more in a *night* than you do in a year," Gregory shot back.

The white boy grinned a face-devouring grin of embarrassment and slunk off. Gregory was arrested a few hours later while sitting in at another restaurant. From the Negroes I was to see in the Movement from the entertainment, business, or professional worlds, Gregory left the strongest impression of self-effacing commitment to his convictions. At a time when so many show business characters were idealizing themselves through public shows of solidarity with the equal rights struggle, he took on dimensions of a man willing to sacrifice, seeking significant action and not the spotlight.

By late afternoon the picket line at Leb's was large and noisy. Numerous Klansmen were around and whites kept bunching up at nearby corners. Suddenly there was a commotion around the door. Pickets had rushed it, trying to force their way inside. Pushing and shoving began as employees held them out. This incident was not in the tradition of nonviolence but very much in ABC's tradition of what constituted news, and I found myself unhealthily elated at the turn of events. My cameraman, Bob Blair, was there and we filmed and recorded the uproar. There was another rush and this time I noticed some whispered conferences beforehand, indicating that it was planned. I spoke to one of the girl leaders on the line and she promised to alert me when the

next attempt on the door would be made. A few minutes later, she sig-
naled and Blair was ready. This time it was rougher, fists thrown on
both sides, and all of a sudden a patrolman, who was trying to come
between the pickets and the defenders was hurtled out through the
crowd. He fell and his head hit the sidewalk at my feet, knocking him
unconscious. Demonstrators scrambled inside and sat on the floor, lock-
ing arms. A white boy across the street shouted, "Let's get the niggers,"
and started across but no one followed. Police began moving in, grab-
bing pickets off the sidewalk and placing them under arrest. Most of
the pickets went limp and had to be carried, screaming, into paddy
wagons. Some protestors kicked at the police and were in turn man-
handled. On and on it went, raw and ugly. Leaving a dozen demonstrators
inside with doors to the toilets locked, restaurant patrons left and the
owner closed the place. Some of the pickets urinated in the restaurant
and later the owner, Charles Lebedin, would hang giant signs in his
window reading:

"Dear Friend: The law forces me to serve communist-led hoodlums
who indecently expose their bodies on top of my tables under the watch-
ful eye of local authorities."

UN members were elsewhere, doing God knows what in discharge of
their role as observers of discrimination and its effects. Eighty-five
demonstrators were jailed that day, another hundred the next as SNCC
kept up the pressure. Mayor Allen lamented that groups were seeking
national publicity at the city's expense. Imperial Wizard James Venable,
heading a Klan that was rival to Grand Dragon Craig's, issued a warning
that the KKK would be in the city within forty-eight hours "to restore
order." New York editors were now getting interested. This was a real
race story. I went along, chronicling the violence, adding up arrests,
chasing the frenzy, and speculating darkly that much worse might be
coming.

What came instead was an intelligent move by the city government
that had the effect of smothering the demonstrations. Mayor Allen
called an emergency city hall meeting of whites and Negroes. He made a
speech detailing the city's racial progress, including some extortionate
praise from President Kennedy for Atlanta's 1961 handling of school
desegregation. He even conceded that orderly picketing in the past
had helped to move the city toward racial justice. But he denounced
irresponsibles who, he said, seemed to be concerned with the "ag-
grandization of their own egos." James Forman was recognized by
him and said:

"There is no malice in anyone who adheres to the principle of nonviolence against any one particular individual. In fact, we love our white brothers even though they may be difficult for us to love. We even love the Ku Klux Klan that was demonstrating against us even though they may not understand this."

"Mr. Forman," interrupted the mayor.

"But this love," continued Forman.

"But Mr. Forman . . ."

"Just a moment, sir."

"I don't like to interrupt you but let's be germane to the subject."

"But sir . . ."

"I'm extending you every courtesy," said the mayor, "but I ask you to speak to the subject."

"Well, I am speaking to the subject because the subject involves the rationale for demonstrations in the city of Atlanta," replied Forman. "Some of us have been called irresponsible and I think it's necessary for the city at this moment to understand some of the reservoir that produces the need for demonstrations. I think it is true that progress is being made in Atlanta, but . . ."

It was hard to imagine another city in the South where a Negro demonstration leader could tell the mayor "just a moment" at a public meeting. The city's posture of tolerance, of being more sinned against than sinning, carried the day as older Negro leaders like Walden stood up to urge a return to the conference table and voluntary action. SCLC's Wyatt Walker, who was arrested at the Heart of Atlanta, commented:

"If we had left it to pure voluntary action, many of us would still be in the cotton fields."

But the street protests collapsed and with it ABC's interest in what the story meant. Atlanta's image stood intact, unquestioned. The violent behavior of nonviolent demonstrators went unprobed. I was left with the frustrating knowledge that not only had I been used as a police reporter but worse, I had behaved like one.

FLIGHT OF
THE BUMBLEBEE

Throughout late winter and into the spring, the South waited in uneasy anticipation for the congressional debate on the Civil Rights Bill and what seemed inevitable passage. The beginning of the end to a way of life was approaching but virtually no rational discussion of it existed once from Atlanta. The time cried for statesmanship and Georgia's Senator Richard Russell, after thirty-two years in the U. S. Senate, could only offer tired negation and sterile alternatives. He was working on a plan, a plan for racial relocation of Southern Negroes into Northern states. American Indians had once been "relocated." So had Russian kulaks and German Jews. In the pre-Civil War days, whites proposed to ship Negroes back to Africa. Although this move would have entailed uprooting families who had been here for centuries, the proposal was given serious consideration by educated men. What had been learned in more than a hundred years? Senator Russell said:

"If the people of the Southern states are to be forced to accept and conform to some federally indicated social order which is wholly alien to them, then I think it is only fair and right that the Negro population be spread more evenly over all sections of the country."

He called it "humanitarian" and said there would be "no trouble getting people to move." The Senator said his Voluntary Racial Relocation Commission would cost $1.5 billion a year, with Northern industries receiving up to $20,000 for each Negro they hired, and families given travel and subsistence grants. Where the implications in such a scheme weren't brutal or implausible, they were laughable. But they were being made by a man who held a powerful chairmanship of the

47

Armed Services Committee and was the titular leader of his eleven-state region of the old Confederacy.

The quality of thinking raised disturbing questions about the Southern capacity to examine intellectually what repelled it emotionally. Southerners rightly bridled at Northern stereotypes of them as illiterate hicks. The South saw in its own cohesive personality, shaped by custom, to take pride in mannerliness and manliness, something infinitely better than the uncoordinated personality of the North, often grasping, vulgar, and hypocritical. And, if race could be put aside for the moment along with inflated Southern notions of gentility, the South comes off well in many comparisons. At his best, the Southerner is capable of a natural friendliness lacking in the suspicious and fragmented Northern personality. I can't conceive of the barbarity of a New York subway rush hour occurring in the South. Good manners are too much a necessity, not merely a way of life. Horns rarely get blown even in the most maddening traffic and the extreme and time-consuming courtesy shown over the right of way at crossroads sometimes drove me to oaths. Self-pride can be a virtue, and it showed itself in such homely ways as repairmen who would come to the house to fix the water heater or oil burner. In New York, their hands would be out and all but in my pocket. In the South they refused tips, a little stiffly; they were doing honest labor for honest pay and wanted no man's gratuity.

I hear a Northern liberal voice protesting: Great! What lovable qualities. They politely get out of each other's way at a lynching.

Southern gracefulness only made more poignant the pity that gracefulness and racial good sense could not have united to supply a needed addition to the American character. That inability was the flaw in Senator Russell and the danger in him. I could dismiss, for example, the mentality of the Birmingham cabdriver who swore as another car cut him off:

"That was probably a damn nigger. They don't care how they drive. Hell, they'd just as soon kill you as themselves."

At the next light, we pulled alongside the car and it was a white man driving.

"No," said the cabbie peering over, "that weren't no nigger. It's a white man. 'Course, we got some white niggers, too."

He spoke from his personal ignorance; but the senator spoke for most of the South. Together they made a formidable alliance, not only against the Negro but against reasonable thinking. What was more warped—a cabdriver calling a man a white "nigger" or a senatorial relocation plan? Such thinking derived from an assumption of white superiority fixed so deeply in the mind of both patrician and proletarian that it could not be dislodged. That kind of thinking had been long developing. Let me quote from Cash again. Cash, the Southerner who loved the South but hated its bigotry, illumines the historical perspective as no other writer does. In the following quotation, he was examining how the plantation system had squeezed, broken, and stratified the poor white farmer:

> If the plantation had introduced distinctions of wealth and rank among men of the old backcountry, and, in doing so, had perhaps offended against the ego of the common white, it had also, you will remember, introduced the other vastly ego-warming and ego-expanding distinction between the white man and black. Robbing him and degrading him in so many ways, it yet, by singular irony, had elevated this common white to a position comparable to that of, say, the Doric knight of ancient Sparta. Not only was he not exploited directly, he was himself made by extension a member of the dominant class—was lodged solidly on a tremendous superiority, which, however much the black in the "big house" might sneer at him, and however much their masters might privately agree with them, he could never lose publicly. Come what might, he would always be a white man. And before that vast and capacious distinction, all others were foreshortened, dwarfed, and all but obliterated.

The price to the Negro had been exacted in blood and humiliation. I would begin to see this price plainly as stories took us west from urban Atlanta and into Alabama and Mississippi, where both white and Negro reality were on the surface, not glossed by image. A voter registration drive in Canton, Mississippi, for example, was being conducted by the Council of Federated Organizations (COFO). This organization, formed to work in Mississippi on the assumption the state was too much for one group to handle, was the agglomeration of SNCC, SCLC, CORE, and the NAACP. A church rally was held one April night before the Negroes were to go to the courthouse. The rallies were primarily designed to put iron in backbones because the walk to the courthouse for most Negroes was a long and fearful one. The church was poor and small, holding perhaps three hundred people on its rough wooden pews. The walls needed paint, the ceiling was flaking and the choir loft, sagging with the weight of years of stomping, held no organ. The scene would be duplicated that year a thousand times in the South—a church whose minister had cast his lot with the new evangelism, the promise now freedom instead of salvation, but Christ still central to the theme; the congregation stirring with new ideas and hopes investing them with purpose never felt before. The people . . . a shambling man about forty stood with sleepy-looking eyes and long arms dangling, oversized hands and feet, an apologetic awkwardness in his body. Twenty years before he might have modeled for a Stepin Fetchit character to delight the white American public who found the lazy and superstitious "darky" so amusing. As he sat listening to the words of revelation, his face and body seemed to acquire a natural dignity. Something Lincolnesque came in those eyes which on closer look appeared more sadly reflective than sleepy. The body seemed more expressive of a life stripped of grace by labor. Wooly-haired old ladies were given to sudden, deep grunts by way of comment on what was being said. Old men smiled a lot in nervousness and confusion and joy that after a lifetime such unbelievable things were coming to pass. And children. Why it should be that the rural Negro child, even into his teens, has expressions of unparalleled innocence and frankness I do not know. But, I felt it true and universal in the South. The eyes, invariably large, seemed impervious to corruption, contained always some hint of deep question, and combined the strength and vulnerability of the innocent. A gravity about the children made them old beyond their years, occasionally relieved by spurts of joy, and their great courage—more than anything else, I believe—accounted for the success of the Southern Movement.

The speaker was a young SNCC worker whose name, unfortunately, is lost to me. He was amateurish in some ways but utterly professional in that he knew his audience inside out. And listening to their response to him, the subjects that roused them to reply, I think we can learn much about what was uppermost in the Negro's mind and heart.

"I noticed a few minutes ago when we were talking about what Freedom Day is," he said, "a group started in shouting, 'Freedom! Freedom! Freedom!' very loud and clear. Feelin' good. Your soul felt good. But then I saw some people out there when the TV lights went on and the cameras started tried to look, you know, cute. I don't want to mention any names but you couldn't say Freedom then. You just sorta frowned. I hear whispers, 'This ain't right for church, yellin' and stompin' like that.' But you know, if you can't do it here, baby, you can't do it any place. (Amen! with laughter and applause) We're taught here how to live so we gotta start practicin' it. You know, we been caged for so long and now we got a way out. So we start it right here at home. This is revival, you know. (Go ahead!) See, I don't know who my grandfather was. He came from the other side of the fence. You *know* no two black people ain't gonna have no grey-eyed, kinky-haired, yeller nigger like me. (Laughter, heads nodding in agreement) How many of you are like me? Hold your hands up. (Hands shoot up all over the church; other hands are clapping) You know, Billy Lord* might be your uncle. But this is

*A particularly disliked police officer.

where it is. Integration has been goin' on a long time. We just haven't benefited from it. (Right!)

"And actually it's goin' on in some parts of the city right now, you know. But when it comes to where we want to stand up and be counted, then we're bad, you see. We're not ripe for it. We cook their food, they eat it. But when you come aroun' and want to sit down and eat *with* them, they can't eat with you. (Hummph, from an old lady) They don't want their children associating with your children. But this is what Freedom Day is gettin' to be about. Between sixty-five and seventy percent of the people in Madison County are folks like you. Kinky hair. Half white. Thick lips. Flat nose. Or maybe some got a thin nose, don't you see. But you don't have anybody representing you in city government. (That's right) Not one policeman. You don't have decent schools. They look good on the outside but when you get inside they don't have much in 'em. (They sure don't) You have one lousy playground in the entire county. You don't have any movie theater the kids can go to, any type of recreation hall. And whose fault is it really? Then they go out and raise hell about the fact niggers are immoral, have illegal kids. A fifteen-year-old girl gets pregnant. What else can she do when she goes out? (Tell 'em!) You know, when the beau comes to your home, mama, and he asks to go out with your daughter, what do you expect him to do? He doesn't have any place to take her. So he drives out in the woods and there it is, she comes back and in a few months you're a grandmother. (Whooping laughter and then serious applause)

"This is what the system does to you, you see. When your kid gets out of high school, you know, where can he go? If he goes to college and comes back to Canton and gets three thousand dollars a year as a teacher, it'll take him the rest of his life to make back what it cost him to go to college. He never gets ahead, you see. So what have you got to offer to him? Or to yourself? Fifteen dollars a week and a little food? It's not worth losin' my dignity for, you see. That comes first. (Yes, that's right)

"Now I hear people talking about, well, maybe if we talk it over with this man downtown, maybe we will have a chance if he'll just listen to us for a while. Listen, he's not gonna let you get up there and register because he knows if you get up there and register you gonna put somebody in the office gonna be fair, you see. What he's really afraid of is when you get in power, you're gonna do him like he's been doin' you. He doesn't want that, you see. (Applause) If he wasn't guilty or had a bad conscience he wouldn't worry about it because he'd know you'd put into office a person who would be fair. If he had been fair he wouldn't have anything to worry about. He's worrying because he's been doin' wrong." (Applause and cheers)

White man's sexual use of Negroes, his double standard permitting black hands near his food in service but barring the black presence from the social ritual of eating, the need for the colored church to get into action, poor schools, inadequate facilities, job deprivation, and the white man's fear of the Negro based on guilt were in the forefront of the Negro consciousness. The Negro now was delighted to hear declared openly in the name of the new evangelism those problems he had whispered about for a long while.

White reaction, official and private, was outrage. The first major crisis of the year came in Tuskegee, Alabama, home of the Negro Tuskegee Institute founded by Booker T. Washington. Tuskegee was in Black Belt country, named for the dark soil that blessed and damned the South's economy and mortality by copiously yielding the cotton that first required the slave, and later the sharecropper. The presence of the Institute produced a preponderance of Negroes better off financially and intellectually than whites in Tuskegee and surrounding Macon County. But the caliber of the Negro made no difference to the so-called elite of Tuskegee who ran the town. I think this concept is important. The Southern segregationist likes to play on Northern sensibilities to gain sympathy by drawing stark pictures of illiterate, smelly, and immoral colored field hands inundating Southern gentility. Black cotton cropper or black philosophy professor are one and the same to him.

In 1957, faced with growing Negro voter registration under Justice Department suits, the politicians gerrymandered voting districts to exclude virtually every Negro from the Tuskegee city limits. Negroes responded with a potent boycott, and a lawsuit that eventually found the Supreme Court upsetting the gerrymander law. Interracial communication, never truly open, collapsed completely. When the Negroes pressed for school desegregation, crosses were burned—although the county did not have a violent tradition. When thirteen colored youngsters were finally admitted to Tuskegee High School, all of the approximately five hundred white students began a boycott.

Governor George Wallace, already planning to make himself a national political figure in the spring presidential primaries, sent in squadrons of state troopers to carry white children to school each morning at nearby towns of Shorter and Notasulga. The twelve Negroes—one was suspended for poor grades—continued attending classes in the nearly empty building for a few weeks and then the governor ordered the school closed. Federal court orders began a now-familiar pursuit of official evasion and by February 5 the stage was set to send half of the Negroes to Shorter, the other half to Notasulga.

Notasulga, consisting of a two-block-long Main Street, a few churches, and the combined elementary and high school serving rural families in the county, was a poor town of a few thousand people. The biggest thing on Main Street was a gas station, old and grimy, with a battered bus abandoned in the back. Some bygone artist had lettered on it "The Boll Weevil Express," and there were bright, crude paintings of cotton plants and a big boll weevil. My crew and I (Blair, a veteran news cameraman who was near sixty, and his soundman, Charles Roberts) drove to the city hall to see the mayor, James Rae. A sign was on the door of the one-story brick building:

"Newsmen are not wanted or needed."

The sign was the most graphic example of the prevailing Southern opinion that newsmen, particularly Northern newsmen, were to blame for much of the South's problems with the Negro. This assumption was true in a way. The films of Birmingham firehoses and police dogs had acted on the national conscience and had helped to produce the pending civil rights legislation. Negroes were often emboldened to demonstrate because the presence of reporters not only publicized their cause but also acted as a deterrent to violence in places where officials feared bad publicity. Where fifteen years before a Negro picketing a Mississippi courthouse might have wound up in jail or on a slab, he now wound up on the "Huntley-Brinkley Show."

In a region where self-criticism was not tolerated, outside observation implying criticism was clearly intolerable. Again, the old incapacity for distinctions did not permit the segregationist to differentiate between straight reporting, biased reporting, or editorialized partisanship with the Movement. Everything that intruded on his psychological province was the same, and his mind clouded at the sight of anyone representing the television networks or Northern papers. Over the course of the year, I saw a number of news people, prejudiced themselves, become the object of indiscriminate attacks. The basic Southerner found a new method of evading the responsibility to think about his way of life. First, he could focus whatever conscious thought he devoted to the system of segregation on outside "nigger" agitators whom he blamed for stirring up the previously contented natives. Then, the Communists in Washington, the Jews and foreigners who were dictating the nation's policies got more blame. And then, close at hand, an appealing target, the newsman, who always seemed to turn up when the "niggers" were stirring, who bothered people with questions that deserved no answers, and who inevitably lied, got the remaining blame.

A clerk, more nervous than hostile, told us that the mayor, whose nickname was K. O., was at the high school. We drove out to await the arrival of the Negro children. About fifty Alabama State Highway patrol cars were parked in a long line around the school grounds and troopers were everywhere. The building itself was a sprawling one-story affair of brick, whose styleless institutional design, so staid and undramatic, stood in sober contrast to the nervous air surrounding it. The school kept making the point: All this because some American children, books in hand, are planning to walk through a schoolhouse door to learn. The troopers blocked passage to the mayor who stood on the doorstep. I thought they possibly had the highest cholesterol level of any police force in the world. Almost to a man, big bodies bulged in their trim uniforms, stomachs slopped over belt buckles, and jowly necks mounted to beefy faces. A majority chomped on cigars, tilting them up aggressively. The act of smoking turned into an assertion of pugnaciousness by grown-up Mickey Maguires. They gave a first impression of being mean men and I never saw anything that altered the first impression. Lillian Smith, author of the controversial book *Strange Fruit,* quotes an aged Negro man who said of unyielding segregationists: "Break their hearts, Lord. Give them tears." I don't think most of these men knew how to feel enough to cry.

Across the road from them were the rednecks, about forty men of Notasulga. Many carried stout canes, although they did not limp. The word "redneck" has been used erroneously and insultingly to mean any Southerner who opposes integration. But it specifically refers to un-educated, violence-prone country people whose manners and morals appall the cultured Southerner just as the urbane New Yorker looks down on the slum denizen. That the cultured Southerner and urbane New Yorker have helped through indifference to create what they despise is a hard truth both individuals seek to avoid.

The troopers ordered us to stand with a few dozen newsmen directly in front of the rednecks, who were mumbling about outside agitators. We were shooting sound. A word of explanation is needed here. A cameraman shooting silent carries a small hand camera which gives him great freedom of movement. A sound camera is a big, bulky affair mounted on a shoulder harness and attached by cables to the sound recording device carried by the soundman. This umbilical arrangement limits movement and increases the vulnerability of the men and record they are trying to make. We waited; considerable tension was in the air.

Across the street was a roving sheriff from Dallas County (about a hundred miles away) surrounded by members of a special posse he used to keep Negroes in line. His name was Jim Clark and he was destined for eventual fame in the city of Selma.

The bus came over a knoll and rolled toward us. A bus carrying school children. That was all, and your stomach knotted. The rednecks crowded in, shoving and cursing. The bus halted directly in front of us, a little cloud of exhaust wafting up, and Sheriff Clark and a man in civilian clothes jumped aboard. The faces of the Negro children, vague behind dusty windows, turned to them and suddenly there were screams and thuds from inside. Somebody threw a firecracker that sounded like a pistol shot. The rednecks pushed into us, swinging canes. One caught Blair on the head, another cracked his camera lens. Someone looped a cane handle over the cables and started tugging, and I grabbed the cane to keep him from cutting the sound.

"Get 'im, get 'im," a redneck yelled.

Bob continued filming, I continued talking into the tape recorder, mike held in one hand while the other tugged at the cane. The racket from the bus was awful—girls' voices crying hysterically, and I thought the children were being beaten. The reality of the scene was hard to believe even as it was happening. But suddenly a slim white youth in his twenties was thrown out the door. He lay on his back, moaning and yelping as a law officer jabbed at his stomach and genitals with a cattle prod, a battery-driven shock device used to get cows moving. Laid on human skin the prod produces excruciating pain. The state troopers watched the youth being worked over but did not intervene. Many were busy pushing us back into the rednecks who in turn pushed us forward. In retrospect, our situation was fairly comical. The white youth finally was permitted to stand up and someone shoved him toward the center of the street. He was pale and shaken. When I got to him to ask what happened, he said breathlessly but courteously, "I'd rather not talk about it now, if you don't mind."

The bus was ordered away and the Negroes' failure to enter satisfied the rednecks. They fell back and we got to our car. The boy was a free-lance cameraman named Vernon Merritt III, twenty-four, and his father was a colonel in the Alabama Air National Guard. He had boarded the bus in Tuskegee, with the knowledge of the county school superintendent. When the colored children got on, and during the trip, he was photographing their facial reactions. Police had radioed ahead to the school, alerting Sheriff Clark. Merritt, a mixture of enterprise and foolish courage, later told me that the terrible thumping was Clark smashing his camera, not beating the children who escaped unmolested. Merritt had anticipated trouble and before reaching the school had secreted one roll of exposed film in his shoe. He sent this by Air Express from the Montgomery Airport to his employer, Black Star. The package, insured for a nominal ten dollars, arrived in good time. But someone at the airport had slit open one end and removed the film. From then on, news cameramen in Alabama insured their shipments for fifteen hundred dollars and film got through.

The Alabamian approach to school desegregation would take still more drastic turns. Notasulga had revealed the capabilities of the rednecks with their canes, the beef-on-the-hoof troopers, and a sheriff with a cattle prod. The children behind those dusty bus windows and the parents who had sent them into Notasulga that morning were still indistinct. Earlier I had spoken briefly to one parent, Dr. Walter Judkins, a veterinarian at the Institute's School of Animal Husbandry, whose seventeen-year-old son Robert was on the bus. He agreed to talk again, although I did not have much time because the morning film had to be taken to Birmingham.

The Judkins lived on a dirt road as a majority of Southern Negroes do because white city governments will not pave their streets. I would learn that blacktopping of roads might be a homelier issue than a motel room, but it held more real meaning for colored families. The house was a modest one-story white frame, clearly feeling the years yet holding the conventional middle-class line. The front yard was sparse with winter grass but extremely neat, the dirt patches looking swept, all of it like a well-brushed, thin old suit. A scrawny dog barked and ran off at a hard stare. Dr. Judkins and his wife invited me inside to a living room spare of things. I recall linoleum on the floor, nondescript chairs, on the walls a few reproductions one looks at, but does not see. The house showed the lean tidiness of middle-class living standards without much money behind them. The Judkins were in their early forties. He was an intelligent, humorless man, at first seeming noncommittal and then turning direct and opinionated. His wife showed a good deal of Indian blood in a beaked nose and long, black hair worn in curls that went out of style with Mary Pickford. Her eyes were dark and mixing an expression of outrage, dull pain, and wariness. That may seem a tall order for one pair of eyes, but I see them now and that is how they were. Our conversation was constrained at first. The conversation was usually this way with Negro adults in the South who did not trust the white presence or motives and had to accustom themselves to an unaccustomed frankness. I hurried to establish my sympathies; they wondered if it all were legitimate or another trick from Mr. Charley; the clock crammed into minutes what hours or days were needed to hold.

"Of course we know there is a risk in sending the children," Dr. Judkins said, after we had talked a while. "We know that. Carmen is going to Shorter, Robert to Notasulga. It isn't easy for them. But we discussed it and they understand why it has to be done and want to do it. There is no point in living like we have been here. You have to take a risk to change things. We were like that dog in the yard to white people, supposed to live on their kindness and lick their hands.

"We had been facing each other for years here in Tuskegee, our education and money on one side, their land and status on the other. Grinning at each other. Hypocritical. They'd say, 'Oh, John, you're a nice boy,' and that was supposed to do you for the things you really wanted in life. There was pseudo-cordiality but it wasn't until the boycott that we began to earn respect. Then white people we had known for years, who we considered friends as far as there were friends within the system, they wouldn't talk to you on the street or in the stores. But they had to respect us when we showed we would not take it any more and that we would do without them."

Disenfranchisement, he said, was at the heart of the Negro complaints. The calculated products were the complicated application forms and literacy tests that whites unofficially said were designed to protect the ballot from the illiterate hands of the "field niggers" who had despoiled Southern legislatures during the Reconstruction. But Dr. and Mrs. Judkins were neither illiterate nor field hands. She was graduated in 1940 from the Institute with a teaching degree and then taught high school. For twenty-one years, she tried unsuccessfully to register.

"You would stand in line all day without being called," she said, "if you could even find out where they were registering people. Sometimes I would be permitted to take it. But they never replied when I asked why I had failed."

Her husband was graduated from the Institute in the same year, spent four years in the service, another four obtaining a degree in Veterinary Medicine, and two more at Colorado State University obtaining a master's. He lost count of how many times he tried to register during that period. The Judkins finally became voters when the Tuskegee registrar's office was placed under a federal injunction. As Democrats, they had to cast ballots stamped with the party symbol—a white rooster circled by the slogan: "White Supremacy for the Right."

"Why didn't we force the issue sooner?" he said, repeating my question. The question irked him; it contained the seed of intimation that the Negro had not been up to asserting himself, the flaw in him as well as in the Southern white. "It's like the bumblebee. He can't fly. Aerodynamically it's impossible to get off the ground. If he believed it. We were like that. We had been told for so long we couldn't. They perverted our history, made believe we had no culture. Made *us* believe it. I've traced my ancestry back to the Ibo tribe of Nigeria, to a royal family there. . . ."

"His great-grandfather was a freeman," Mrs. Judkins said. "An ironmonger. A man of property. He bought his own way out of slavery, bought a farm. You get tired of hearing white people say what they did for us."

"But none of that made any difference to these people," he said. "I remember once my father saw a white man beating up a colored boy. The man stopped and said to him, 'You don't like it, do you?' And then went back beating him. No, he didn't like it. But there was nothing to do if you wanted to stay alive.

"They say that Wallace is responsible for this trouble over the schools here. I don't believe that. No one can create the hate there is here. Men aiming guns from inside a store as the school bus with my son drove by. Can you imagine it?"

"The white mothers say, 'If only my little Jane can stay away from Negroes,'" Mrs. Judkins said. "But when they're small and there's no one to play with, they'll tell the cleaning woman to bring her kid to keep the white children company.

"Now they say, 'You have a good high school already, why do you want to come into ours?' It's true, the colored Tuskegee Institute High School is good. But our children are going to live in a world with white people when they get out. They should get used to each other, competing with each other and helping each other so you don't have an unnatural situation in life."

"But you can't get that through to them," said her husband, "because the effect these people's racial attitudes have on them is outside all logic. They tell a story that Booker T. Washington was on a speaker's platform along with President Teddy Roosevelt. A Southern white man who knew Washington came up on the platform, said hello and shook his hand. Then he started off.

"'Wait a second, Mr. Jones,' said Washington. 'Aren't you going to shake hands with the President?'

"And the man replied: 'I haven't said a word to him since he invited you to dinner.'"

He gestured hopelessly.

"And still," he said, "when the white man here wants to be your friend, you don't have a friendlier person in the world. Out in rural communities, white and black help each other, often on the sly. Simply people helping each other."

Their son, a tall, loose-limbed boy with the gangly grace of a basketball player, came in briefly to say hello.

"It wasn't so bad," he said. "They didn't hurt us. Just the photographer."

He seemed to have a dead center of absolute reserve and calmness. His parents did not want him interviewed because of pressures already on him but their attitude did not seem so much parental anxiety as the concern of equals in a mutual effort, an adult interplay of understanding. A year earlier the bomb in the Birmingham church had extended the limits of white violence deep into childhood. Since neither church nor childhood was inviolate, the Judkins had a clear estimate of risk. Clearly they would persevere. We said our goodbyes and I left them in their modest house on their dusty road, impressed by something more than their courage: Here were the favored among Southern Negroes, people who had traveled from ignorance into education, from subsistence into enough. But learning, a decent standard of living, even the ballot was not sufficient. The totality of human need demanded nothing less than total assertion that their humanity not be equated *to* white humanity but coexistent *with* it. The bumblebee's determination to fly was irresistible.

Conversations like that one, so necessary to an expanded consciousness of why the Negro pressed as he did, unfortunately were curtailed by the nature of television newsgathering—or, at least, as it was practiced at ABC. To begin with, we operated with a policy of crisis reporting, moving on a story as it boiled up, quickly dropping it the moment its supposed public interest had died, and racing off to a newer crisis. Much of this procedure was inevitable, given a small staff in competition with the armies fielded by the other two networks which could afford the luxury of sparing a man to go to a story early and stay late. Our procedure crimped perspective and often substituted the superficial glance for the needed long look. Additionally, from the correspondent's point of view, television coverage generally consumes great amounts of time, that should go to the story, in travel and physical preparation of the films. Time, of course, is a factor in all reporting but in no other area of journalism is it so dominant. Unless the story occurs in a city large enough to have an affiliate capable of transmitting the film report over special telephone company lines to the network in New York, the correspondent must fly from the scene to the nearest affiliate. The day after the bus incident was typical.

During the night, the Notasulga water works burned down. Mayor Rae promptly decided that miraculous coincidence made it necessary to close the high school because, without a workable water works, there would be no water to fight a possible fire in the school. We left early from Birmingham to fly to Opelika. We had to load the twenty separate pieces of equipment television cameramen must carry into a charter plane, unload it in Opelika, load up a rented car, drive twenty-five miles to Notasulga, unload again. From the moment of arrival at the scene, the clock began hurrying backward toward us. At 4:30 P.M. the day's report would have to be fed to New York for the six o'clock evening news. The feed time was 5:30 in New York, but Alabama was in the central zone. Sometimes, during Daylight Saving Time, two hours were lost.

To have the film ready by 4:30, we had to leave the scene by 1:00 P.M. at the very latest. The trip to the airport took half an hour. Leave one hour for the forty-five-minute flight to Birmingham because we might hit a headwind or get stacked up for two or three circles of the field, and these things subtract minutes. The station in Birmingham was a good twenty minutes from the field in normal traffic. Forty-five minutes were needed to develop the film, providing nothing was ahead of you in the developing machine. Then you had to hope that a film editor would be available and not engrossed in cutting advertising segments into the Pat O'Brien-James Cagney Marine Corps film to be shown later that evening. If you were lucky, he could begin immediately pulling out the scenes you wanted, timing them, cutting, splicing, and recutting so the piece would hang together properly. If all went well, the editing would take forty-five minutes. And then fifteen minutes more in which to write the script, catching up meanwhile through the teletype machines on all that had happened after you left at one o'clock. So many things could and did go wrong in this process that I feel anxious remembering them again. Weather could delay you. Film that you counted on turned out underexposed or with faulty sound. Developing machines would break. Cutters got nervous and fumbly fingered. Or the reporter, quintessence of professionalism and epitome of aplomb, could make mistakes in judgment of timing that cost minutes. All of this was for a piece of film that might run one minute if virtually nothing else were happening on the globe that day.

We were back in Notasulga filming the gutted brick building that had been pumping the town's water until coincidence struck a spark. The mayor had promised by phone to make himself available for an interview about eleven o'clock. While the cameraman was filming, a rawboned man in shirtsleeves came up and began chatting in a friendly fashion about the fire. He did not have a cane; he did not even seem to have any animosity when he learned I was a reporter. He was a minister from the Baptist church in Notasulga, a simple-spoken man and country poor from his dress. He did not think the school desegregation was a good idea because people were so set against it. Desegregation was bound to create problems, children might get hurt. But was the life of God something different? Would he accept a Negro at a service in his church?

"*I* would, yes," he said. "I believe we're all children of God. But I couldn't do it. If I ever did, you see, the people would run me off."

I wanted to get him aside and have a long talk about the people in his church. I wanted to gather his insights about whites in their relation to a white God and the black man. But the appointment with Mayor Rae was pressing. And better to be early than risk missing him. He was late, apologetically so. The mayor was in his late thirties, paunchy, open-faced, prematurely bald, and he spoke in tones of a man being put upon. He had been elected just in time to inherit the school crisis and he was not happy. After all, the men with the canes were his constituents and although he was a lawyer, he had to answer to mentalities that answered to something more basic than law. The sun kept going in and out, delaying the filming. I would start on a question, he would warm up to his answer, and the cameraman would cut us off as a cloud made shambles of his exposure. Eventually, we pieced together some observations by Mayor Rae. "We have a quiet town here. We live quiet lives. We're certainly upset about the situation that has developed." And the fire in the water works?

"Well, of course, our first thought under the circumstances was that it was probably set. So we immediately called on the state fire marshal's office." The official indication? "A bad electrical outlet in the ceiling. We've known for some time that the wiring was bad and a complete rewiring job is included in our program."

Who would deny that what Notasulga needed was a complete rewiring job? The mayor's lateness and the erratic sun had now pushed us close to one o'clock. I wanted to try to talk to a local school board official whose barn had reportedly been burned, apparently because he voted to obey a federal court integration order. White parents needed to be sought for their reactions and Negroes in Tuskegee Institute with an intellectual view of realities in the area. So many persons with so much intimate knowledge. But no time. We had time only to rush back to Birmingham with ruins of a fire in a quiet town and an upset mayor.

The procedure was the same all spring, hit-and-run attacks on a story that had not yet focused, barnstorming from one impression to another and hoping that what was glimpsed might someday fall together in understanding. My log of those days summons up pictures:

Freedom Day in Hattiesburg . . . rain drenching Negroes on a courthouse step as a squad of hastily assembled auxiliary police in helmet-liners hup-hups along the main street, soggily out of step . . . about thirty Negroes, led by Forman, bunch up before a door, not allowed to stand inside while they wait to enter the registrar's office . . . an old white townsman observes the Klan was good enough for their grand-daddies and it's good enough for them . . . a Negro girl in her twenties looks through the door glass and says to a deputy, "You stand there and look at me like you never seen one before. But you have, you got one in your house right now. I know because I worked for some of you. Now all we ask is one vote." . . . white ministers, including a son-in-law of Governor Nelson Rockefeller, picket carrying "One Man, One Vote" signs . . . the old townsman says, "They might look white but you can be sure they got nigger blood in 'em" . . . Forman knocking and demanding to be let in while I marvel at his audacity and later realize that is part of it, to demand . . . Negroes, like the man with frizzled gray hair in his seventies, who stands in the beating rain for an interview and says, "I lived in Hattiesburg since '23 but never voted. No, sir. Why? Well, I come down to register once three or four years ago and they said they wasn't registering any—you know—colored folks."

Freedom Day in Greenwood . . . pickets marching in vivid sunlight past the courthouse entrance, past the granite statue of a Confederate soldier mounted on a tall columnar pedestal honoring the Civil War dead . . . the atmosphere is subdued in this city where one year earlier white men machinegunned a car carrying SNCC's fabled Mississippi pioneer Bob Moses and a local boy named Jimmy Travis who was wounded and almost died . . . it is the hometown of Byron de la Beck-with, accused of the ambush killing of NAACP leader Medgar Evers . . . but today the weapon is a paint brush that draws a bright yellow line on the sidewalk beyond which the pickets cannot pass . . . it gleams there, fresh yellow paint laid on this jot of Mississippi called Green-wood, and eyes of police and reporters fill with yellow as the pickets' feet approach, turn, approach, turn and finally pass . . . the arrests are orderly as pickets are led into a school bus turned into a paddy wagon, but one of the Negro jail trustees, whose scarred and brutal face rebukes the notion a God of love exists, wants to show the white jailer what he thinks of "nigger" troublemakers and pushes a Negro girl sprawling onto the floor, in that push sending himself further down into the oblivion of hate his way of life has created . . . and finally, after the bus leaves, city attorney Stanny Sanders, who helped defend de la Beckwith, takes me into the registrar's office and shows me the pathetic inability of most Negro applicants even to write their names and addresses on the application form . . . "Do you see" he says, "what we have to put up with? Would you let them vote?" I shake my head, sigh, "No, they obviously can't qualify," and my cameraman zooms in on the Negro scratches on the forms.

The office of a high official at the University of Alabama . . . the university has had racial crises in the past when Governor Wallace stood at the door and tried to turn away a Negro student. Now all is relatively calm and in the large, pleasant office there is no academic severity but tasteful informality of a desk cluttered with doodads, books piled here and there. The official is fortyish and urbane, clearly at ease with the Yankee press, seems like excellent material from which to make a business executive with his evenly handsome face nicely balancing youth and maturity, his voice sonorous with friendship and conviction. . . . We are making small talk, grandly demonstrating our mutual goodwill, and cameraman Blair comments on the loveliness of the campus, which *is* lovely: staunch brick buildings, distinguished old trees gracefully blurring vistas, pretty girls clutching books to bosoms already demanding kindlier embraces, a buzz of youth promising, promising. "But," says Blair, "I am kind of a bug on antebellum homes and I know this is an old university and I was surprised not to see any." The official smiles wryly. "I'm afraid," he says, "that the Union forces burned them all to the ground when they came through in 1864." I feel an urge to apologize for the depredations of those vanished Yankees and I shake my head as I did at the Greenwood voting lists. "But why," I ask, "did they burn down college buildings?" The official opens his hands in an easy, tolerant gesture at the inexplicability of human behavior and seems to implant a moral with a look into my eyes; he seems to say: "Why don't you excuse our excesses as we so graciously excuse yours?" Before we leave the campus we stop at an historical marker which describes the university. It says: "Used as a school for the training of Confederate officers until destroyed by Union Forces in 1864."

All these were snippets of reality, some trivial, some important. We had no chance to develop these pieces in the rush of movement from story to story, some with civil rights themes and others the normal run of news. The log for a two-month period tells of flights to Fort Benning, Georgia, where Cuban officers were quitting the U. S. Army because we would not reinvade the island; the Jimmy Hoffa bribe trial in Chattanooga; a week in Mexico for the visit of General Charles De Gaulle; Huntsville, Alabama, where Lady Bird Johnson toured the rocket sites and confessed she hadn't the foggiest notion what Wernher von Braun was explaining to her; a cold snap blights the Georgia peach crop; a Negro lawyer in Albany, Georgia, E. B. King, decides to run for Congress; Negroes parade in Tuscaloosa, Alabama, and in the morning Blair and I joke with a hotel waitress about Groucho Marx's line that elephant hunters like to go to Alabama because there the tusks-are-loosa and in the afternoon he is knocked down by rednecks during my absence and his film confiscated by police.

For those months, we flew as if the "Hound of Heaven" were in pursuit. We loaded and unloaded those damned twenty pieces of camera equipment from commercial flights to charter flights, cabs to rented cars, in and out of motels. All our great motion seemed to signify accomplishment but most of it on the police reporter level. The beat enlarged, the issues intensified, but the reporting still ladled off only the surface. At one point, we were flying charter every two or three days in Georgia, Mississippi, and Alabama, and one of the regular pilots offered to teach me to fly. Those runs were boring; the enervating, droning sameness of flight, and I was glad to do something. He had instructed me to the point of taking off and landing by myself when one day he flew off on another assignment to Akron and, carrying four passengers, disappeared without a trace over Lake Michigan.

Apparently with all our frenetic maneuvering, we were really getting no place. I remember one day when commercial flights were grounded because of poor weather and I had to bring film from Canton to Jackson. Most of Mississippi was covered with low and sullen clouds—the ceiling perhaps a variable 400 feet. Assuming that New York would want the story after it was processed, I was very pressed for time. This acceptance was doubtful because it was a voter registration drive which by now was old hat. The pilot was a rawboned, laconic type with a country bumpkin accent, but with a certain quality of competence when he said he would get me there in time. And he did, flying low enough most of the flight to follow highways lying under the cloud layer, so low that we occasionally passed radio station towers whose tops disappeared into the clouds above us. I felt this was the stuff, getting the news through, risking your neck, hell-for-leather derring-do. But that night, after New York had not used the story, I thought that the effort was like the scene in *A Tree*

Grows in Brooklyn when Katie Nolan and her children have been playing Arctic explorer. Under the pretense they are awaiting rescue at the North Pole, the family stretches what little food there was in the cupboard. Young Francie says after one game that explorers go hungry to achieve something big, but all they seem to be doing is going hungry. And her mother says sadly:

"You found the catch in it."

So for all the mad dashes, the swindling of minutes, juggling of film and script, I was finding the catch. At the end, the great salami slicer awaited. Perhaps I'd get a minute and ten seconds, perhaps fifty seconds, perhaps nothing if the order is already filled to the satisfaction of someone "up there." Even when something like the Greenwood interview with City Attorney Sanders got on, what did it achieve? That kind of interview gratified segregationists, infuriated liberals, and did nothing for the limbo mind, except perhaps plant in it the conviction Negroes were dumb. The complicating factor of Negro undereducation in Mississippi, of registrars who helped whites with their forms, of colored apathy toward education and politics, all had to be examined at length before I or a viewer could know what Greenwood was really about. Instead, we were reducing to shorthand something that only full exposition could make intelligible. Documentaries, not merely a lone half-hour but many, were needed to help prepare America for this confrontation with itself. But all suggestions to New York went unavailing, for the producers would neither develop the interest nor make the time.

Still, at every opportunity, we were whetting public interest in the sensational aspect of the story by using the phrase "the long, hot summer" to describe the coming civil rights drive in July and August. The words throbbed with an undertone of violence, conjured images of clashes in the streets, blood spilled in the dry blast from Southern suns and under steamy Southern moons. I was as guilty as the rest. The coverage smacked of the old yellow journalistic trick of denouncing vice in order to print photos of naked women. Did we unconsciously desire the coming of inflamed days with the excitement of death, beatings, white and black openly in combat? Some of this contention, I am sure, was in the prevailing mood. Even civil rights leaders, who should have known better, kept hammering the phrase into the public mind. Later, in McComb, Mississippi, newspaper editor Oliver Emmerich told me that many Mississippians—and not all of them rednecks—actually came to expect the approximation of armed invasion. If Walter Judkins and "the grey-eyed, kinky-haired, yellow nigger" in Canton would persist, white men were prepared to prevail against them. All these white men were not of the same aristocratic stripe as Senator Russell with his grand plan of relocation. Throughout the South, Ku Klux Klansmen were preparing their version of the long, hot summer.

Those Klansmen I had seen in Atlanta were part of a so-called Invisible Empire, totaling perhaps twenty thousand men divided into eight or nine loosely affiliated Klans. I had difficulty knowing whether or not to take seriously men addicted to alliterative mumbo jumbo, their sacred book, the Kloran, their Klaverns units and their chaplains—of all things—Kludds. The Klans had enjoyed two eras of past prominence. Their terroristic attempts to cow Negroes and chase carpetbaggers during Reconstruction were glorified by D. W. Griffith in the movie *The Birth of a Nation*. The Klan choked on its own excesses and became moribund in the thirties. Now, it was on the rise again.

The crew and I went to Tuscaloosa where the United Klans of America, Inc., had its headquarters in a turn-of-the-century office building on the main street. The elevator was one of those clanking metal cages that should be descending into a coal mine, and the young Negro who ran it could have been taking you down to the mine or up to the Klansmen for all the apparent difference it made to him. His expression was impenetrable, his attitude verging on torpor. The hallway was narrow and dismal, the kind suited for the office of an abortionist or sleazy detective agency.

An attractive brunette lady in a black cocktail dress and high heels opened the door to a pine-paneled room with modern office equipment and planters. She was Mrs. Robert Shelton, wife of the Imperial Wizard, who emerged from an inner office wearing a business suit. His purple-and-white robe hung in a zippered plastic clothing bag; he declined to wear it for our interview, but otherwise offered a wary brand of cooperation. He was a former tire salesman, an unsmiling, smallish man, with a spare face and flat gray eyes which seemed incapable of relaxing into casualness or losing their somberness. He told me that the news media was creating a distorted picture of the Klan as a group favoring violence and bigotry.

"They are trying to bring about the understanding of the Klan today as though it was living on a pedestal of history and yesteryears," he said. "Because the Klan today is entirely different in operation than it was in the years of 1865 to 1875. In that area of our history we had no laws that was protective of the white race or the chastity of womanhood. Therefore, it was the only method of self-preservation of the members of the Klan and for it, as a body to, on occasion, what it would appear to be break laws when only they were creating laws to give them protection because they were under an occupied force of carpetbaggers, scalawags, and under the heel of a black tyranny here in our South.

"The Klan today is definitely an organization devoted to upholding law and order for the purpose of maintaining segregation of the races and using all legal methods that we can use at our disposal. However, we are not a group of people that will sit back and allow our organization or allow our members or the citizenry of our country to be trampled by this Communist conspiracy that is using Nigras as a tool and pawning them off on the white race to bring about this animosity and ill will that we have in America today."

I asked whether he believed Negroes should be ill-treated or the subject of derogatory remarks.

"No," he said. "By using the demagery [sic] remarks as to what a Nigra should be called or any other individual will not bring about the association of advancement of any organization we have desire to be building. We are not innermotional [sic] type people that will go for this type of speech or rampaging demagery remarks. Because this is the caliber of people that are immediately seeking action to let out inner emotions."

Shelton said that Negro crime rates showed the race was immoral. He described his repugnance at using interracial restroom facilities because of the high colored venereal disease rate. He seemed to be confused on the subject of racial superiority, although the basic tenet of the Klan—like that of the Alabama Democratic Party—is white supremacy. I asked whether low whites were better than upper-class Negroes.

"Well," he said, his tone verging on expansiveness but not quite making it, "we have the lower class of people, so to speak, in all races whether they be Negro, white, Jewish, Italian, or what have you . . . that is not capable to sit into the society of one other class of people. This is something that has to be on a selective basis with the individuals themselves giving him the choice of association. And not on the basis of race being denied his rights because he cannot associate with another race that is not his national origin."

I wanted to ask Shelton what the hell he was talking about, but instead decided to present a hypothetical case that might clarify his outlook. Supposing a Negro who was a college graduate, a lawyer earning, say, $25,000 a year and very clean, especially clean, wanted to use a white restroom. Would the Imperial Wizard object?

"In the first place," he said, and I saw the only grudging indication of a smile during the interview, "if there was a Nigra with all that, he would have the financial ability to build a restroom of his own."

He had no "second place" and the interview concluded shortly after he predicted that the Communists would assassinate Martin Luther King in 1964 because he had outlived his usefulness to their movement. The interview was never used because the sound was off speed. We were always having camera problems of one sort or another at ABC. As an artist friend of mine used to say, "A portrait is a painting in which there is something wrong with the mouth," so I came to look on our reports as news coverage in which there was something wrong with the film.

The Klan, publicly joining in the vogue of imagery, had its new image of respectability. But how deep did it go? Back in Atlanta I soon had an inkling. The newspaper notice said:

Stand up for God, our homes and America.
Attend United Klans of America, Inc., Rally
of Americanism, Sunday, March 22, 1964, 2 P.M.

The park was a sunken acre-sized swatch of green laid down at the fringe of the business section. Mayor Allen had opposed its use by the Klan because the U. S. Attorney General's subversive list carried a Klan organization and he wanted to know whether the two Klans were the same. The American Civil Liberties Union took a stand, arguing that the Klan damn well was entitled to use the park and what was free speech coming to, anyway? One of those typical American philosophical-political crises was arising from a people basically unsure of itself or the real nature of the democratic system they so passionately espoused and sought to impose on others. The Atlanta aldermanic board, a group of nonentities and political hacks, finally granted permission for the rally "providing it does not conflict with other activities at Hurt Park, such as the Tulip Festival."

Ruth came with me, as she had on other Atlanta stories. We arrived to hear the public address system blaring the record of a lugubrious-voiced gospel singer who warned:

Someone will die tomorrow
As many have before,
Maybe it's you, and then
Maybe it's me.

The people didn't seem to let the prospect worry them. About three hundred Klansmen, ladies from the Klan auxiliary and their families attended. Facially, most were of a characterless yet not displeasing cast, the kind of unremarkable, basically Anglo-Saxon countenance I imagine was found on the early pioneers going West. White satin robes gave off a creamy effulgence in the sunlight. Here and there gaudy purples and greens and maroons signified degrees of potentatehood. No one was masked, but the inverted cone headdresses stood up like a combination phallic symbol and accommodation to pinheadedness. A fat old Klansman in a green robe embroidered with a Chinese dragon held a pretty blonde girl in his arms. She was munching an ice cream cone, her face smeared with chocolate. It made a fine picture.

There were Grand Dragons from six states, and Georgia Grand Dragon Craig was keynote speaker.

"We've seen these agitators," he declared. "Now, ladies and gentlemen, I wanna quote you this as I feel it. You seen white people demonstratin' up there with these Negroes that everyone of them looked homosexual or looked like a common queer. (Cheers) They're only outcasts of their own race and I certainly do not admire the Negroes for picking them up out of the gutter. If they fall in the gutter, let 'em lay in the gutter."

His speech was meandering as most Klan speeches are, and generally mild, as most are not. Craig was careful to say "Negro," as the press listened, and at one point, while attacking the Atlanta officials, said he didn't blame city Negroes for complaining about their poor sewage facilities. He almost lost his audience with that one. The crowd stood silent and puzzled, only revived when he returned to the safe ground of communism. An unexpected element was introduced when about six white and colored SNCC workers walked into the park in a test of police protection and display of bravado. Knots of Klansmen surged toward them, but Craig ordered them back.

"We're certainly glad to know that the American people have a right to use this park," he said, "because we feel Martin Luther King and his cohorts, all connected with the Communist party directly or indirectly, have the right to use this park then we the American people should have the same right."

His followers reluctantly gave ground; the new Klan public respectability triumphed. About this time, I lost track of Ruth who was down in the crowd while I taped the speeches on the platform. The rally went its predictable course—the speeches dully repetitive and the listeners soon getting bored and drifting away. A Kludd finally closed the program by asking God to bless Klan officers. I did a piece of commentary for the camera in the emptying park; still Ruth did not appear.

Not until the park was deserted did I see her coming up the street where our car was parked. She was clearly upset, and with reason. Among the SNCC party had been a Negro girl Ruth had spoken with one night during the Leb's picketing. The girl recognized her, said hello and asked what she was doing at the rally. They exchanged a few innocuous remarks, said goodbye, and the colored girl walked off. Immediately, a half dozen Klansmen surrounded Ruth. They accused her of being a "nigger lover," asked her how many colored men she had had in her life, and pursued their interracial speculations with rich biological detail. They herded around her, and she was quiet but frightened when one of the Klan's so-called security guards came up. He suggested she leave for her own safety, and she did. The Knights' mask of respectable protector of womanhood had slipped, revealing a more lurid face.

I did not know it at the time, but standing up for God, home, and America at that rally were two other Klansmen who soon were destined to cast further light on the Klan image. Their names were Joseph Sims and William Meyers from Athens, Georgia.

New York, however, was not interested in examining the phenomenon of the new Klan and the report was not used. Two weeks later, while Alabama Governor Wallace was running in the Indiana Democratic primary, the Notasulga High School was destroyed one night by fire. The ruins of the building were still smouldering when we arrived the next day. A brick shell surrounded the ashes heaped over metal frames of what once had been school desks. Mayor Rae told me that he thought to believe both the water works *and* the school fires could be accidents was stretching coincidence. He reluctantly supposed the fires were arson. He did not tell me that a few days before the city had removed all the street lights from around the school grounds, making them obscuringly dark at night. I began the piece.

"While Alabama Governor George Wallace is instructing Indiana voters on civil rights, there are a few civil rights problems back home that merit attention."

But New York was not interested in this report, either. If Wallace were to be put in any kind of perspective as he wooed the Northern right, the history of his involvement in the Tuskegee and Notasulga school struggle, that now had taken this drastic turn, should be examined. Irresponsible hands might strike the matches, but what were supposedly responsible minds doing to prevent it? About a week later, all correspondents who were to play a part in covering the political conventions later that summer were called up to ABC, and now I had an opportunity to form opinions about some of the men who were directing the news operation. I was not reassured.

For instance, I talked one day with an executive who was in overall command of the day-to-day coverage. The World's Fair had just opened and certain Negro groups had threatened a stall-in to block traffic. The stall-in had been a sodden failure, but the networks had spent tens of thousands of dollars with camera crews and remote transmitting facilities preparing to cover it.

"What I want to know," the executive said, "is how long we are going to keep jumping every time they say 'Boo'? They're using us, goddamn it, and I resent it."

A peculiar vehemence in his words seemed to go beyond the World's Fair incident. The word "they" turned into something blackly all-inclusive. He clarified it in a few moments.

"Look, I don't have to show my credentials on civil rights. I'm a hundred percent for it. But the pendulum is swinging too far, that's all, and goddamn it, I think it's time we stood up and said, 'Whoa.' Let's look at somebody else's rights for a change."

Two nights later, a news department dinner was held for all the convention coverage people. ABC had recently hired its first Negro television reporter, a former newspaperman, Mal Goode. He was late for the dinner, and we all had been drinking deeply on the company scotch by the time he arrived. My executive bounded up from the head table when Goode came in the room and rushed to meet him in the center of the floor. He bear-hugged him, patted him on the back (he did not rub his head) and gave him the hearty "You-old-son-of-a-bitch, where-have-you-been" treatment. Goode was plainly embarrassed and, as a Negro, obviously understood the effusiveness that never would have been shown a new white staff member.

In *Othello,* Emilia says, "I will speak as liberal as the north." The modern aptness of the phrase had long been apparent to me. I too often applied the speech to myself. To consider its hypocrisy in the abstract was disturbing enough. But by now I had seen faces of its reality. On one hand, a watcher of pendulum swings, a back-slapper of the "nigger-taken-to-supper"; on the other, an old man who had never voted standing in the rain outside a Mississippi courthouse, men burning a school so that children could not use it; mothers in a church listening to the pregnancies of their unmarried daughters analyzed. The executive's approach, as well as the approach of many of the editors and producers, was that they would measure the importance of the Negro crisis in the context of their own limited intellectual and social experience which by and large had excluded Negroes. They used old personal and journalistic standards to determine how much "play" to give this news. If television were to be more than a recorder, the crisis was beyond such handling. They could not see this concept or, more accurately, they would not attempt the necessary thinking that could produce the vision. Were they prejudiced men? I think no more than most. Their basic inclinations were good; but their knowledge of reality—like the knowledge of most whites—was totally inadequate. Was I, after four months in the South, possessed of the wisdom and infallible judgment to know invariably where truth lay and to avoid the partisan tone, to strike the precise balance between both camps? No.

I returned to a South still hanging on every word of the civil rights debate in Congress and bracing for the summer of discontent. During May, I spent ten days in Panama during the presidential elections. The network provided shooting and New York lacked interest. The progression of frustration continued for me—at home or away. After a few days in Atlanta the Cuban exiles in Miami let it be known that a new "secret" move against the island was underway. By this time, the exile groups were so discredited among those who understood the realities of Castro's Cuba, that to dignify the exiles with coverage compounded their own self-delusions of significance and further confused an American public long misled by Washington on the possibilities of Castro's overthrow. The new move turned out to be another abortive nothing. Some exile press agent in Miami got the idea of using an IBM computer to decide which of the many splinter groups might gain a popular mandate to unify them all. An ultimate absurdity, I did not cover it. The proposal appealed to one of our producers, and he was displeased that we did not have it. An IBM machine tabulating Cuban exiles meant something; an American high school burned because Negroes attended it did not.

Before leaving Miami, I called the Atlanta office of SCLC to see if anything was stirring. An aide of Dr. King advised me to head for Saint Augustine immediately; a major effort was getting underway. I headed there on May 27, thinking it had damn well better be major or the trip was a waste of time. All I knew about Saint Augustine was from a childhood trip. I remembered that it had an old jail and the water tasted of sulfur.

Spring

SCHIZOPHRENIA
BY THE SEA

I. Moment of Truth in America's Oldest City

The moon-washed moment on the street corner of America's oldest city had been coming for more than three centuries. On the dark Cordova Street sidewalk leading back from the center of Saint Augustine to "Niggertown," a line of nearly two hundred Negroes stood silently. Around the corner, out of their sight, lines of white youths and men had formed a corridor down King Street leading to the bayfront and the Old Slave Market. The whites carried sticks, pipes, chains, and axe handles. Some men seated in cars parked along King Street had shotguns cradled in their laps. The whites were quiet, too.

The Negroes intended to march to the Old Slave Market and to hold a prayer meeting beginning a series of demonstrations against racial discrimination. On the corner, police officials in white riot helmets talked in low voices to the Negro leaders. The words were vivid in the silence that seemed to insulate the corner of King and Cordova from the rest of the world, to insure that on this warm nighttime stage this drama would be played out with no interruptions.

"You're gettin' ready to get a bunch of your people hurt an' hurt bad," said Police Chief Virgil Stuart.

The Reverend Andrew Young, an assistant to Dr. King, replied: "We've been hurt for three hundred years."

"No," said the chief. "No. You ain't been hurt like this."

Three hundred years. And now in minutes, a decision had to be made. . . .

Inside the red-brick Baptist Church it is stifling.

Black hands, in a practiced, Southern way, flutter cardboard fans bearing advertisements for a colored mortician—a rapid, genteel fluttering before sweating and smiling and singing faces. Television lights burn with insane heat on Dr. King, the catalyst for the Saint Augustine movement, who has told the congregation:

"You are proving to be the creative spiritual anvils that will wear out many a physical hammer."

The phrase is a favorite of Dr. King. Already he has spoken it to congregations in Georgia and Alabama who have looked to him for the word. But here in Saint Augustine it is new, and the people savor it as *their* word. The local leader, a tall, serious young dentist named Robert Hayling (youngsters in the church carry signs reading: "Let Freedom Ring with Dr. Hay-ling") sits next to him, listening to the last speaker, the Reverend C. T. Vivian from King's Southern Christian Leadership Conference . . .

"When I saw the cover of *Time* magazine, I knew that we'd come a long way. I realized how far we had come. That out of us, out of a people that had been degraded and placed on the second level . . . out of us, a people that had been given a second-rate education . . . out of us, came the man of the year. We've got the man. And we've got something more than that, we've got the message. We've got the message, really. We've got a better message than anyone's got. The bigots and the segregationists don't have a chance. And do you know why they bomb the churches? And do you know why they beat you? Because they don't have a message. We've got the message . . ."

The preacher is tall and slender; his voice mellifluous, compelling, and somehow cool in that steaming, sweating church.

". . . whether you're going to surrender or whether you're going to stand up in dignity. Whether you're going to march on with a sense of strength and fortitude. Whether you're going to hold your head high and show the world the raw power of righteousness. We've got something to march about tonight. How many are ready tonight?"

A cheer. It seems all are ready. Young and old file out to the street, singing, "Which side are you on, boy, which side are you on." Outside, there is an excited, picnic spirit among the young, who have been preparing for this night in classes conducted by the SCLC. The faces of the older people are not so certain as they line up with their children, a hump-backed granny with frizzled gray hair and an old man in overalls who keeps putting on a smile, but there seems to be confusion in his eyes, which have seen Saint Augustine for seventy years but have never seen anything like this. Rev. Young takes a megaphone and says:

"I don't care what happens, we want you all to remain nonviolent. (Got you, calls a voice from the line.) Now, I don't know how often you pray but I want you to pray tonight. (I prayed tonight, honey, a woman tells him.) Now we believe that we shall overcome. But we won't overcome by trying to be as mean and hateful as our enemies. If we overcome, it will be overcoming through love. If anybody curses you, you walk straight ahead and say a prayer for them. If anybody says any kind of mean word to you, I want you to pray for them. If anybody should throw anything at you, I don't even want you to look evil at them. Okay?"

A few young people who have not gone to training classes and committed themselves to nonviolence are spotted and picked out of the line. They try to save face, swagger over to join street corner hangers-on who indicate by smirks that all this is stupid, beneath them. The line, with a vanguard of newsmen, moved out through "Niggertown." On porches of small frame houses, dark faces look out through darkness but say nothing. The line grows quieter as it reaches the beginning of white territory on Cordova Street. The line passes front yards grown with palm and magnolia. A tropical smell, vegetal, both sweet and bitter, is heavy on the air. Not a word is spoken in the long line. From King Street the bark of a police dog chops the silence. Feet shuffle methodically forward. Not a word . . .

About forty whites, mostly young, were bunched inside the Old Slave Market. Lights had been extinguished but the axe handles curved whitely in the moonlight. By day, the Slave Market is one of the points of interest for tourists to photograph in a Southern town that dates back four hundred years. Clip-clopping buggies driven mostly by quaint old Uncle Remus Negroes take visitors to the oldest schoolhouse in the United States, the oldest home, what passes for Ponce de Leon's Fountain of Youth, and Robert Ripley's "Believe It or Not" Museum, which is not very old but which has great appeal for the kind of family tourist who comes to Saint Augustine. The Slave Market, in fact, might make an exhibit for the museum. Once Negroes could not walk freely from it; in 1964 they could not walk freely into it. Local custom reserved the market for old white men who played checkers.

Now the tourists were all tucked in their beds, sunburns oiled, cameras dormant, and at the Slave Market a boy about twenty years old with long black sideburns and head already balding, said: "Just let them sorry niggers come."

"Wouldn't you love to see Martin Luther Coon come down that street?" said another. He spat. "Put 'em to the sword."

Standing in front of the Market was a pot-bellied forty-five-year-old man named Holstead Manucy, dressed in a black T-shirt and a battered black cowboy hat, his trademark. Friends, including Chief Stuart and St. Johns County Sheriff L. O. Davis, called Manucy by his nickname, Hoss. Hoss, powerful for all his fat, was absolute authority to hundreds of local men who belonged to the Ancient City Hunting Club, which in some minds was considered synonymous with the Ku Klux Klan. In any event, he was a special deputy and extra-special judge on what would or would not be done·on the Saint Augustine streets.

"We're better organized than the niggers," he said. "That's 'cause us white people have to stick together. We're not tied to the Klan. Not that I'm knocking it. The Klan is a wonderful organization."

Privately, the better white people of Saint Augustine would disavow Manucy and his followers, who ran heavily to fanatical and semi-literate men dedicated to white supremacy, and in whose narrow-chested bodies and pinched faces could be read an old Southern story of the economic deprivation suffered by poor whites that sapped soul along with substance. No one would speak out publicly for two reasons. First, Manucy and his types coerced businessmen through fear. In March, when the first wave of demonstrations brought arrests to hundreds, including the mother of Massachusetts Governor Endicott Peabody, one leading restaurant owner desegregated for one day. The next night his windows were smashed and his life threatened, and he resegregated.

St. Augustine segregationists were proud of their Easter victory when arrests of demonstrators seemingly broke the protest's back, and intended that it would endure. Behind his desk Sheriff Davis displayed a sign:

St. Johns County famous jail.
Mrs. Peabody of the Boston Peabodys
stayed here two nights
Reasonable fines . . . $35 and up.

The second reason was more insidious. For generations, "better" white people bent on maintaining segregation had used trash to run interference for them. They themselves remained aloof from violence against Negroes, but their silence was a clear stamp of approval. This theory held in Saint Augustine. Negroes had been the targets of shootings, beatings, house burnings, and leading citizens said nothing. Men like Mayor Joseph Shelley, a doctor, only bemoaned the public dissatisfaction of the colored at a time when the city was preparing an international quadricentennial celebration.

"We've been made a target," he said, "simply because we are the oldest city. They know they'll get publicity." As the worst racial crisis in Saint Augustine's history approached, Mayor Shelley went on vacation.

After inspecting America's historic antecedents in Saint Augustine in Mayor Shelley's city, a Negro tourist could eat in *one* colored luncheonette or sleep in *one* colored boarding house. A chain-owned motel on the highway sometimes supplied lodging with advance reservations. One Negro policeman was on the force. His beat was "Niggertown" and "Niggertown" only. Five Negro youngsters sat in desegregated classes. The home belonging to the parents of two of them had been burned to the ground, the car of another family destroyed. Now, after the Easter attempt and with the Civil Rights Bill approaching law in Washington, outsiders like Dr. King were again organizing the local Negroes to protest. The whites had gathered under the moon to make certain things clear. Many of these same men had also gathered at a Klan meeting outside of town the previous September, when the Negroes first began stirring . . .

The burned cross, sticky with creosote, is cold. But the speaker, a minister, is warm, and the robed Klansmen and their ladies are bright-eyed with admiration while tourist cars sweep past on U. S. Route 1 a mile away, unaware of this local color.

". . . the Klan is on the move again, and it is not going to let the niggers and Jews take over the country." (Whoops and cheers)

The women are very enthusiastic. They are mostly scrawny and dried out, worked out, worn out by childbearing. Their dresses are overlong. Their breasts are flaccid and their elbows sharp. The speaker tells how the FBI had been questioning him.

"Then they said to me, 'Do you know who bombed the church in Birmingham?' And I said, 'No, and if I did I wouldn't tell you.' But I'll tell you people here tonight, if they can find these fellows, they ought to pin medals on them. Someone said, 'Ain't it a shame that them little children was killed.' Well, they don't know what they are talking about. In the first place, they ain't little. They're fourteen or fifteen—old enough to have venereal diseases, and I'll be surprised if all of 'em didn't have one or more. In the second place, they weren't children. Children are little people, little human beings, and that means white people. There's little dogs and cats and apes and baboons and skunks and there's also little niggers. But they ain't children . . . and if there's four less niggers tonight, then I say, 'Good for whoever planted the bomb. We're all better off." He finishes and the cheers are frenzied. The words excite and comfort, because the threat is here and now, the local "niggers" picketing, trying to move out of their place. Another speaker begins but hc is not so thrilling and the night's excitement starts to trail off until suddenly, unbelievably, the cry "Niggers" goes up. Men swarm into the bushes and march back four Negroes at gunpoint. Among them is Dr. Hayling. Dr. Hayling has lived in Saint Augustine for three years with his wife and two children. He has been county jail dentist and fifty percent of his private practice has been white. He is the first Negro accepted into the state dental society without reservations. When he became local NAACP president, customers dropped off and his home was fired into, his dog killed. Whites say he is arrogant and city manager Charles Barrier calls him an atheist. "I don't blame God for a lot of things that man does," Dr. Hayling has said, "and I don't look to God to solve all of man's problems. But I have become extremely disillusioned with religion as it's practiced in America." Tonight he has bravely or foolishly tried to reconnoiter the meeting from the highway. Klansmen chased his car down a side road until he and three men with him were caught. Those at the meeting surge forward, and he recognizes in the crowd a patient, another man whom he considered a good friend, and the city's official photographer. The beating begins. The men are pistolwhipped, punched to the ground, and kicked. A woman cries, "Kill 'em! Castrate the bastards." A white minister, observing the meeting for the Florida Council of Human Relations, hurries off to call the sheriff . . .

Whites waited at the Slave Market and on King Street, Negroes on Cordova. Both groups were aware of what the Klan had done months before, now both wondered what was next. Word has spread back along the line of Negroes that toughs and Klansmen were waiting for them. No one moved. Seemingly no one even spoke once word was passed. On the corner, the police dogs betrayed the constant anxiety their training for violence had worked into their nerves. They panted, fat tongues lolling out, and their eyes glittered, sweeping back and forth, unable to hold anyone in focus unless commanded. Rev. Young, a slender, light-skinned Negro in his early thirties, saw what was down King Street and understood its potential. Married and the father of two children, he had helped to lead the children of others into the night's march, and he knew how some whites looked on Negro children, on the Birmingham children . . .

"Don't come any further," Chief Stuart told him, "unless you prepared to get in serious trouble." A flashbulb popped. "Don't turn that camera on me," he warned. "I don't want my picture taken. You take my picture, you'll go to jail." The chief had a reputation for a bad temper, also the reputation for being a good police chief when faced with anything other than racial disturbances where his private passions came into play. His voice tight with anger at this unaccustomed role of counselor, not authority, to Negroes. He said to Rev. Young: "It's my strong advice to go on back."

"We kind of feel," said Young, "that the only way we'll ever really have any respect or . . ."

"Now—now listen. I'm not gonna argue with you at all. My advice is for you to go back. If you don't, my firm conviction is that some of you are goin' to get hurt and some other people are goin' to get hurt. It's my job to protect this city. Now you've gone just as far as you'd better go. We can't protect you any further."

Chief Stuart had a force of only eighteen men. Four or five were in evidence and they were soon to disappear from the scene. Technically, he was correct in saying that his small force, even if it cared to try, was inadequate to prevent violence. Practically, the Negro leaders felt this was another form of legal intimidation, part of a Southern pattern which ran: Don't call out county or state reinforcements when threatened by mob action; fall back on the excuse that Negroes will be hurt if they protest; frighten them into inaction. So the corner of King and Cordova Streets was literally and figuratively a crossroad for Saint Augustine Negroes. Rev. Young had to decide whether to lead his column back, back into "Niggertown" and further, or lead it between those twin white lines.

"The trouble with this town is," says the white restaurant owner who comes from the Mediterranean and has some English problems and some alien outlooks, "is that everybody is afraid. They afraid. No guts. Nobody is gonna say nothin' about this integratin' because they afraid some of these bums will crash in their windows or shoot their house. You can't call the police. They think like the KK's. So are they gonna help you? What, are you kiddin' me? An' this—what do you call 'em—this power structure, you know, the rich men, the bankers with the mortgages for every goddamn business in town. Don't you think they could do something if they wanted? Go on, sure they could. They pass out the word and fftt—it's law. Better than Washington. But no, they take the nigger's dollar all week, they go to church on Sunday, an' they don't say nothin'. Why should they? They don't wanna change, they like the old way. An' they got theirs. A business goes fftt an' they foreclose the mortgage. So the town is goin' to hell, the tourists are afraid to come. You ask a restaurant, a hotel man to tell you the truth an' he'll tell you it's off thirty, forty percent. But these big power boys don't care. Listen, back at Easter we had the chance. Listen, I'm be frank with you. I don't serve niggers here since I been in business, twelve years. That's the way it is so I do it. But I know it's wrong. Sure it's wrong. Jesus Christ, why shouldn't they eat? All right, but I'm not gonna start somethin' an' get my business blown up. No, sir. But back at Easter when we had the troubles an' the governor's mother she got arrested. Then we could've done it. Bang. Fftt. Open the doors an' it's all over. The niggers—okay, the Negroes—they come, they eat, everybody gets used to it. But the people what run this town, this mayor, what do they do? They run an' hide. They think it will go away. One man tries to desegregate an' these bums almost put him out of business. So now you see them take over the streets an' you watch, somebody will get killed yet. An' these, you know, good class people, the power structures, they say: We don't like it one bit but you got to control the niggers. They say they're afraid of the niggers. You know, they not afraid of the niggers. They afraid of their conscience."

Hurt for three hundred years but not yet hurt like Chief Stuart says they are going to be, the Negroes marched back from the corner across Cordova Street to a parking lot and formed a wide circle. Some of them could see the whites who waited down King Street. The town gave up its dark silence to the Florida sky and the sky returned an infinite silence. Rev. Young stood in the middle of the circle and addressed his people in a firm voice, very calm.

"Tonight is the night we decide if you want to be free. For three hundred years we've been kept in slavery through fear. If you can keep a man afraid, you can keep him from being a man. Because a man who's afraid never stands up for any of those things which God has ordained for him. Now from the time of slavery until the present, whenever Negroes have tried to get their freedom, there have been some people . . . sometimes in sheets, sometimes even in police uniforms . . . who have tried to keep us from getting our freedom. And they've done this by putting fear into our hearts. The chief of police has advised us not to march down in the block of the Slave Market. He said he's not sure he'll be able to protect us. Well, I think we've been living this way for some time now. And I think this is really one of the first times I've *ever* been in a situation where a Deep South police chief was even concerned about protecting me."

Light laughter. Nods of agreement. Cameramen are taking crowd reaction. A small Negro boy and his sister smile hugely—not a worry in the world.

"And so frankly I've lived all my life depending on God to protect me.

Now we're not asking anyone to go on and risk danger. There may be some, there may not be. I've been in situations that looked dangerous before and somehow we've come through. There may be some physical hurt. But I know if I get a broken arm it will be healed in six weeks. I know if there's a cut or a bruise in a few weeks' time that will go away. But the scars that are placed on the minds and hearts of Negro people throughout the Southland for having to live under fear and intimidation for all their lives will never heal.

"And so tonight we have to decide whether to stand back and give in to fear, or whether we really mean the words that we sing, 'Before I'd be a slave I'd be buried in my grave, and go home to my Lord and be free.'"

A murmur of approval came for the young preacher who did not once falter for a word or raise his voice. The level calmness gave re-assurance; something stronger than the borning visions of disaster began to take hold.

"Now I'd like to ask the camermen if they would stop for just a minute, if they would give us time to think and pray a minute. I think this is a decision that every man has to make in his own heart. Nobody can make it for him. And so I want you to think how many of us will go on and keep the movement alive, and assure ourselves of an oppor-tunity to gain our freedom. For if we stop now we can give it up, per-haps forever, in Saint Augustine. I'd like to ask again that we all bow our heads for a minute, if each person could pray silently in his heart to see if you are ready to go on. Let us pray."

Superimposed on the still night came the unearthly silence of prayer. Unheard, the prayer seemed to hang palpable in the air, loft up past the graceful reach of the palm trunks into the sky. A pressure built in an observer's chest, a suffocation of emotion wanting some word, some sound to give outlet. And at last Rev. Young began speaking again:

"Thou who hast called us to be Thy sons and Thy daughters, we come before Thee like empty pitchers before full fountains, confessing our fears, confessing our doubts and yet knowing, dear God, that Thou has ordained us to be Thy sons. We ask you this evening for courage. We ask you for strength, we ask you for wisdom. We ask you, dear Father, if you would not only melt our hearts and mold them in Thine image and give us the strength of the prophets of old . . . and give us the strength and the courage of children and adults of all ages who have stood their ground in order that man might be free . . . but we would also pray, dear Father, for those who would stand between us and our freedom. For we know they are not to blame. We know they are only saying and repeating those things they have heard for generations . . . and we have silently adhered to . . ."

Then, he led them in the Lord's Prayer and when it was concluded the assembled voices, ragged at the start but strengthening at the end, "For Thine is the kingdom, and the power, and the glory forever. Amen." The circle closed tight, hands and arms linked, fathers pressing children to them. They sang a moving and beautiful hymn, in sweet and sweeping rhythms, "God will take care of you, In every way, All through the day . . . (Yes, He will, a woman sobbed. God will, oh yes.) God will take care of you, God will take care, take care of you."

The circle slowly broke. A man in his forties, face wet, wrung his hands and kept repeating:

"These beautiful people, oh, all these beautiful people."

Boys in their teens who served as marshals to keep the line in order grouped briefly, joining hands in a mound like a football team before it goes onto the field. No weeping, their voices were young and clear.

"We're gonna show these white folks that it's all over now."

"It's all over."

"Man, it's *all* over."

The decision had been made without being articulated. A handful, very young, very old, dropped out. Rev. Young said:

"May we march . . . line up again."

Without another word, the march began. No policeman was in sight—not one policeman. A long description could be written of the progress of that march. How a churchbell slowly tolled eleven just as Rev. Young in the lead began passing the first whites . . . how a crowbar was dropped to clang a warning . . . how every ear tensed for the first shot or rebel yell. The black column advanced in silence, two by two, holding hands and looking straight ahead, passing so close to whites the two skins were almost touching. The marchers wound past the Slave Market, past Hoss Manucy, like some surrealistic dream, up the other side of the Square, back to King Street, onto Cordova and then toward the safety of "Niggertown." The word "nigger" had been hissed a few times, not often, and that was all. The white faces had watched, set in contempt and threat, and that was all. As the Negroes returned to the church singing: "I love everybody, I love everybody, I love everybody in my heart, There's no doubt about it, I can't live without it, I love everybody in my heart." Other nights soon would come with stonings and beatings. Marchers, including Rev. Young, were kicked and cursed;

cries of hate and terror filled the Square. Later, remembering it, Rev. Young said:

"I think there were two reasons we made it. One, the whites were awestruck by the quiet and the prayer and the dignity of the process. And the other is quite cynical, that the whites were operating under orders from the local police, that it served their purpose there would be nothing that night. And I don't know which was which. I would imagine both might be true."

A girl in the line had her own explanation for the blow that never fell. "Only God stopped it," she said.

And the Movement went on.

II. The Town That Lied to Itself

Cameramen were a prime target of white mobs that began harassing demonstrations the night following Rev. Young's march. Over the next weeks, heads were bloodied and cameras smashed. Once the sun went down, law and order sank with it. The crew and I dreamed up a hypothetical situation that was very funny to us at the time. A tourist who has not been keeping up with the world around him (that is, a typical tourist) rolls into Saint Augustine with his family at dusk, oblivious of the racial tension in the air. They drive along the Matanzas bayfront, exclaiming over Nature's twilight palette on the waters, breathing in the salt breeze gently nudging the tranquil palms, and perhaps delighting over the slow motion homeward plod of the colored cabman and his faithful horse. In front of the Slave Market, they see a statue of someone pointing and to the father that spells a probable historical lesson for his children. He cannot wait to record it, for light is falling fast. He jumps out with his movie camera, hurriedly reads his light meter, lifts the camera to his eye—and is promptly hit over the head by a segregationist.

No one who was in Saint Augustine during those days would say positively that such an incident could not happen. We must be lenient with the tourist for not realizing that something was wrong in the city. After all, American tourists—mostly from the North—thinking everything was all right, had been coming there for fifty years. They had sat at quaint restaurants built on sun-bleached piers over the bay and decorated with fishnets and conch shells. They dropped bread crumbs to fat mullets bumming in the clear water below, and never wondered at the absence above water of certain other diners. They had swum from beaches of sand so white it looked fresh-mined from pure ocean depths, and had not noticed someone missing from the water. They had, in short, accepted without question the fact that American Negroes were for some reason not present in America's oldest living city.

If tourists from all over the country did not notice that something was wrong, then who could blame the white people who ran the city for insisting that all was well and that anyone who said otherwise was an agitator bent on creating chaos? A non-touring reporter might observe some seeming contradictions in Saint Augustine. For instance, a quadricentennial chock full of pageants, floats, and fireworks was being planned for 1965, yet no Negro had been invited to participate. The whites said they got along perfectly well with the Negroes, but this did smack of racial exclusion. I asked Florida State Senator Vergil Pope about the exclusion. He represented the Thirty-first District which included Duval County, and in 1961 had been chosen by fellow Florida legislators as "the most valuable man in the legislature."

"Let me ask you a question," intoned Pope, a handsome, white-haired man who sounded and acted like Senator Everett Dirksen with a drawl. "When did the Spaniards arrive here?"

I subtracted four hundred from 1965 and came up with 1565.

"All right," he said. "And when did the first Negroes come to America?"

I was proud to remember from history that it was in 1619.

"Well," he said, smiling at the clarity of it all, "it would be rather incongruous, wouldn't it, to have Negroes playing a role when they weren't even here yet? You can't pervert history for the sake of social change."

I wondered if you could pervert social change for the sake of history. The city manager of Saint Augustine was Charles Barrier, a young man slightly pudgy in his seersucker suit, who also replied to questions with questions. Of course, I said, there are deep-rooted white customs here. But did he think it was right that in 1964 a Negro resident or a Negro tourist should be turned away from a restaurant in such a prominent city?

"Well, let's say you were back in Atlanta," he began. "And you walked into a nice restaurant, like the Dinkler Plaza, without a tie and coat on, and the manager asked you to leave. Wouldn't he be within his rights? It's the same exact thing."

In his sixth floor office (highest in town) atop his Exchange National Bank, septuagenarian H. E. Wolfe looked old and weary, a subtle pallor in his suntanned face and a tremor in his fingers. He had dominated the city's finances for three decades, amassing millions, making people happy by lending them money and sad by foreclosing on mortgages when they could not pay back. A cartoon in his outer office showed a formidable-looking chairman of the board saying to its members: "Those opposed? But that's silly, isn't it?" Wolfe denied exerting any control over the city's racial policies despite his powerful position, and he could not understand why Negroes complained because not a single colored clerk, bank teller, or secretary was employed in the city.

"I honestly believe Negroes are being accepted and employed to do any job they are qualified to do," he said. "And I don't think it helps any to talk about the matter of equality. Take John D. Rockefeller, for example. If you were to say I wasn't equal with him, well, I would know that I'm not. But saying it wouldn't help our relationship any. Patience. If there's one word in life I love, it's patience."

That was the word Negroes could no longer abide. Dr. King and his high command had calculatedly chosen Saint Augustine as the sunny catalyst to make sure a Civil Rights Bill with hair on its chest was passed. If Southern whites were peddlers of image, Negro leaders were salesmen of symbol. And the tourist city was a made-to-order symbol of segregation on a nationwide scale with the bonus of international implications. What better example to place before Congress of the need to apply interstate commerce controls to insure open access to motels and restaurants than the oldest city in America where a Negro couldn't buy a meal? And here was Saint Augustine promoting a quadricentennial with the theme "Bridge to the Americas" when it would be worth the life of any dark-skinned Latin visitor to dip a toe into a motel swimming pool.

A grand jury summoned during the demonstrations handed up a presentment that contained the sentence:

"The local racial problem confronting the city of Saint Augustine is no greater a problem than that of many other communities throughout the entire nation."

This contention was true. For that reason the grand jury and the vast majority of white residents felt that Saint Augustine should not be singled out for special attention. They seemed to assume that prominence should give immunity, when a logical mind—segregationist or otherwise—should have seen that the opposite would be the case. A militant movement of limited resources like SCLC naturally seeks the most likely target, is frankly opportunistic, sometimes dissembles, and does not care particularly if innocents get hurt in the process. Only white liberals in advanced stages of racial guilt ascribe all saintly scruples to Negroes. Why expand energies bringing Boll Weevil Junction to the national consciousness when storied Saint Augustine is already there, needing only a demonstration or two to change its Fountain of Youth into a wellspring of bigotry? Saint Augustine never understood this reasoning, never addressed itself to what was right or wrong within its confines. The city retreated from reality into self-delusion, especially as the reality grew uglier, and its civic personality split in half—charm by sunlight, terror under the moon. The "good people" would not dirty their hands on a problem that threatened the life of the city. They abdicated responsibility to the rednecks (called "jarheads" in the local parlance) and then blamed the ensuing violence on outside agitators. The mayor went off to play golf, the priests and ministers preached of God and ignored moral breakdown on their doorsteps, and the businessmen floundered between their desire to make a buck at any price and their fear of jarhead retaliation if they tried to exert leadership. The result was unbelievable.

The night after Rev. Young's march another was scheduled. During the day, fifteen whites and Negroes had been arrested trying to sit in at segregated restaurants. Young said that overtures toward beginning talks aimed at settlement had been made to the mayor. But Mayor Shelley, according to SCLC, said that this was a matter for the businessmen of the city and any intervention by city hall would not be in the American tradition of free enterprise. That night the march was cast to the same pattern—the long black column advancing through grim silence until police, a few state troopers now on the scene, and dozens of deputized civilians spotted it and started the dogs howling; the whites waiting around the square; the long, nerve-shredding walk around that square with the deputies looking more threatening than the jarheads. The mob was noisy, yelling insults, spitting on the marchers but concentrating on the press rather than on the Negroes. My cameraman now was Marty Schmidhofer, a rubberfaced former vaudevillian. We had hired a husky skindiver from Jacksonville, named Terry Phillips, to carry his lights and look out for him in general. The tempo of the mob's agitation increased as we neared the entrance to Cordova Street again, the last leg to the safety of "Niggertown."

Then rebel yells broke, punches sailed, a shot was fired, and cameras began being smashed with crystalline shatter and glassy tinkle in the dark. The Negroes ran and made it safely around the corner while police and deputies stood by, watching or participating. A policeman jumped on SCLC's Harry Boyte. Boyte had been taking pictures, and the cop put a stranglehold around his neck and threw him to the ground. Young whites closed in, kicking, their faces gleeful. In the ensuing melee, I had a tape recorder torn off my back and Marty, unable to get the police to protect him, ran around the corner into a walled parking lot. Skindiver Phillips reported later that he was engaged in a losing tug-of-war for my recorder while Marty was running for safety. Nevertheless, this muscle-flexing young Floridian adept at karate proved to have a strange inability to deter other young Floridians who descended on us. The pay was good, but I don't think his heart was in it.

Marty meanwhile was crawling on hands and knees to a dark corner and probably wishing he had never left vaudeville. He hid his equipment, worth a thousand dollars, behind an oil storage tank and then ran back to our car. The mob finally dispersed. NBC cameraman Irving Gans, the back of his head opened by a tire chain, was sent to the hospital. When things calmed down, Marty, Phillips, and I went over the parking lot foot by foot with a flashlight, but the equipment was gone. During the night, Marty called everyone from the police chief and sheriff on down trying to get the camera back, but no one supposedly knew anything.

Next morning we learned that after the attack, Boyte and his nineteen-year-old son had been getting from their car at a motel when someone fired a shotgun blast through the rear window. The window was blown out and the windshield broken by pellets. Gunmen were busy away from the central area, too. Dr. King had been using a beach house loaned to him by a white New Jersey doctor and his wife. During the night, the now-empty house was riddled by rifle and shotgun fire. We drove out to film it and while we were there Boyte arrived to inspect the damage—broken windows, splintered walls. He called the sheriff's office and gave a matter-of-fact description of what had happened.

"Was anybody hurt?" the man asked.

"No," replied Boyte. "A light was left on so it looked occupied. But fortunately the people had left during the day."

"Then what are you getting excited about?" said the deputy, and hung up.

Unbelievable.

That day the Saint Augustine City Council banned night demonstrations. While SCLC was appealing this in federal court, a lull lasted nearly a week. During that time, Sheriff L. O. Davis, a bald, pot-bellied former football coach with smiling eyes and genial air, was amusing himself. The sit-in demonstrators in his county jail—white and Negro, men and women—were kept outside all day in an uncovered exercise pen under a molten June sun that hit ninety by 10 A.M. and went up from there. A hole dug in the ground was the common toilet.

"They were doing a lot of singing at night, you know," said the sheriff who had a picture of himself dressed as Santa Claus on his office wall. "This way it's more healthy for them to be out in the air all day, getting exercise. Makes 'em sleep better at night."

Although the ABC news producer was lukewarm on the story—an account of the Boyte shooting and the attack on the house was used only after a stiff argument—executives had been busy protesting to officials about the loss of equipment and danger to personnel. On Wednesday, a week after it disappeared, Marty got his camera back intact— save for the film and its record of violence. A story about its return appeared in the *Saint Augustine Record* which had editorially blamed newsmen for sparking violence by their presence.

"Both the city and county law enforcement officials," said the editorial, "have done an excellent job in prohibiting serious violent actions during the latest period of unrest . . ."

In its story on the camera, it reported: "Lieutenant E. J. Irwin said that the police department received a tip that a Negro had hidden something behind the Cordova building Thursday night. A police dog trained by Patrolman George Thorton found the camera, the police said."

Interesting reading. Marty, crew cut and pale with fright that night, looked as much like a Negro as Hoss Manucy. And the "trained" police dog—we speculated if it were trained especially to find 16-mm cameras. Was there such demand for that sort of sleuthing in Saint Augustine? Or did the force permit itself the luxury of having canine specialists on hand for any contingency? Of course it was all a sham. Police found the whites who had stolen it and designed their story of recovery to preclude any prosecution. I later learned that my recorder, battered to junk by a steel pipe, had been thrown into the bay.

Unbelievable.

A silver-haired and courtly federal judge, an Old South man named Bryan Simpson, revealed another dimension of truth about the city of Ponce de Leon and the picturesque buggies that went clip-clop. The white mobs that kept assembling in the city had a degree of cohesion. Many were members of the Ancient City Hunting Club, headed by Manucy, and, in the minds of the best local observers, either part of the north Florida Klan or close cousin to it. On at least one occasion, I saw Manucy give an order to the mob not to attack passing Negroes and the order was obeyed. His followers drove around the city in cars equipped with Citizens Band radios, oversized antennas whipping; that guns rode with them was common knowledge. We were staying at the Monson Motor Lodge, which was to figure prominently in the Saint Augustine story. Every day a tall, thin old man with wild eyes and dirty tongue used to walk along the seawall, a long fishing pole in hand, muttering condemnations of Negroes and reporters. He never fished so we dubbed him the Klan's walking antenna. His fish pole as he spied on us, really keeping him in contact with the jarhead network. Our hearts were young and gay.

That Manucy, who had played football under Sheriff Davis in high school, was not only the sheriff's friend but also a deputy was not laughable. Knowing that scores of the other deputies came from Manucy's hunting club and that none of them could be depended on to give protection to a demonstrator or to a reporter in that city was not laughable.

The Jacksonville courtroom, mellow with sun strained by window shades and filled with the inhibiting gravity men build into churches and courtrooms, was so remote from Saint Augustine and its mad square that it was hard to believe the past nights had happened. Judge Simpson asked Sheriff Davis how many deputies he had. The sheriff said thirty-five or forty. The judge then had him read off an official list of his deputies. The list had 169 names.

"It might be simpler," observed Judge Simpson, "for me to get a list of people who are not deputies."

The judge interposed again when Manucy's name was read, pointing out that he received a felony conviction in that very courtroom.

"But he's good enough to be a deputy?"

"He never was a deputy sheriff," replied Davis.

"The card you issued says he's one," snapped the judge, and the sheriff looked aggrieved.

Davis explained that he began deputizing men after the Easter demonstrations. He followed a simple procedure.

"When anybody came in and asked for a badge, did you issue it to them?" Simpson asked.

"Yes, sir," Davis replied.

Men walked around with deputy cards that were licenses to use guns. Many of these men, to a moral certainty, were members of the KKK.

"Are you a Klansman?" the judge asked the sheriff.

"No, sir," the sheriff replied, and Judge Simpson took him at his word. He had heard enough from Davis and other witnesses, some of whom had told of guns and ammunition being taken from members of the mob only to be given back the next day. He ordered the "cruel and unusual" punishment of the exercise pen halted. He lifted the city's ban on nighttime demonstrations. The white reaction against the ruling extended even to many correspondents. They criticized that it was inviting violence in order to please King. They did not see the basic issue: In the civilized American state of Florida mob violence or the threat of it could not be permitted to intimidate constitutional guarantees of free assembly. This contention seemed like a lofty and impractical notion to many, judged against the reality of threat. But a constitutional democracy lives or dies in relation to how well such guarantees are made a part of the life of its people. Saint Augustine had not been taken unawares. At Easter, two months before, Negroes served notice that they wanted the system of segregation ended. A few wise white heads had counseled that some agreement should be reached in the name of good public image if not morality. The respectable citizens would not listen. They would not confer the equality of discussion on Negroes. They hoped the matter would all somehow go away. When the jarheads came in during those chaotic days that followed Judge Simpson's decision, the respectable citizens took no stand against them. This inaction is why Manucy and his followers, detestable though they were, did not merit the role of arch villains that we of the press bestowed on them. They were so easy to hate and to despise—Manucy with his gross body, his slit eyes with their wealth of shrewd suspicion and poverty of understanding, his dull mouthings about "niggers" and "Martin Luther Coon." The truth is that Manucy was a cipher raised to the value of substance by his social and intellectual betters. The people of Saint Augustine, who wouldn't let a Hoss Manucy in their front door, allowed him to run their city.

What followed was unbelievable to me.

The Negroes marched again as soon as the Simpson ruling came down. Young led it, and I watched him get knocked down on three street corners around the square, punched, blackjacked, and kicked. In each case, policemen intervened only after the whites had vented their wrath. Half-a-dozen demonstrators were beaten that night and carried to segregated Flagler Hospital for treatment. The march was eerie to watch, to stand in the night in this famous city and see people you respected walk down a sidewalk and to know that it was a matter of minutes before someone would knock them down, and to know that the police would not prevent it, and you could do nothing.

Young later told a churchful of Negroes:

"I for one last night witnessed the power of nonviolence in one of the hardest hearts this city has to offer. For as we crossed the street the first time, I saw a young feller who hauled off and hit me. What happened when I got down on the ground I don't know, but he was one of those over me kicking me. I got up and we went down to the next corner and there he was again. There was a policeman standing right between him and a friend of his, but he hauled off and hit me in my stomach and when I bent over he attempted to kick me. We stopped and we didn't fall, even though Reverend Taylor and I were hit by a fellow with a blackjack. You continued to follow us and we walked together down the side of the park. And there at the foot of the park was the same guy waiting for us again. And we walked up to him and we didn't break stride and we looked at him and continued to smile, and I was waiting to get hit again. And he just barely kind of pushed me aside a little bit. And we turned around and passed it back, don't touch him. And I know something happened in the heart of this young fellow. Now he was a fellow not any bigger than me, the kind that before I heard of Martin Luther King I would've enjoyed eatin' up and spittin' out the pieces. And yet, that wouldn't have done any good because I would've only made an eternal enemy. Yet tonight I'm sure in the heart of this young man some of the spiritual turmoil is taking place right now, not only for him but for the whole city of Saint Augustine."

He may have been right about the young man, but he lost count of the knockdowns and his Christian estimate of Saint Augustine was dead wrong. My crew and I now were part of the rhythm of the city. By day when nothing was happening we swam in the Monson pool, swilled beer, let the sun drill into our brains the golden fiction that life was rational and beautiful. A Confederate flag on the motel staff and owner James Brock, a self-made little man with balding head and rimless glasses, trying to hold onto his nerve as sit-inners made periodic calls and the tourist business went to hell and his sensible inclination to desegregate was cancelled out by fear of the jarheads whom he and his fellow businessmen had allowed to take over the city—all were demurrers to both rationality and beauty. That night following Young's beating, as we prepared to cover the next march, our faces pleasantly tight with sunburn and redolent with coconut oil, a Colonel Miner arrived at the motel. He was a kind of unofficial civilian liaison man between the police and reporters, and he brought sealed white envelopes.

"There's boric acid inside," he said. "We heard rumors some of them downtown have mustard oil to throw. Now if it gets you in the eye, run down the end of the square near the public library. There's a water fountain there. Just dilute the boric acid and wash out your eyes. You'll be all right."

I said:

"This seems a little backwards, colonel. Why don't you arrest the ones with the mustard oil?"

"Now we're just trying to cooperate," he replied. "It might be just a rumor. 'Course we'll stop 'em if we see 'em do it. But in the meantime we're not taking chances."

Just before the march reached King Street that night, we passed a Jewish tailor's shop. The owner was standing in the door smiling nervously. As we passed he said in a rich East Side New York accent: "Watch out for the Klooxers!"

We tried to. I saw no one "mustard oiled." But Marty was slugged again by a kid who jumped over a wall, hit him, and ran off. The cameramen were the most vulnerable of all because their vision was directed on the filming and they could not see approaching attackers. Some, including Marty, were quite brave in doing their job although they did not want to. Others were callow, broke and ran on occasions as when the whites pried up bricks from the park behind the Slave Market and began heaving them. I play and replay the tape of that night in America's oldest city and see it all again: the stones lofting out of darkness, the column breaking into a terrified run, thuds of stone on pavement, a young colored boy about ten hit and falling down, women screaming, the damned police dogs yapping but doing nothing constructive, cameras breaking, rebel yells. A big goon rushed me and I threw him off and a policeman came up and told me I'd better stop fighting. The next day Colonel Miner came around again. In the interim, Marty had been threatened on the street and our car followed by a group of jarheads with clubs. I bought a gun, a 25-caliber Italian automatic, the first weapon I had ever felt the need for, including the hectic times of Latin American revolt. The colonel commiserated with us on our problems. His role was obviously to soothe the savage press. I remember telling him:

"Colonel, we're fed up with platitudes. Any good cops could control this if they wanted to. These bastards are threatening us and I'm telling you—and you can tell them—I've got a gun and if they come around bothering us I'm going to shoot the sons of bitches."

In retrospect, I sounded overly dramatic. But in defense, it was getting hard to know how to behave. A grim Alice-in-Wonderland atmosphere existed in those days; bizarre things were done but with a kind of

grotesque logic. An editor named Elliot Bernstein had come down from
New York to help with production. Jimmy Brock felt he was vulnerable
and graciously gave him an eight-inch length of pipe to carry in his
car should the jarheads attack. State troopers looking for troublemakers
stopped Bernstein and found the pipe. Was he arrested? No. They
politely took it from him and wrote out a neat receipt, noting under
"Item," one eight-inch pipe.

"You can pick it up," they said, "after this mess is over with."

Beyond such personal involvement was a philosophic one. Reporters
are supposed to revere objectivity, a quality which has never existed
or can exist when perceptive human beings are trying to tell others
truthfully what they think they have seen happen. I tried to tell both
sides as far as there were two sides to tell. But how would you report
a Dachau or a Buchenwald? By faithfully expounding Hitler's thesis of
the Jewish problem, so much space for the international conspiracy of
World Zionism, so much for descriptions of mothers leading children
into gas chambers? Or would you equate the words of Pastor Niemöller
with those of a district Gauleiter? The contrast was not so extreme in
Saint Augustine, unless inhumanity to man is everywhere and always
the same degree of mortal sin, but it was vivid enough.

Nothing revealed the contrast so clearly as the white countermarchers.
These marchers were basically organized by J. B. Stoner with the help
of Manucy and Ku Klux Klansmen. Stoner was an Atlanta lawyer and
head of the National States Rights Party, an anti-Semitic and racist
organization that offered among its many publications what it called a
"spoof" entitled *The Diary of Anne Fink*. Stoner himself was a pear-
shaped, jowly man of about forty who walked with a decided limp and
had the reputation of turning up when racial conflicts took violent turns.
This night a crowd of about two hundred whites gathered in the Slave
Market for the countermarch. Men, women and children bearing Confederate flags and smiling slightly at themselves, at the strangeness, the
audacity of the plan to walk through "Niggertown." The first speaker
was a Klansman, a big, darkhaired and moustached man identified only
as the Avenger. I thought of Superman, Captain Marvel, Submariner
from childhood comics.

"The Klan in the South is like the dew," he said. "It covers the whole
South."

The slogan of McGill's liberal *Atlanta Constitution* boasted that the
paper "covered Dixie like the dew." I wondered if the Avenger had
appropriated the slogan. He was followed by a wiry little preacher who
ended each sentence with, "Hallelujah!"

"I want you to know that God made the separation in the eleventh chapter of Genesis. Hallelujah! He made twelve tribes. Hallelujah! I want to be just one of those twelve tribes. Hallelujah!"

And on and on. Since they controlled the area, we had to ask permission of the jarheads to photograph Stoner. To defer to them was humiliating, but if one wanted pictures rather than a fistfight, there was no alternative. Stoner had a highpitched voice and an often breathless delivery. The crowd generally enjoyed his oration, individuals frequently calling out responses as the Negroes did in church. He began with an attack on King George III, who apparently still was something of a villain in Saint Augustine.

"You newspapermen watching our sign, it says: 'Don't tread on me.' That's what we say to all the race mixers. (Amen!) It's the slogan of the American Revolution when this country won its independence from England because we were no longer willing to suffer tyranny under the British monarch. (Yeaaa . . . a cry of great enthusiasm from one man apparently still nursing a grudge.) Now one great American, Patrick Henry, said, 'Is life so sweet or peace so dear as to be purchased at the price of slavery?' He said, 'Forbid it, Almighty God.' And that's what we say today. We're not gonna be put in chains by no Civil Rights Bill now or any other time. (Amen! Yeaaa! Whoop!) There's nothing in the U. S. Constitution that gives Congress the authority to tell us that we've got to eat with niggers, that we've got to go in swimming with 'em, go to school with them or anything else like that. (That's right!) We have a communist-backed Supreme Court that is much more tyrannical than King George the Third ever was." (That's right, from the man who had not forgiven the fat king.)

While individuals in the crowd frequently yelled approval, the group was incapable of giving concentrated attention, lapsing into private conversations, skinny girls in shorts and halters whispering to husbands and boyfriends, men restlessly prowling in and out of the crowd, boys sucking in their stomachs and looking hard at cameramen. This inability to maintain focus on a speaker for more than a few minutes at a time was a trait common to such rallies. Speakers could only draw them back with increasingly extreme or provocative remarks. So Stoner got a whoop by saying we had "a bunch of communist nuts up in Congress."

"Our ancestors who wrote the Declaration of Independence," he continued, "in many cases were slave owners. And when they said that all men were created equal, they weren't talking about niggers. They were talking about white Americans, white Englishmen and white Frenchmen. Of course, I can understand why Martin Luther Coon (Yeaah!) and CORE and the rest of them want to associate with white people. It's because they're tired of associating with filthy, sorry niggers." (Great! Brother, you got it! Tell 'em about the Jews!)

Stoner described the birthright that needed protecting in the name of "our ancestors who maintained the purity of the white race." And who made the mulattoes? No questions, please, to mar this excursion into dementia. He gave instructions for the march to the men who had been throwing punches, cobblestones, kicks, and perhaps mustard oil for two weeks:

"Under no circumstances should you panic," he said. "If some nigger calls you a bad name pay no attention to him because what a nigger says doesn't matter anyhow. (That's right . . . Yeaah!) You don't need any weapons with you for protection because we have good police officers with us who will protect the procession from any black savages that desire to attack us."

Sheriff Davis and Police Chief Stuart, who pulled his men off the street the night of Young's march, were to lead the white column through "Niggertown." The good people of the city did not protest this participation by their leading lawmen, marching with a man who ended his address:

"Why do they want to integrate on the beaches, swimming pools and places like that? It is because they want our white women. That's the main thing that the black man wants. He wants our white women and I say we would be better off dead than to let those savages have our women." (Booming applause)

The whites moved off under heavy police guard, cigarettes dangling from lips, arms swinging in pugnacious arcs, fists balled up. "Niggertown" was dark as poor sections are where city fathers skimp on street lamps and people conserve electricity. Policemen guarding the marchers swept their flashlight beams down the street as the column turned into the enemy ground. The beams revealed the enemy standing along the sidewalk, brown faces staring into the street, singing, "I love everybody, I love everybody, I love everybody in my heart. There's no doubt about it, You can't make me doubt it, I love everybody in my heart."

The singing had been planned, of course, and the element of a slick propaganda maneuver was about it. Negro youths, with excessive courtesy, reassured the marchers that nothing would happen to them, that they were welcome to come in peace to the neighborhood. Yet the reception *was* in harmony with the character of the Movement and the philosophy behind it. The incident carried to a logical extreme everything that the Negroes had been trying to say to the whites about Christian love and brotherly cooperation. The white marchers smirked at the singers, made jokes to each other, swaggered. Still the song, softly chanted, came at them from up ahead where the flashlights poked into the privacy of homes, from behind where the street was settling back into darkness. "I love everybody in my heart . . ." I think the singing got to them and confused them. A rock sailing out of the dark they could understand, even welcome, since it would enable them to retaliate. But this being sung at. One of them finally had an idea.

"Okay, boys, let's show these niggers some singin'," he cried, and began: "She'll be comin' 'round the mountain when she comes . . ."

Those around him laughed explosively. Some joined in for a few raggedy bars. But they were nervous as all inhibited people are at singing in public, their voices quavered. The song quickly petered out before the end of the first chorus; even the man who started it did not know all the words. The marchers continued on without incident. But as they passed the Negro Blue Goose Café, some patrons came out who were not singing and whose faces did not seem to love anybody. I heard a hefty girl with hard eyes say to the man next to her:

"I'd like to take a machine gun an' kill them all."

The expression was a little crude but refreshing.

On the following night when the Negroes received permission to use the Slave Market under heavy state trooper guard, SCLC's Rev. Vivian, standing on the same spot where J. B. Stoner had condemned "filthy, sorry niggers," delivered one of those extemporaneous, yet eloquent, speeches so often produced by the Movement.

"This tragic situation," he said as a police dog barked on a policeman's cue but did not rattle the speaker, "brought those who came marching into the Negro neighborhood last night expecting a fistfight. But there was no fight. Because we didn't come to fight with fists and clubs but we wanted to raise great ideas up to the level of conscience where men will deal with them. We want to raise issues, not guns or knives; these have no meaning in our society today and we cannot live in a society controlled by violence, no matter whose it is. But we want to live in a society where we can come to men and women and say to them, 'These are the things for which we struggle, not with brutality but with the truth of the human spirit, with the heart filled with understanding. And who would have more understanding than the Negro because who has suffered more than we have suffered?'

"Those who came into our neighborhood were largely the underprivileged, too, and we could feel for them, for they were as poor as we are.

They had been cheated out of an education just as we had been. You could tell that most had come from the backwoods. And what is good for us is good for them, too. And so they came into our neighborhood and found that we sing to them, 'We love everybody in our hearts.' And out of this sense of love we want to create a new kind of Saint Augustine where everybody can be safe. . . . What are Negroes really marching about in this city? We march for some basic things. Things like jobs are at stake. We live in the kind of society where a man who led the march to the Negro neighborhood said, 'Let's chase all the Negroes out of their jobs.' What kind of heart, what kind of mind is this that says, 'Let's take jobs away from people so they can't feed their children, so they can't hope, so they can't aspire, so they can't become part of the American dream'?

"We don't say take jobs away from anybody. We say, 'Let everybody have better jobs, Negroes included, poor whites included.' All of us. For God's sake, we all need more in this Southland. They say 'Negroes steal.' Yet segregation takes thirty billion dollars a year from Negroes and other minorities. With that thirty billion we could see the Southland flower as it's supposed to be. The thievery has come from higher up, from the system of segregation itself. You see, if we were really inferior, there wouldn't have to be a system of segregation to keep us down because we wouldn't be able to aspire. My God, what kind of people can there be that break a man's leg and then blame him because he limps?"

The ears of educated white Saint Augustine were closed to such language. The city preferred to write off any complaints as mindless outside agitation, to see nothing wrong with a social structure that permitted a police chief to march along with Manucy, to lie to itself that all was well and try to foist that lie on the outside world. Respectable citizens put on a false face of reasonableness. They felt if King left or if the newsmen left, things would be all right. Talks might be arranged if the insufferable Dr. Hayling stepped aside, taking his arrogance with him. I spoke to Dr. King about it one day in the house where he was staying in "Niggertown," a comfortable old house with a screened-in porch where we talked in the languor of the drowsy mid-afternoon. I asked if Hayling might be the stumbling block, and for the first time since I had known him I felt his somewhat pompous ministerial front give way to real, not church meeting, anger.

"This is the old story we find every place," he said. "They never want to deal with the local man who began the movement because invariably he is a true leader and a dynamic force in the community.

What it really means is that they don't want to deal with anybody they can't control. We went through this in Birmingham with Fred Shuttlesworth, in Albany with Slater King. It's an evasion. They don't want to come to grips with reality. They want a cooling-off period. To cool what off? People have waited long enough. They don't want to be cooled off when they realize it isn't to serve a constructive purpose but merely to blunt the thrust of the movement."

He went over the Negro demands which had been formally presented to the white residents in a letter—some additional police and firemen, unrestricted hiring, immediate desegregation of public accommodations, and the formation of a biracial commission.

"They want to wait until the Civil Rights Bill passes to desegregate," he said, "but this is morally wrong. We want them to admit that segregation is evil and take it upon themselves to rid this city of it. But they won't do it. All they want to talk about is outside agitators."

He stared out through the screen, this epitome of the outside agitator. I looked at his profile in the porch shadows. He was and remains enigmatic. For centuries, American Negroes had looked for and failed to find a prophetic leader and now they had it in this man with a face more sensual than spiritual, a reserve that should divorce him from the masses but somehow did not, a personality intolerant of criticism, slipshod to the extreme when it came to administering his organization, yet with a razor-fine intuitiveness when deciding how and when the American Negro and America should be moved.

Although his speeches were repetitive and often delivered with a curious air of detachment, he had a power to galvanize audiences. The night before when a battered column returned to the church he told them:

"You held yourselves together with such a beautiful dignity. You proved yourselves to be that kind of spiritual anvil that will wear out many a spiritual, I mean physical, hammer in this community. We go on with the faith that unearned suffering is redemptive."

Most of the Negroes listening hadn't the foggiest notion what the word "redemptive" meant. But they knew what King meant. He was the word made flesh and despite the deficiencies my white eyes noticed, to Southern Negroes he was "the man." He articulated their sufferings and hopes from a level sometimes above them, but more often in catch-phrases that touched his listeners like shocks, exciting them to joyous shouts of affirmation. "We're sick and tired of being sick and tired. . . . Put on your walkin' shoes 'cause we're on our way to Freedom Land an' we're not gonna stop until we get there. . . . We will hew out of the mountain of despair the stone of hope. . . . Children, don't you get weary."

His formal declarations could be painfully overblown. When a Saint Augustine grand jury handed up a presentment demanding his leaving town during the proposed cooling-off period, he said in a statement that Saint Augustine could not "prolong the timetable of freedom in the hope that the narcotics of delay will dull the pain of progress."

Always in talking to the Negroes, King brought to life their God, a tangible God, not some metaphysical concept, but a God who in the words of the hymn "will take care of you, in every way, all through the day." The literalness of this belief might strike the sophisticated mind as childlike. The belief might also be considered truly Christian in an age that had lost its Christianity. King's own belief in God, which I believe was deep, despite sins he might have committed as a man, enabled him to be fatalistic about the threat of death. Yet even this noble aspect of him had its modifications. He never led a night march in Saint Augustine because the probability was too great that someone would shoot him from the dark. I don't believe fear stopped him, but nice calculations of gain and loss to the Movement if he were killed weighed against the need to risk it. He was continually involved in such calculations and his success is a measure of his judgment and the judgment of men around him, like the Reverend Abernathy.

By June 11, they had decided the time had come to get arrested and so they went to the Monson Motel. When they weren't falling over each other, squads of newsreel cameramen recorded the scene. Owner Brock —a frightened man covering his fear with bluster—refused the protesters service. The Civil Rights Bill was in the final stages of debate in the Senate and the fourteenth arrest of Dr. King would dramatize anew the need for passage. Before police could arrive, a half-demented white man shoved King aside and walked in. Later we learned that he had talked of killing King, and he could have upset the nice calculations in that moment if he were so inclined. Instead Police Chief Stuart came to make the arrests and later when he was asked if there had been any difficulties, replied:

"Nothin' to it. We had a Cub Scout signed up to handle it but we found out at the last minute he didn't have a driver's license."

Wise-guy remarks when the city needed wisdom.

The city could not learn, seeming instead bent on compounding the economic and moral disaster upon it. On June 17, with tourism off fifty percent, a group of businessmen was inclined toward reasonableness. The fear of antagonizing the jarheads was such that the move was doomed before it started. Twenty-six businessmen pledged to obey the Civil Rights Bill if it were passed and to support a study of community problems. Brock, a motel operator named Eddie Mussalem, and Senator Pope held a press conference. The conference began with Mussalem calling Mayor Shelley "one of the great living Americans," and criticizing newsmen for not printing his side of the racial story. A howl went up. No newsman had been able to get near the mayor as he golfed away the crisis. Mussalem looked confused at the reaction.

Senator Pope took over, lecturing the conference on "the invasion of human rights" by demonstrators, but never discussing the broad aspects of Negro demands to be treated like other citizens of the city. He praised the police work to men who had suffered under it. He complained that trouble had come when the city was trying to "build a bridge of culture with Latin America that would make a contribution to better world understanding." No one laughed outright. But the image of the dollar-hungry entrepreneurs of Saint Augustine as culture bridge-builders made some smile.

"We find ourselves beset by outside forces," he said sternly, "when we had thought our race relations were among the finest."

The statement, probably true of what they believed, was only an indication of the unbelievable gap in understanding that separated the races. The three men were obviously under extreme tension because their words—however dissembling or naïve to us—their gratuitous pledge to obey a federal law, if it were passed, was going to mark them as compromisers to the jarheads. Pope would have the windows of his law office smashed and Brock's lounge would later be firebombed. But they still did not seem to see that by permitting the violence-prone the run of the city, they had lost control of Saint Augustine, and of their right to speak freely as Americans. The situation was pitiable.

The very next day, the Negro Movement in Saint Augustine found the precise picture it had been seeking to project on the American conscience. Again, the target was Brock.

A white worker for Dr. King named Al Lingo rented a room at the motel, and then four young Negro boys and girls drove up in bathing suits and jumped into the small swimming pool. Brock ran out, beside himself, only to be told by Lingo that he had the right to invite friends to swim with him. A mob of segregationists quickly gathered. Black bodies in a pool with whites touched sexual nerves. State troopers held a thin line between order and violence. Brock was almost hysterical. He ran to the pool with gallon cans of muriatic acid, a relatively harmless disinfectant when diluted, and dumped them in.

"Oh, hold me baby, I'm scared," a Negro girl wailed to a Negro boy, and they clung together in the water.

Television cameramen, previously alerted by SCLC, captured all the wildness of the bizarre scene. Across the street under a palm tree, Dr. King, released from jail on bail, calmly watched. Finally a city policeman took off his shoes and dived into the pool. He put an arm lock on Lingo and forced him out. The others followed with police bestowing occasional kicks and cuffs.

"Let's kill the goddamn niggers," a jarhead cried, and if desire were deed it would have been done.

Brock, weeping with frustration, feeling betrayed after his moderate gesture of the day before, ordered the defiled water drained. Before this was done, two county deputies arrived from one of the tourist attractions, an alligator farm, with two big cartons. Each held an alligator about four and a half feet long. After the pool was drained, scrubbed, and refilled, it was understood that alligators would be thrown at the next dive-in demonstrators. Police dogs in Birmingham and now a year later, alligators in Saint Augustine.

Although the next week saw violence intensified on the streets and on the beaches, the alligators never got to use the Monson pool. But on June 25, the Senate passed the Civil Rights Bill and President Lyndon Johnson was soon to sign it. The bill probably would have passed without a Saint Augustine but then the country would not have had the chance to see a certain part of itself. How much true insight was gained cannot be judged; unfortunately, we suffer from a retention deficiency along with our short attention span. I would like to think that tourists today in the old music instruments shop hear echoes of "I Love Everybody" and "She'll Be Comin' 'Round the Mountain"; that the pop-up prisoners in the old jail recall Sheriff Davis's exercise pen for real, live human beings; that Robert Ripley's "Believe It or-Not" inspires the visitor to ponder on the believability of what happened in America's oldest city. Americans had so much to think about in those days that some oversights are understandable. Summer volunteers were about to enter Mississippi and that certainly was thought-provoking. With a sunburned headstart on the long hot summer, I left Saint Augustine and headed for Mississippi where tragedy was waiting to be played out.

Summer

SUMMERTIME

The list of the Mississippi summer volunteers had the geographical ingredients of one of those groups Hollywood loves in its war movies: the cross-section squad—an aggressive but lovable Jew from Brooklyn, a readyfisted Boston Irishman with a heart of gold, the peppery Italian from a California vineyard, the stolid, dependable Chicago Pole, and some practically pure Anglo-Saxons from everywhere. I did not know their personal qualities but I counted volunteers from eighteen states on the list handed me that Monday night on June 22 in the Jackson COFO office. Listed were a Hogan and Cierciorka from California, Tessaro and Moore from Illinois, Perkins from Massachusetts, Young from Hawaii, Lavelle from Pennsylvania. The cities represented have those names that Thomas Wolfe used to love to pry from American maps and inset on his pages for the exotic sounds in them—Callicoon, New York; Winnetka, Illinois; Exira, Iowa; Prairie du Chien, Wisconsin. Appropriately, with six volunteers, the nation's greatest city had the most names next to it. The second name on the list was Andrew Goodman.

I arrived, sand from Saint Augustine still in my shoes, in the Jackson COFO office late, about ten o'clock. 1017½ Lynch Street. The irony in the address had not been deliberately sought out by COFO. Lynch Street was the main drag through the Negro section, and the offices of NAACP and the Masonic Temple from which Medgar Evers was buried were directly across from the one-story converted store housing COFO. Police cars on surveillance were parked on the street, virtually deserted, since the next day was a workday. The Mississippi night was quiet and

107

balmy, but latent with the murderous heat of the day past and the day to come.

The office looked as though everybody had gone home—leaving behind cluttered desks, littered floors, empty Coke bottles beside a sagging leather sofa with stuffing drooping out through various holes. In an inner office I found a white boy on the telephone, his pallid face dirty with dark beard stubble and his melancholy, Semitic eyes filled with concern. I recognized him from an earlier trip to Greenwood. He was Bob Weil, a twenty-four-year-old staff worker from the Columbia University graduate school in Asian studies. A boy serious to the point of somberness, he had been working in Mississippi for three months. We had talked once about the dangers and he admitted being afraid for himself and others. He had stressed the lack of protection by local authorities and the attitude of the Justice Department and FBI agents which, he said, bordered on indifference. When I asked why he had come in the face of this attitude, he said, without outer swagger or any underplay of bravado in his manner:

"I felt simply that I had to be here."

When he got off the phone, I began to explain that a camera crew and producer were flying in from Chicago to do a story on the newly arrived volunteers. A different story had developed during the time I had been in transit from Saint Augustine to Jackson. He explained that three civil rights workers had disappeared more than twenty-four hours ago in the city of Philadelphia, Neshoba County.

"It's very bad territory," he said. "A lot of Klan. Yesterday when we called the jails up there everybody denied knowing about them. Now it turns out that they were arrested Sunday afternoon in their station wagon on a speeding charge and then supposedly released that night. But they never went back to their base in Meridian, never phoned. They know how important it is to maintain contact and they never would drop out of sight this way unless something happened. The only hope is maybe they got chased into the woods or something and are hiding. But it's been a long time now."

Weil said that after hours of inertia following the first report of the disappearance late the previous night, the FBI and Justice Department finally had entered the case. He showed me log reports made about midnight Sunday to H. F. Helgesen, Jackson FBI agent, and a Mr. Schwelb, a Justice Department lawyer in Meridian.

> Robert Weil from Jackson COFO called Schwelb and gave him the license number of the missing car and further information on the addresses of the missing people. Weil requested an investigation. Schwelb stated that the FBI was not a police force and that he was not yet sure whether any federal offense had occurred, so

he could not act. He was informed of the provision in the U.S. Code providing for FBI arrests; He still insisted he did not have authority.

Weil also called Helgesen at this time [the first call to him was made at 10 P.M., six hours after the disappearance] . Helgesen took in the information curtly and did not allow a chance for further conversation. Weil also called the Mississippi Highway Patrol with similar results.

By six o'clock Monday morning, the respected John Doar of the Justice Department said that the FBI had been invested with power to look into the case.

The missing were a twenty-year-old white volunteer from New York City, Andrew Goodman; James Chaney, twenty-one, a Meridian Negro; and Mickey Schwerner, twenty-four, a goateed white New Yorker affiliated with CORE who had been working with Chaney on the Meridian staff. They had driven to Philadelphia to check reports that whites had burned the colored Mount Zion Methodist Church outside the city and had beaten members of the congregation. The summer "invasion" of Mississippi was now two days old. Goodman had been in the state one day, arriving on Saturday from a COFO training school in Oxford, Ohio.

Anxious because Weil—who was mature enough not to waste anxiety—was anxious, I lit a cigar. From what I had seen of COFO, many members had a strong strain of excitability untempered by common sense. A young group involved in deadly serious business, its exuberance pervaded the office. The disarray was youthful—kids not having parents around to tell them to straighten up, and so not straightening up. The signs: "Anything left on this desk subject to immediate destruction"; pasted on a filing cabinet: "I am an FBI agent"; a photograph tacked on the wall showing Attorney General Robert Kennedy with a phone to his ear and ironically captioned: "In constant touch." The implication that the Justice Department was loathe this night to listen to civil rights complaints assumed a sharper edge.

Two boys and a girl drifted in and began talking about the disappearance. One of the boys, a Negro named Alvin Packer, was already discussing Schwerner in the past tense.

"A very brilliant young man," he said. "One of the best we had in the state. We were told by the Negroes and whites that if we were to come to Philadelphia, make it in the daytime because it wouldn't be safe at night."

"Schwerner was very friendly, very popular, liked by the people," the white boy said. "Somewhere else he'd be mayor."

What did he think had happened?

"Well, I know he wouldn't just go off somewhere without notifying us. He knows the ropes too well."

"I think he's dead," said the girl.

The crew arrived about 12:30 and the producer wanted to go ahead with plans to do a feature story on volunteers at work. He was skeptical of the validity of the disappearance.

"You might sit up there all day and have nothing happen," he said. He was for the first time in his life in Mississippi and ignorant of realities, but afraid to question a preconceived company plan and arrogant in his ignorance. I took an hour persuading him that the next day Philadelphia, Mississippi, would be a world dateline and we must be there. The next morning when the crew and I began driving north to Philadelphia on Highway 51, the sun was barely up but already the air was saturated with humidity and the cloudless sky was filling with heat. Delta land is flat and fertile, green and black after spring rains, mile after mile of earth sexual in its fecundity. Cotton fields studded with plants repeated Mississippi's old agrarian story. The fields, levelled out from either side, were still empty of black workers hoeing and cultivating, or of tractors, while ravaging the pastoral tableau, doing their work more efficiently. This kind of Mississippi land unrelieved by hills and with few lakes to slake the thirsting eye of summer is monotonous, but a primal beauty exists that complements lives spent simply and harmoniously on the tranquil earth.

The city's name loomed on a tall water tank grey against the blue sky. A wooden road sign, with something on it about Philadelphia being the heart of the Choctaw Nation, flashed by. I glimpsed Indian words and in English, "Heap big welcome." Philadelphia, from a rise near the water tank, looked small, neither pretty nor ugly, prosperous nor poor. In stretches the main street had old-fashioned high sidewalks which were unusually populated for a workday. Men in groups stood, talked, stared. The courthouse across the street was their principal interest, but each car that came along was closely scrutinized. The phrase "tension in the air" generally refers to a feeling not in the air but in the breast of the observer aware of conditions making for tension. In Philadelphia that morning, someone who did not know of the disappearance might have driven through, barely noting the place except perhaps for its quaint Indian sign. We felt the tension, a miasma of brain-clouding hostility hanging in that bright morning sunshine, distrust for the outsider, century-old anger that someone was presuming to interfere in "their" world.

We stopped at the courthouse, whose front lawn had a big sign listing all the churches in Philadelphia, and I went inside to the sheriff's office past a cluster of old men with weathered faces and eyes alive with country suspicion—an evil thing to see. Sheriff Lawrence Rainey, a big, overblown man with a moonface and pendulous stomach, but withal strength suggested underneath, was in his outer office. He wore a modified Stetson and cowboy boots, and one cheek bulged as if he had a billiard ball inside his mouth. The bulge never moved as he spoke, and I later learned it was chewing tobacco. At the time I thought he had a toothache or a tumor. He was nominally friendly, which was more than I had expected. I said that reports now stated that his deputy, Cecil Price, had escorted the three from town after their release late Sunday night.

"Naw," he said. "That's wrong. He didn't escort nobody. He was drivin' along an' just happened to see their car turn off on Nineteen toward Meridian. There wasn't no escortin' about it."

Also reports from COFO said the boys had been beaten in jail.

"You go on over the jail yourself an' ask the jailer, Mr. Herrin," he said. "He'll tell you it didn't happen. Go anywhere you like. We got nothin' to hide here."

Well, what did he think had happened?

"I'll tell you what," he replied, not smiling but opening his eyes owlishly. "I bet they're off someplace drinkin' beer an' laughin' at us."

He did not want to be interviewed on film or with the recorder. I left after he assured me that Philadelphia had no "nigger" problem and that he would bend every effort looking for the three boys. The jail was a neat little one-story red brick affair with ivy nearly overgrowing the word "Neshoba" blocked out in concrete. I remember holding back the vine so that the cameraman could film it. The side door had curtains and looked just like a door to any residence. A massive lady opened the door onto a small living room with linoleum on the floor and bright plastic flowers stuck here and there. She was Mrs. Herrin, the jailer's wife. She had small dark eyes in a doughy face and black hair pulled into an old-fashioned bun. The sum of her appearance, forbidding in its parts, was somehow maternal. She was very nervous. A thin bird-eyed old man, who perhaps came up to Mrs. Herrin's shoulder, walked into the room. Shouting to me that he was pretty deaf, she introduced him as her husband. He smiled and fixed birdy eyes on me.

Mrs. Herrin explained that they had rooms in the front of the building with the jail in back off the kitchen. She said they tried to run a good jail, treated everybody the same, same food, same attention. Of course, local custom called for separate cells—for whites, Negroes, and Indians. But, well, that was the way it was. Roaring at Mr. Herrin, I asked why COFO had originally been told that the missing boys were not there when it turned out that they were. He shook his head and pointed to his ear. Before I could roar again, Mrs. Herrin explained that a niece had answered the phone and had not known of the arrests.

"But let me tell you what happened," she said. "We got hold of the justice of the peace after a couple of hours and he told the deputy sheriff it would be a twenty-dollar fine. So Mr. Price came around and he went back there and told the boys. He says, 'I found out how much the speeding ticket's gonna be. It'll be twenty dollars. You-all got twenty dollars? I'll let him pay that and I'll release you boys.'"

The explanation was an astounding display of accommodation from a Mississippi deputy sheriff to three rights workers. They would not even have to go to the JP's house.

"This colored boy didn't have it," Mrs. Herrin continued, "and he asked this black-headed boy, I don't know which one it was, I didn't get 'em separated, if he had it. An' he gave my husband the twenty dollars. We just released them all. They all left at the same time. This is the receipt my husband gave 'em and this here is from the justice of peace. He turned the money in yesterday morning."

Had the boys been, well, roughed-up any?

"There weren't a hard or a cross word between them, nor the deputy sheriff," she said. "There hadn't been any hard words. Not any."

I wondered why they had left the jail at night since this was in violation of all COFO rules on night-driving in Philadelphia. Did they seem apprehensive about leaving?

"They didn't seem to be," said Mrs. Herrin. "They got their billfolds and their drivin' license an' everything back and they put them in there and just walked on out and I reckon just got in the station wagon and left."

I wanted to film the cell with the couple inside but Mrs. Herrin seemed reluctant. Was there some rule against it, perhaps? "No, it wasn't that," she said, but the way they were dressed, her husband without a coat and tie, her in a working dress. But if I could wait, they'd change and come right out. Foolish vanity at such a time was doubly incongruous in this gross woman. Yet, the vanity was also reassuringly human on a day when all signs pointed to an act of inhumanity. They emerged resplendent, she rouged and powdered, he combed and coated, a Neshoba Mutt-and-Jeff team except that tall was also stout and they were man and wife. Mr. Herrin, talking for the first time and with pride about the electric door controls, let me inside the cell where the three had been. Not a bad cell, moderately clean, but smelling, as cells do, of urine on stone. I looked for some sign of the boys, message scratched on the wooden table or some writing on the Salvation Army religious tract lying there, but there was nothing. Three lives had been in there and had gone out into the Mississippi night. . . .

"They didn't give us a minute's trouble," Mrs. Herrin said as she stood proud in her good dress in the white glare from our camera light. "Ate a good supper. I had green peas, and a green salad, and fresh mashed potatoes, sponge cake and corn bread and iced tea. All ate heartily. They cleaned their plates up."

Like good little boys, I thought.

We thanked them and left the jail to talk to Art Richardson, the public relations man for the Mississippi Highway Patrol. He was very courteous and gave me a Philadelphia Chamber of Commerce pamphlet.

"A visitor to our community," it read, "finds an old-fashioned welcome and a degree of friendliness that exists in no other place."

Richardson said that an intensive search was being conducted, although we had not seen a single patrol car on the highway coming into town. And curiously, he said that Deputy Price had escorted the boys from the city, although Sheriff Rainey had insisted this was not so. About ten miles from the city, the Mount Zion Methodist Church lay off Route 16. On the street, I asked a clean-cut white boy in his early teens how to get to Route 16.

"Find it your own fuckin' self," he replied.

Well, chambers of commerce sometimes exaggerate local hospitality, I thought.

The church was one mile off the highway down a rain-rutted dirt road, past modest Negro farmhouses and uneven farmland. Only a chimney remained standing, grey ash and blackened metal covering the ground under some pine and a big sassafras tree. A small graveyard lay behind the ruins, a few stone markers, crosses of wood, bottles stuck in the earth holding dried-out flowers. One headstone said:

"Just Sleaping."

Two New York white boys and a Mississippi Negro had stood together before the burned church. The vast quiet of the country and its warm green odors mixed with the acrid smell of fire. Their thoughts and emotions interplayed; young blood keenly alive to the elements of nature and the works of man. . . .

Witnesses to the churchburning, Mr. and Mrs. T. C. Cole, lived down the road. I did not see them that day, but later the Negro couple told me their story of the night white men beat them and burned their church.

"When we come out of church, they was out there in the yard," said Mr. Cole, fifty-nine, a lifelong county resident who owned his small farm.

"They asked me where was my guard. I said, 'We don't need any guards, we're havin' a church meetin.' He said, 'Damn you, liar.' An' he just take me by the car and just struck me."

"One man clubbed him with a pistol." Mrs. Cole said, "He say, 'You better say something,' an' he hit him again. I said, 'He cain't say nothin', he's unconscious.' He never did say a word because the first lick they got him out unconscious. They said, 'Search him an' git it' . . . and they stepped up to me an' said, 'Come out here, old woman.' An' they just snatched me on out. They said, 'What you got in this purse?' I said, 'Not anything but school literature.' He searched it and threw it back in the car.

"They was beating my husband an' I was just prayin', prayin' to the Lord to spare his life. Well, there was a crowd just ahead of us and I heard a lady, Miss Burch, screamin'. An' I was just figurin' whether next time was my time. A man came up an' snatched me aroun'. I started to say somethin' and every time I started he'd say, 'Shut up.' I said, 'Well, will you let us pray? Let us all pray.' One man says, 'You better pray.' Another says, 'It's too late to pray, it's not gonna do you any good.' I said, 'It's never too late to pray.' I just fell on my knees there in the road an' begin to pray an' put up a petition to God to spare my husband's life. An' one said, 'That's enough, leave him livin', load up.' An' they loaded up and left. Twenty-five or thirty of them, some of them dressed in uniforms. But I didn't know them. Kind of lead-grey color an' with pistol belts. After they left my husband, I went an' held his head up. I thought he was dead an' I was rubbin' my hand over his face to see if he was dead. An' I called him an' he answered me. I held his head up on my lap to wipe the blood out of his face. When I held him up, he slumped down and then I lifted him again but then he fell to his knees."

Mrs. Cole said that three local white people had driven to their farmhouse later to say they were sorry it had happened and one offered to carry Mr. Cole in his truck to a doctor. I asked how bad the injuries were.

"Just bein' black," said Mrs. Cole, "hurts the most."

I stopped in Meridian en route back to the Jackson station and talked to some volunteers who had come in with Goodman. I spoke to a girl with a Bryn Mawr accent and an intellectual Jew from New York . . . each in his own terms—one with a cool Brahman concept of duty, the other with an involuted explanation of personal psychological needs and pressures—explained why they were there and why they would stay no matter what had happened to Goodman. They spoke of his qualities, of friendship and mutual respect that just had been starting. A Negro boy about ten years old listened. His face was locked in woebegone sadness disturbingly different from the momentary griefs of childhood. He was

James Chaney's brother, Ben, and I, impelled by witless desire to get twenty feet of heart-rending interview to complete the day's package, pointed the microphone at him and asked what he thought about his big brother. He looked at me with the young-old hopelessness of a Mississippi Negro kid who knows the score. Although he did not cry, he could not answer.

New York used fifty seconds that night. The Chicago producer did not deem the interviews with the volunteers important, despite my feeling that in the volunteers' attitudes lay the heart of the story. An old problem to divert energies that should have been concentrated on the story was brewing again. I flew back through a thunderstorm to Meridian. Tornadoes had been hopping around the state all day and the weather was ferocious. CORE's James Farmer was to arrive that night and the order was to film him. Of course, the story would be too stale for use on the next night's show. At the airport, NBC correspondent Dick Valeriani told me that the volunteers' station wagon, destroyed by fire, had been located late that afternoon outside Philadelphia just off a road near Boque Chito River. Apparently the car had been there for a day although Indians, who fished the river, had on Monday passed the spot where it was found, and said nothing. That action was in keeping with traditions of the happy community where the Indians avoided talking to whites, whom they hated, while disdaining the Negroes as beneath them.

On his arrival, Farmer, eyes glittering their customary look of outrage and his overly articulated speech verging on pomposity, made an interesting observation which gave some perspective to the disappearance. He said:

"I feel untold shock and disbelief that this could happen in our country. Our young people, black and white, go all over the world in the Peace Corps. They work in Ghana, they work in Nigeria, all over the world, teaching people, helping them. But are we to say they cannot work in one state in our country?"

Where did he lay the blame?

"Oh," said Farmer oratorically, "the blame is on all of us."

At this point, a British correspondent from the *London Daily Mail*, said:

"I mean, you're basing your statements on no facts yet, are you?"

"What's that?" snapped Farmer. "These people have disappeared."

"Are you basing your statement on fact?" continued the Britisher. "This could be a propaganda trick, you know."

"A propaganda trick by whom, sir?"

"Well, on both sides there are extremists."

"Two of these men were members of my staff," said Farmer coldly. "I can assure you this was no propaganda trick. We don't anguish the families of two young men for the sake of one headline."

"They just vanished into thin air, eh?" concluded the reporter, nothing daunted.

Perhaps, I am being too hard on an alien. Governor Paul Johnson, who should have known better, said: "They could be in Cuba."

The next day was desultory. Searchers moved through swamps said to be infested with water moccasin and surely cloudy with mosquitoes; townspeople glared at all outsiders; depression reigned at COFO headquarters in Meridian. On this day, personal and professional differences with ABC reached a climax and with much long-distance shouting on both sides, I quit.*

Americans and their government, predictably, were shocked at the disappearance and the probability that murder had been done. CIA chief Allen Dulles was sent to Jackson by President Johnson. Editorials in Northern newspapers were chesty with indignation that a state of the union should harbor such darkness. Tragedy had been clearly forecast both by contemporary events and the evidence of history. The Southern Regional Council, a private group that has been laboring for decades to better race relations in the South, compiled a carefully documented record of civil rights violence in Mississippi since the beginning of 1964. In each

---

*I would have been more satisfied with the break if some transcendent principle had been involved. The break was a combination of old conflicts and aggravations stemming mainly from arbitrary decisions made by New York editors who simply did not know what the hell was going on in the South but were not deterred from behaving as if they did. The problems with the Chicago producer worsened until that day he decided I should go back to Jackson to listen to some statement from Governor Johnson. I argued that the story still was in Philadelphia where much digging into what might have happened remained to be done, and that's where I was going to stay. He complained to New York and an editor called and told me to do what I was told—team play and all that. The discussion escalated until he told me to go to Jackson or lose my job. I told him in graphic terms what he could do with the job. With a mutual slamming down of phone receivers, I quit and he fired me. In retrospect the incident is all kind of laughable. The next day to try to resolve things, a news executive had me fly up to New York. I told him that any resolution had to include my immediate return to Philadelphia with no interference from that Chicago character. My request was, I know, an impossible challenge to the chain-of-command system, and so the quitting-firing stuck. The loss of ABC paychecks was a blow, but my wife, Ruth, immediately got a secretarial job, enabling me to try free-lancing articles with newspapers and magazines. For the first time, I had some freedom to set my own journalistic standards and priorities. That freedom made some tough financial times worthwhile. I never regretted that explosive telephone conversation. Team-playing is fine if you like the team and respect the manager. When you don't, the best thing to do is say goodbye, walk away and don't look back.

case, the accounts carried in newspapers were checked before their inclusion on the list:

Canton—COFO alleges, over denial of sheriff, that George Raymond, voter registration worker, was beaten and bloodied by police in January. (*Jackson Daily News,* 1/5/64)

McComb—Armed night-riders shot into six Negroes' homes, wounding young Negro boy. (*Atlanta Daily World,* 1/16/64)

Amite County—Louis Allen killed by two shotgun blasts, on January 31, in front of his house. Allen had been a witness to the 1961 slaying of Herbert Lee, active in voter registration, by E. H. Hurst, then a state legislator (ruled justifiable homicide). (*New York Times,* 5/30/64)

Jackson—Two voter registration workers, Arthur Harris and Will Galloway, badly beaten by police in February. (*Mississippi Free Press,* 2/15/64)

Neshoba County—Twelve crosses burned throughout Neshoba County around 10 P.M.; one at county courthouse and three in Negro section of Philadelphia; others in scattered communities. (*Jackson Daily News,* 4/7/64)

As summer approached the tempo of violence increased. Here are samples from a three-week period before the disappearance of Goodman, Chaney, and Schwerner:

Canton—Pakistani instructor at Tougaloo College (interracial) hauled from car and beaten by whites. (*Washington Post,* 5/31/64)
CORE Freedom House had explosive hurled against building in pre-dawn hours. (*Baton Rouge State Times,* 6/8/64)

Summit—Three white free-lance writers reported being forced from their car at pistol point and beaten by three carloads of whites. (*New York Times,* 6/10/64)

Hattiesburg—Catholic parish meeting hall, which had been used by Negroes, destroyed by fire. (*New York Times,* 6/21/64)

Neshoba County—Mount Zion Methodist Church was burned down. Armed white men, some masked, some in law enforcement uniforms, had allegedly earlier surrounded church and brutally beaten three Negroes who were attending a church meeting. (*New York Times,* 6/21/64)

This kind of violence was in the Southern tradition—not that violence is a Southern phenomenon. Peculiarly, the South stamped violence with social, if not legal, sanction.

Mark Twain fictionalized the fact in *The Adventures of Huckleberry*

Finn when the Sartoris figure of Colonel Sherburn faces a mob after he has killed the Snopesian Boggs.

"I know you clear through," he says. "I was born and raised in the South, and I've lived in the North; so I know the average all around. The average man's a coward . . . your newspapers call you a brave people so much that you think you *are* braver than any other people—whereas you're just *as* brave and no braver. Why don't your juries hang murderers? Because they're afraid the man's friends will shoot them in the back, in the dark—and it's just what they would do."

Twain's pre-Civil War Missouri is not the South today. Roots into this historical South remain, and nowhere were they so tenacious as in Mississippi. The state boasted of having the lowest crime rate in the country —but law was a sometime thing.

I remember, for example, a spring night in Jackson before the volunteers came. The second trial of Byron de la Beckwith for the murder of Medgar Evers had ended, as did the first, in a hung jury. Two policemen from de la Beckwith's home town of Greenwood had placed him in the town at the time Evers was being ambushed in the driveway of his Jackson home. The prosecution could not do much about that testimony. The night of the verdict I went out to the new Jackson municipal auditorium, a multimillion dollar structure with the colorful look of a carousel. The architects who had built gaiety into the design had also built-in segregation. Entranceways and seats were planned for Negroes. The night before, a white volunteer named Eli Hochstedler was arrested when he and a Negro tried to buy seats in the white section. More attempts were anticipated. I stood outside talking with two city policemen while white people went in to see an ice show. One cop said:

"Whoever killed Charlie Evers made a mistake because he was one of the good ones. We grew up together right close by here."

"That's right," agreed his partner. "Charlie Evers helped us raise money to build a Catholic Church and he wasn't even a Catholic."

"Still," said the first, "those police in Greenwood owed it to their community to protect a man from up there."

"Oh, yeah," replied the other. "There ain't no doubt about that. Like if somethin' happened up in Greenwood, I wouldn't stick my nose in where it don't belong."

Precisely at the hour we were talking, Hochstedler was placed in a cell at Jackson's Hinds County Jail. He had already been sentenced to six months for breach of the peace. His cell was filled with common prisoners, and the jailers made certain they knew of Hochstedler's crime. Here, in his words, is what happened:

"At about nine o'clock a dozen or more inmates gathered in the cell. I was told to get out of my bunk. After talking and trying to reason with them for some time, I was told that they were going to show me and other people from the North thinking about coming down to stir up trouble what would happen to them if they came. I had been sitting on the lower bunk. When I stood, a prisoner, who weighed about four hundred pounds, hit me near the left eye. I fell to the floor. When I got up, he hit me and knocked me down again. After one or two repetitions, I fell into a lower bunk. My face was bleeding. He then stopped hitting me. One of the prisoners ordered me to get back on my bunk and to roll up my mattress. They threatened to kill me if I didn't follow orders. I did as I was told. After laying on the steel bunk ten to fifteen minutes, I was ordered to get down and lean over with my head on a lower bunk. Another prisoner then began whipping me with a leather belt. I had on only my underwear. After about eight lashes I was ordered to lower my shorts. He then continued the whipping. All during the whipping I kept repeating, 'Father, forgive them because they really don't know what they are doing. Oh, Lord, help me to take it.' After sixteen or eighteen lashings, I screamed and stood up. Somebody then hit me hard on the right jaw and nearly knocked me out . . ."

At least one voice raised in Mississippi verified and condemned such behavior. Pulitzer Prize winner Hodding Carter's *Delta Democrat Times* editorialized:

> With monotonous regularity civil rights activists in Mississippi claim they have been beaten either by law officers or prisoners bribed by the officers to attack them in various jails. Some of these protests can be discounted as so much propaganda. . . .
>
> But too many are not fabrications. Too many are simple truth. Even one would be too many; there have been far more than one. Again, we have personal knowledge of this. . . . The jackboot approach to law enforcement—or to the preservation of the status quo—can only result in the creation of a brutalized public as well as police.
>
> . . . the midnight beating and the old-fashioned third degree are still too prevalent, especially where Negroes and civil rights "outsiders" are concerned . . . and while all-white Mississippi juries have refused to convict lawmen in several trials involving beatings, the evidence has been incontrovertible that the beatings occurred. . . . it is more than a coincidence that the only prisoners who are consistently coming out of jail with bruises and black eyes are civil rights activists. This isn't law. It is sadism hiding behind a badge.

On July 10, FBI Director J. Edgar Hoover arrived in Jackson to open an expanded bureau office and to talk with Governor Johnson about Neshoba and the days ahead. Scores of FBI agents now were working on the disappearance and Hoover said he was convinced the three were dead. COFO criticism of the FBI role in Mississippi had grown increasingly bitter and Hoover's public statements did nothing to allay the contentions. Meeting with the press and Governor Johnson, Hoover said there had been an "overemphasis" on the civil rights situation in the South. He said the FBI "most certainly will not" offer protection to rights workers. And he introduced Governor Johnson as "a man I have always admired from a distance." That same day in Hattiesburg, a white rabbi was battered by two white men using steel bars. The day before, in Clarksdale, the chief of police had told three civil rights workers, including a minister, to get out of town. The day before that three bombs had been exploded in a McComb Freedom House. And the day before that, in Moss Point, a nineteen-year-old Negro girl singing at a church rally had been shot in the chest by shots fired from a passing car. The Negroes who chased the car were arrested for attempted assault. Mississippi law enforcement could not be depended on if one were involved in civil rights work. The workers could not understand why the federal government, through the Justice Department and the FBI, seemed loathe to safeguard the lives of United States citizens and to prosecute their attackers. In January, 1963, the Mississippi Advisory Committee to the United States Commission on Civil Rights said:

> The Committee finds that the federal government has not provided the citizens of Mississippi the protection due them as American citizens. The Department of Justice has acted in good faith, but the present interpretation of the function of the Civil Rights Division of the Justice Department is unduly and unwisely narrow and limited. . . .

Since 1961, the Justice Department had filed twenty-one voting rights suits against Mississippi counties and cities. Only one, in Panola County, had been effective in increasing Negro registration. The other suits languished in various stages of judicial delay. As far as intervening in violence, Director Hoover and his men kept reiterating that they were an investigative, not a law enforcement body. This belief was strictly true, although the Notre Dame Conference on Congressional Civil Rights in 1963 had observed:

> To contain and disarm lawlessness, a clear federal presence is required at the first outbreaks. We think the Attorney General has the power, in the face of determined lawlessness supported by an acquiescent or conspiratorial community, to send federal marshals and agents of the Federal Bureau of Investigation for on-the-spot protection of the exercise of federal rights.

The United States Criminal Code seemed to provide broad legal ground beyond the more limited language of the three civil rights acts. Title 10, Section 333 gave the president the power to use militia, the armed forces "or any other means" to suppress domestic violence or con-spiracy that deprived any part or class of people of "a right, privilege, im-munity, or protection named in the Constitution" when the consti-tuted state authorities "are unable, fail or refuse to protect that right, privilege or immunity." Title 18, Section 241, made it a crime "if two or more persons conspire to injure, oppress, threaten or intimidate any citizen in the free exercise or enjoyment of any right or privilege se-cured to him by the Constitution or laws of the United States, or because of his having so exercised the same."*

Civil rights leaders complained that their objection was not so much a question of law but of attitude, from Hoover on down to the agent in the field. The FBI could not physically be on the scene to prevent each slug-ging or bombing. Civil rights leaders widely felt that agents, often on friendly terms with local lawmen with whom they cooperated in crime investigations, reflected local antagonisms toward the rights workers. For example, on February 28, 1963, a car carrying Robert Moses, Randolph Blackwell of SCLC, and SNCC worker Jimmy Travis was ma-chine-gunned outside Greenwood. Travis was severely wounded. An FBI agent named George Everett later questioned the survivors.

"I felt," Blackwell told me, "like it was a Klansman talking to me, he was so cold and hostile. I don't mean that he was a Klansman, but we were the victims and he acted like I had done something wrong."

Everett later was elected district attorney of Greenwood's Leflore County.

This incident may have been an extreme case, but—rightly or wrongly —rights workers felt it typified FBI attitudes. If Mississippians had been interfering with United States mail trucks, they argued, agents would not have hesitated in taking direct, on-the-spot action without waiting for consultations with Justice Department lawyers. But FBI action was less imperative when bombs or billy clubs were used against Negroes trying to vote. If the FBI could get John Dillinger, then why couldn't it apprehend certain sheriffs robbing citizenship instead of banks? Cyni-cism extended to the Neshoba investigation. Scores of agents were working and working hard on the case. But what if the three had been all-black instead of two whites and a black? Rights workers thought they knew. On July 12, the bodies of two Negroes sawn in half were found in a river near the Louisiana-Mississippi border. One had been involved in

---

*On June 26, 1964, the FBI did make use of this section in arresting two white men in Itta Bena on a complaint they interfered with voter registration workers. Little further use was made.

racial protest at the Negro Alcorn A & M College in Lorman, Mississippi. No swarms of agents descended on that case, and the FBI critics, pointing to a history of official indifference to violent black death in the South, reasoned that two New York white boys plus national hue and cry in an election year had made the difference in Neshoba.

The steaming weeks of July went by without a trace of the three. In Philadelphia, Sheriff Rainey and his deputy Cecil Price, who had arrested the three men, were busy harassing the COFO workers in their Freedom House. They would race past at night with sirens blaring, shine lights into the rooms, threaten arrests and dispossessions. A world away in New York City. violence in the Northern tradition was beginning. Harlem's dormant hate for the white man came awake, fed on slum air, heavy as a vile broth, was warmed by Manhattan's July heat, which is as blood-prickling as any the Mississippi Delta can produce. Night after night, rioters ranged the streets.

All this had happened before, in fact and fiction, and if America was aghast (particularly since the Civil Rights Act had been passed, what did the Negro want anyway?), America should not have been surprised.

> I was one of the mass, moving down the littered street over the puddles of oil and milk, my personality blasted. Then I was in the next block, dodging in and out, hearing them somewhere in the crowd behind me; moving on through the sound of sirens and burglar alarms to be swept into a swifter crowd and pushed along, half-running, half-walking, trying to see behind me and wondering where the others had gone. There was shooting back there now, and on either side of me they were throwing garbage cans, bricks and pieces of metal into plate glass windows. I moved, feeling as though a huge force was on the point of bursting.
>
> . . . a mounted policeman charged through the spray, the horse black and dripping, charging through and looming huge and unreal, neighing and clopping across the pavement upon me now as I slipped to my knees and saw the huge pulsing bulk floating down upon and over me, the sound of hooves and screams and a rush of water coming through distantly as though I sat remote in a padded room, then over, almost past, the hair of the tail a fiery lash across my eyes.
>
> ". . . This is some night," one of them said. "Ain't this some night?"
>
> "It's 'bout like the rest."
>
> "Why do you say that?"
>
> "Cause it's fulla fucking and fighting and drinking and lying—gimme that bottle."

The excerpt is from Ralph Ellison's classic *Invisible Man* written twenty years ago. This following excerpt came from *Time* magazine for July 31, 1964:

> The nights shook with gunfire. Police exhausted their ammunition, and had to send out emergency calls for more. False fire alarms rang through the area.

Mounted police heaved back against the mobs with their horses. . . . A Negro woman lay down on the sidewalk and muttered through her drunken stupor: "They walk all over me in Greenville, South Carolina, and they might as well run over me here." An onlooker cried: "Did you see that? They shot that woman down in cold blood."

Ellison's account was a fictionalized version of the Harlem riots of 1941. Like Twain's fiction, it was grounded in fact. Parallels between the 1964 riots and the imagined ones were striking. Both riots held two black and bloody catalysts—Ellison's young Negro Clifton, slugging a cop who was arresting him, was killed by the cop, reality's fifteen-year-old James Powell who allegedly came at a cop with a knife and was shot to death. In book and real life, extremist elements seized the chance to mobilize black hate into violence. In Ellison, Ras the Exhorter mounted on a black horse and dressed as an Abyssinian chieftain. In life radicals screamed, "We don't have to go to Mississippi because Mississippi is here in New York." Indiscriminate looting, purposeless violence against police, unfocused goals—the embodiment of Ellison's riot and Harlem '64 and Harlem '41 and Chicago '38. Nothing had changed. That absence of change was the point for America to grasp. Nothing had changed in Harlem over those years except the area had gotten bigger, which meant the border to the outside world was that much farther from the center. Jammed inside were people who had the vote but were spiritually disenfranchised, morally impoverished, and psychologically indentured to a system as destructive to the soul as Mississippi plantation life. A free man in a ghetto is not free and is stymied as he seeks to become free or to obtain what he conceives to be a state of freedom. New York was paying for more than half a century of bottling up people, sticking in an economic stopper and leaving the mass to decay, releasing in fetid tenement doorways and odorous alleys the volatile gas of frustration that finally popped.

Northern whites had chosen to pretend that the ghetto Negro did not exist, while Southern whites were pretending their Negro was contented. South he was not contented; North he did exist. A few years earlier, I had done a series of television interviews for NBC in Harlem. I talked with families struggling to stay decent in the midst of depravity, with families coasting with the social tide, with street gang members so probing in their cynicism that my middle-class answers to their questions about how the nothings in America could achieve something sounded like Horatio Alger—and as believable. The interviews were taken in winter. The furnace in the tenement in the West 140's had broken—leaving the residents without heat or hot water for three days. The family I interviewed, a man and a woman and three children, was paying $120 a month for three rooms. In each room portions of the ceiling had caved in from rain water on the roof. Roaches ran wild in the kitchen. Holes and rats were in the wall. The sixteen-month-old baby had an ugly little scar on his upper lip from a rat bite suffered a few months before. As I interviewed the mother, who was not married, the squeaking of the rats in the walls could be heard clearly over the television soundtrack.

This one family, what it was morally and economically, and why, is an intensely complex story that cannot be oversimplified. One cannot just say that white avarice buttressed by white indifference made Harlem. This assumption is true but only part of the truth. Other truths exist about the economic structure that has created this country, truths about the mass Negro and the criminally inept leadership he has received (fostered) in Northern sectors like Harlem, and his own generally feeble efforts to remake his situation when he does not fly off into the escape of a place in the white scheme of things. These truths cannot be put down in shorthand without doing mischief to full understanding. In this book we are concerned with the South. The South's reaction to the Northern riots—even as searchers poked through Neshoba County for the three missing workers—occupies us. If the North, blind to the inevitable moral chaos its silent sins of prejudice were creating, was appalled by the black lightning that struck in Harlem, Rochester, and elsewhere, the South was gleeful.

"Those Belgian paratroopers did so well against the Congolese," a letter to the editor was to say in the *Jackson Clarion-Ledger*, "that we need to fly some of them into the dangerous jungles of Washington, Harlem, Philadelphia, and other crime centers where black savages wage a reign of terror."

That terrible incapacity for making distinctions prevented most Southerners from seeing that the windows smashed on New York's 125th Street were not proofs of inherent Negro inability to handle freedom—and parallel inability of the white Northerner to handle *him*—but sorry evidence that in both the North and the South, white America was failing, each in its regional way, to resolve a racial dilemma unique in the world.

"I think the riots are very unfortunate," Dr. King told me on July 22, as he and the Reverend Abernathy left Atlanta for a tour of Mississippi. "I abhor violence whether it's from the white community or from the Negro community. I do not think that the Negroes of Harlem should seek to solve their problems—and they do have many problems—through violence. There are other channels of peaceful protest open and these are the channels that should be followed."

That belief was well and good for Dr. King and his God-directed Southern Negroes still marching down an emotional Freedom Road that so far had none of the twistings and turnings that come with political sophistication. I think he would have been hooted down on a Harlem street corner by people who didn't love anybody and who knew damn well that God would not take care of them. As they neared the first corner, Southern Negroes still had sweet dreams. The Mississippi Freedom Democratic Party was trying to gather enough momentum to dislodge the regular Mississippi Democratic delegation from the August 24 convention in Atlantic City. To that end, the first Negro political television program in Mississippi history was to be taped for replay at WJTV, the CBS affiliate in Jackson. Since Negroes charged they were systematically excluded from programming, both WJTV and the NBC affiliate had been under scrutiny by the Federal Communications Commission. License renewal was coming up, so the CBS station decided to demonstrate its goodwill by giving the Negroes a free half hour. To placate white Mississippians, the story was given out that the Negroes paid for the time and the station was forced to accept the arrangement. This explanation, like so many things in Mississippi, was not true.

Dr. King, who had done little personally in the state, was to appear along with Aaron Henry, president of the state NAACP, and other leaders of the Freedom Party. Dr. King planned to enter Neshoba County after the taping on July 24. I was invited to be the unpaid moderator for the show and to accompany the King party into Neshoba. I was happy to do it. To moderate is not to advocate and since no payment was involved, I did not see my free-lance position compromised by participation.

The station was heavily guarded by police but no incident occurred. White television viewers in the Magnolia State had a limited tolerance for dissenting opinions entering their living rooms. The rival NBC station preceded its network news show from New York with the announcement that the news show represented "managed" Northern reporting. Officials and technicians were courteous when we entered the station, but they handled us gingerly and speeded up our stay as a restaurant owner might who was called on to serve a band of typhoid carriers. After a five-minute "rehearsal," the discussion began. The program was to be called "Challenge" and I said:

"Sometimes in these United States of America, an election year comes along that offers a particular challenge to Americans. Nineteen sixty-four is such a year. It is a year when the Civil Rights Law has opened the gateway to full citizenship for millions of American Negroes. And here in Mississippi, a new political party called the Freedom Democratic Party wants to play a role in this election year. What is it? Why is it? How does it work and who can join? These are some of the questions this panel is going to discuss . . . so that the citizens of this state, both white and Negro, will have a better understanding of the Freedom Democratic Party. The aim of this discussion is the truth, and the truth is not always easy. But there is no freedom without truth, and no truth without the freedom to express it."

Hardly revolutionary words—except in Mississippi. The panel took great pains to explain that the party did not want to take over Mississippi elections but only to join in them. The party explained over and over again that it had been formed because black Mississipians could not enter the regular Democratic Party. They said the party was designed to show that if they were given the chance to exercise constitutional rights, Negroes wanted to vote and to participate in the political life of the state. The members made it clear that because they believed the regular white delegation was illegal, they would demand representation in Atlantic City. The concept was an anathema, of course, to white Mississippi. And, as events were to demonstrate, too rich for the political blood of President Johnson and a lot of other Americans whose life experience did not include being black in Mississippi.

After the taping about twenty-five cars gathered for the trip to Philadelphia, a hodgepodge cavalcade of civil rights leaders, state police, FBI men, and correspondents. One month had passed since the lone station wagon with Chaney, Schwerner, and Goodman had entered the city. Now townspeople gaped at the new intruders bringing their lawmen with them. With wheels spinning in fast turns that sent up dusty clouds, we cut across the railroad tracks onto the dirt roads of the colored section. We moved with assurance. Philadelphia could not intimidate our brave procession. The mind kept returning to that lone station wagon that dared to come without protection—three young men with no FBI to guard them or correspondents to chronicle their drive. . . .

No arrangements had been made for the arrival of Dr. King and SNCC's John Lewis. We stopped outside a pool hall, the recreation center for the colored community. The pool hall was an oversized box of cinder blocks near a ramshackle frame building that had once been a ten-room hotel and was now the Freedom House. Some curious colored kids gathered around the cars; "Niggertown" had never seen anything like this. COFO workers scurried around to houses summoning people to the pool hall. A crowd of fifty, mostly children, a few women, finally was assembled. I did not see a single adult Negro man. Women and children first; black breadwinners had to use discretion in Philadelphia. Rev. Abernathy stood by a pool table, its green felt bald in patches, and delivered a warm-up spiel. His very dark face glistened with sweat in the humid room. ("You know why they call 'em shines, don't you?")

"We want to commend you for your courage in spite of threat, intimidation and violence. So we have come down here to be with you and make a first-hand investigation of the situation here in Philadelphia. We've said all along that Negroes want freedom all over the state of Mississippi, including Philadelphia. (Applause) Senator Eastland says the Negro is satisfied with segregation. Is that right? (No-o, cried loudly) Isn't that wonderful? And are you willing to fight for freedom? (Ye-es, cried faintly) Isn't that marvelous? We're so happy now to present to you the leader of our race, the leader of our people, the leader of the non-violent revolution. . . ."

The spiel smacked of cornpone evangelism. Make way for de Lawd God Jehovah. The kids' faces in a dark cluster about the table seemed to expect something big and exciting, something beyond the dingy pool hall, beyond their black lives, a few magic words of bolster, and maybe Rev. Abernathy and Dr. King knew the incantation.

"I could not conceive of going to the spot where the church was burned," Dr. King said, "without visiting you. They have probably given their lives for your freedom and mine. I see a lot of young people here. Now you have been born into a world that presents you with so many conditions that cause you to feel that you are inferior, that cause you to feel that you are less than any white man. But if I can leave anything with you this afternoon, I want each of you to feel that you are just as good as anybody else that God created in this world. I want you to know that you are somebody and that you are God's children."

The old-innocent eyes stared at him without expression.

"Now the second thing I want to say is this: With all the conditions you live with there is the temptation for you to be afraid. But if we are gonna be free as a people we've got to shed ourselves of fear and we've got to say to those who oppose us with violence that you can't stop us by bombing a church. You can't stop us by shooting at us. You can't stop us by brutalizing us because we're gonna keep on keeping on until we're free."

They came alive at that remark. They had been reached, and he took them along a little further in a talk about voting, asking them to tell their mothers and fathers to get behind the Freedom Party.

"We will come to that day," he concluded, "when all God's children in this state will be able to live together as brothers. So I say to you keep on. Cooperate with the Movement, children. Don't you get weary, 'cause there's a great day comin'."

The visit to the burned-out church seemed anti-climactic. Our mass journalistic assault on the ruins seemed an intrusion onto ground sanctified by the past presence of men on nobler missions. Dr. King gave a lackluster talk about the role of the church in the Movement. John Lewis recalled that ten churches had so far been burned in Mississippi.

"In America," he said, standing on a remnant of tin from the roof, "we have the religious slogan, 'Worship at the church of your choice.' It appears to some of us that the slogan is, 'Burn the church of your choice.'"

Lewis' statement sounded inappropriately wiseacre from someone who was a dedicated, serious man, not given to glibness. Words were not needed anyway. The setting, which had been a magnet for men of humanity and for their opposites, said it all.

On August 3, on a farm outside Philadelphia, the FBI found the three who had visited the church a month before us. They were under twenty feet of Mississippi red clay, earth piled for a dam under construction above them. Deputy Cecil Price, sweating in the 100-degree heat of the August sun, helped carry the bodies. Each of the young men had been shot, and Chaney had been beaten. Dr. David Spain, a pathologist from New York with twenty-five years' experience, examined Chaney:

". . . the jaw was shattered; the left shoulder and upper arm were reduced to pulp; the right forearm was broken completely across at several points; and the skull bones were broken and pushed in toward the brain. Under the circumstances, these injuries could only be the result of an extremely severe beating with either a blunt instrument or chain. . . . It is impossible to determine whether the deceased died from the beating before the bullet wounds were inflicted. . . . I have never witnessed bones so severely shattered, except in tremendously high-speed accidents such as airplane crashes."

The FBI had an informant who had witnessed the murder and directed them to the grave. No immediate arrests followed. The discovery of the bodies had no noticeable effect on the violent-minded men of Mississippi. The next night a church in Natchez was burned to the ground. Shortly, the bombs began going off in McComb and the beatings continued here, there and everywhere. In New York, Andrew Goodman's parents grieved. His father read a statement to the press:

"For ourselves, we wish to express our pride in our son's commitment and that of his companions, now dead, and that of his companions, now alive, now in Mississippi, acting each hour to express those truths that are self-evident."

Mickey Schwerner's widow, Rita, said through her attorney that she hoped the sacrifice of the three would bring redoubled efforts to secure civil rights in Mississippi. And in Meridian on August 7, the shattered body of James Chaney was buried while his mother and brother Ben, no longer dry-eyed, watched him enter the same Mississippi earth that stretched to another black resting place, to the Mount Zion churchyard and its pile of ashes and its headstone: "Just Sleaping."

THE INVADERS

Unfriendly critics of the civil rights volunteers who went into Mississippi have accused them of everything from interracial lovemaking to Communism. Charges that they were guilty of these two deadliest of sins originated in the South but soon spread to the North, where the remarks were welcomed by the same unselective minds that earlier had accepted Southern reports of widespread Negro contentment in Dixie. Segments of the press aided in this indictment of the volunteers and catalogued lesser specifications: They were beatniks; they did not bathe or cut their hair; they were arrogant and contemptuous of established values, and they caused unrest, instead of truly advancing the cause of civil rights. That elements of truth existed in most of these charges disturbed even some independent minds. An American trait demands unblemished heroes. I think the accusations say more incisive things about America than they do about the volunteers.

For instance, assuming the accusations were one hundred percent true, questions are immediately raised: If only the sloppy, the subversive, and sex-mad invaded Mississippi, where were the prim, patriotic, and Puritan-minded young Americans who supposedly believed in democracy? Were they back on the campus, getting neatly barbered, then hilariously smashed at beer parties, and showing their scorn for bourgeois values by plotting panty raids? Samples of Madison Avenue's—and Main Street's—dream of what young America should look like were in a minority among the workers. Not so many robust boys with golden crew-cut blond hair and even smiles, or girls joyful in the pretty bloom of their smooth-skinned faces and curving bodies, sexual but "nice," came to Mississippi.

I remember many discussions with reporters reciting how repelled they were by the appearance of the CORE and SNCC people. The slack-shouldered boys, acne-faced girls, the evidence of personality problems in tight faces, their hostility and suspicion, their irritating efforts to "out-basic" each other. More and more focus was placed on the personal aspects of the volunteers until an image developed of the average boy volunteer being bearded, smelly, and probably Jewish, and the average girl a lank-haired, flat-chested neurotic horror who, with a folk song on her lips, jumped from one colored boy's bed to another.

When I would talk to visitors from the North or people in Atlanta about the workers, their questions indicated a fascination with this personal side, combined with almost superficial interest in what the kids were really doing. The soul of American conformity seemed outraged and quick to accept the worst suggestions about the behavior of youngsters who lay outside the Norman Rockwell model for our times. Of course, segregation was wrong. To inflict a bunch of loudmouth psychic misfits, who were probably rebelling against their parents, on a hapless Southland that, Lord only knew, had problems enough wasn't right either.

This reasoning demonstrated a desire on the part of the American public opinion while commiserating with the South to believe the worst about civil rights forces. The Southerner is seen as a man who has sinned, yes, and suffered for his sins, yet he is somehow more reassuringly American in a better, older sense than these unwholesome, guitar-toting rebels gone South to dissipate as much as to agitate. Did COFO workers fornicate among themselves? Did black and white have intercourse? Yes, a lot did. Well, wasn't that proof that the whole thing was, in the delicate language of McComb's Mayor Gordon Burt, "just a damn screwin' orgy"? No. Most of the volunteers and staff were of an age when sexual juices are flowing abundantly and the imperative to make love is irresistible. From what I saw in various Freedom Houses where I stayed, a good deal of lovemaking was performed under ideal conditions—no parents or damning adults around to interfere with graphic proofs that interracial equality was a reality. Negro boys made love to many, but by no means all, white girl volunteers. White boys had young colored girls, in the ranks and out. While this admission is true, it can be misleading unless one accepts lovemaking as a fact of life rather than interpret it as a proof of depravity.

Anyone with a taste for interracial lovemaking did not have to come to

Mississippi to satisfy it. It would have been safer to establish liaisons in Chicago or San Francisco or New York, where life was not endangered and the living was materially more pleasant. Did some persons take advantage of the sexual freedom and concentrate on indulgence? I think so. Certain Negro boys I kept running into over the months seemed to spend most of their time hanging around the COFO offices, trying to maneuver the girls, white and black. White boys had dropped like gods into black rural communities where sex was as natural as sleep. Little black girls were eager to show their gratitude in ways the boys were pleased to accept. While all this "loving" was done in the name of equality, I sometimes found it morally disturbing. Some of the adult Negroes in the communities also found it disturbing. No, the white planter wasn't taking their women, but a white boy bringing freedom.

In the ranks of COFO were the sordid, the bizarre, and the stupid. A couple of white boys wore earrings and talked like faggots from *Naked Lunch*. A Negro girl in Greenwood thought Goldwater-Miller was one man, not a ticket. One night in the Hattiesburg office I saw a runtish white boy with a sickly beard pawing a scrawny and unclean Negro girl with razor scars on her face. Both of them were glassy-eyed drunk. Another night in the Jackson headquarters, a drunk Negro teen-ager broke a Coke bottle over the head of a Negro worker and threatened all the white workers who—adopting their habitual attitude in Mississippi— deferred to the Negro.

I would become periodically enraged when trying to get information from self-important adolescents who were both ignorant and arrogant. Slovenliness among many was a badge of honor, and this statement is said after making allowances for youth's cavalier disregard for neatness. I slept in Freedom House beds on sheets that would give pause to a resident of a Bowery hotel, and washed in bathrooms unfit for human use. Intelligent discussion was impossible with many of them, particularly the girls, because of their shrill insistence on speaking in terms of absolutes, no shadings or modification allowed to touch their pure and precious beliefs.

And yet . . .

"You must not wonder," said the Abolitionist Samuel May, "if many of us who have been left to take up this great cause do not plead it in all that seemliness of phrase which the scholars and practiced rhetoricians of our country might use. You must not expect them to manage with all the calmness and discretion that clergymen and statesmen might exhibit.

"But the scholars, the statesmen, the clergy had done nothing, did not seem about to do anything. And for my part I thank God that at least any persons, be they who they may, have earnestly engaged in this cause; for no movement can be in vain.

"We are what we are," he concluded. "Babes, sucklings, obscure men, silly women, publicans, sinners, and we shall manage this matter just as might be expected of such persons as we are. It is unbecoming in abler men, who stood by and would do nothing, to complain of us because we do no better."

As you probably suspected from the language, this quotation is old, more than a hundred years old. Other writers have called attention to the similarities between the present Movement and that older one, notably Professor Howard Zinn in his book, *The New Abolitionists*. America had gone through all this protesting once before, the parallels so poignant that as I read the history of abolition, I am continually substituting SNCC or COFO in the text and they fit neatly. Still something about our national mind, despite self-liberating advances, can recognize a social evil yet look askance at those who agitate to remove it. John Jay Chapman, who acutely observed the workings of that mind during the eighteen hundreds, wrote:

"The North died for the slave with condemnations of the Abolitionist on its lips."

I found the more I understood these latter-day Abolitionists, the more I understood myself and this country. This understanding made the volunteers troublesome to the American soul. They raised moral questions that would not go away. Sooner than probe profoundly into regions of ourselves where unpleasant surprises might await, we simply dismissed them as beatniks. Besides, what adult wants to see his inadequacies revealed through a youngster? Such revelation is galling. Well, about these galling creatures, what were they really like and what did they really do?

When SNCC and CORE cast a net of conscience over America to recruit for the summer project, the groups had to take just about anything that was gathered in. If a force big enough to achieve results were to be recruited, extreme personality cases that might cause problems were thrown back, but run-of-the-mill personality deficiencies had to be accepted.

A joke spread that anyone who wanted to come to Mississippi had to be crazy anyway. Coming to Mississippi was not so much of a joke. Anyone who came had to have a fatalistic nerve beating in him, a taste for suffering and denial, and a conviction that he was right and would prevail against frightening evidence to the contrary. The workers did not have average egos, and were, for the most part, not the average kids from next door.

Aside from a universal commitment to nonviolence, which was an absolute prerequisite, the range of personality was tremendous. Kids came down who didn't like their fathers, mothers, congressmen, or anybody else who stood for authority; kids overflowing with the dialectics of Marx, Sartre, or Christ but without the foggiest notion of how to handle realities; kids who knew it all and knew nothing. Among them were also sober-minded young men and women with quiet capacities for intense commitment, intellectuals anxious to test theory, and some very average ones who for the first time in their lives felt a call.

"Most volunteers who came to Mississippi," Bob Weil once said to me, "came to free themselves."

Bob was a volunteer who came early, stayed late, and ranged the state continually, sharing talk sessions that went on night and day among the volunteers—sessions that were as much group therapy as they were strategy meetings. What these young people were freeing themselves from varied in particulars. Generally they were freeing themselves from the American Way of Life.

The Mississippi Way of Life for the white volunteers began by their placing themselves under the control of Mississippi Negro veterans. This way of operating was a survival measure and a psychological necessity: Negroes had to begin calling the shots for themselves. I saw one indoctrination meeting in the basement of the Masonic Temple in Jackson that I think was typical. Mack Cotton, a twenty-two-year-old Negro, veteran of a dozen arrests and one of the original Freedom Riders, was in charge. Unless you believed a sprinkling of beards, guitars, and sneakers was proof of inherent instability, the group looked level-headed and capable. Any who might have had delusions about their new environment were quickly brought down to earth by Cotton, whose ironic eyes in a handsome chocolate face would have smiled at the notion any surprises were left in this life.

"Some people might think they're smart and socially conscious," he said. "They might think they can go down on the corner in Ruleville or Holly Springs, and reason with the white people. Well, don't. Physical violence is king in Mississippi and you never know what will happen."

In every group trying to learn something, always one person feels compelled to ask questions to establish his presence. Here he set his face grimly at Cotton's warnings or laughed too loudly at his jokes, and interrupted always with questions.

"You're going to tell us what our specific assignments are, aren't you?" he asked as Cotton tried to explain the program.

"Yeah, we'll get around to that," Cotton replied. "But first you have to know what the hell you're doing down here."

The questioner was not daunted. He asked the population density of certain counties. He observed that nonviolence was a "challenge to the whole history of social change." He asked whether the Citizens Council could be contrasted with the Klan in terms of opposing power structures. Cotton tolerated him but in his face was the contempt of the Doer for the Talker. He held the black knowledge earned by beatings and jailings that salvation could not be entrusted to white dilettantes.

By the time an unassuming young girl asked, "What rights have you when you're arrested?", Cotton's irritation at the blabbermouth broke through, and he smiled without humor and said:

"You have two rights in Mississippi. You can keep your mouth shut and maybe nothing will happen to you. Or you can open it and anything can happen. The United States Constitution stops at the Mississippi border."

A middle-aged lady from Greenwich Village, one of the very few older people who came down, was already having some second thoughts.

"Let's say you disappear," she said, although she did not like saying it. "Will the office here call? Will anybody look into it?"

"They will," Cotton said.

"You say that with a big smile," replied the lady. "It's important to me because I've left bail money with my lawyer in New York City and he wants to be notified immediately."

"Well, sometimes," said Cotton, "they don't know in the office whether you've been arrested or whether somebody has taken you by the head down to the river."

The statement was cruel, all right, deliberately so. Cotton was saying clearly that the lady's noble sentiments might better have taken her into the Peace Corps, perhaps for a rewarding tour of duty in a less dangerous place than Mississippi, such as bandit-infested Colombia or one of the Southeast Asian countries. She was later assigned to an office job in Jackson. After Cotton read out their assignments, the others left for towns and cities in which the hazard, though varied, was never without risk.

The woman's attitude demonstrated why the volunteers had to be young. Only youth could take the absolute chances Mississippi demanded without absolute guarantees or assurances. Only young people could have reached the black boys and girls of Mississippi who were the backbone of the Movement, could have won them over so swiftly and completely to ideas that often set their parents trembling. I think the almost chemical intuitiveness of youth was at work. A white boy from Chicago, a colored boy from the Delta are culturally light years apart. Yet both are creatures of youth, hypersensitive, alternately frustrated or wildly confident, hungering to confide immensities of feeling or agonizing when personal trifles slip out. The devastating rejection of race prejudice can be felt more keenly by young people who are dogged by rejection of their precious persons or sensibilities in a world they never made. They understand better what it is to feel bereft than adults who have found some emotional sanctuary or whose wounds are scarred over. The young whites who came down were vibrating to the same universal chord of hope and despair as the blacks awaiting them. This similarity made all that followed infinitely easier than if age had plodded in to lead and lecture rather than to accompany on the Mississippi adventure.

What was the adventure to accomplish? Get Negroes registered at their courthouses for the Freedom Party elections. Make colored farmers aware of their rights under federal subsidy programs and support them as they organized to exercise those rights. Teach young and old in Freedom Schools what citizenship was all about and give tutorial help to youngsters mentally rickety from the starvation education diet Mississippi provided Negroes. The grand design was to demonstrate to Mississippi Negroes that they were no longer alone, that other Americans cared and were willing to help them learn how to stand on their own.

Given the impediment of Negro fear and apathy, and universal white opposition, the summer crusade was an ambitious program. Sometimes it seemed overambitious, considering human and physical resources. Sometimes I felt the workers unconsciously were setting impossible marks so that the built-in inevitability of failure could be used to explain away efforts that fell short of the mark. The concept and the execution therefore would not be questioned, since failure came from paucity of means. Mixed in with this subtle hedging was the apparent opposite, the cocksure bravado of youth. The young could do anything. The fact that something like the summer crusade hadn't been attempted before was all the more reason to try. Watching the kids bravely fan out over the state after the indoctrination, I felt they must be depending mostly on raw nerve to carry them through. The organization of COFO did not inspire confidence. Authority and direction were loose from the top, from men such as Bob Moses, Lawrence Guyot, and Stokely Carmichael. Between the loose leadership and the centers in the various communities, the Freedom Houses, as crisis after crisis arose, loomed a great gap that had to be filled by local leadership, self-imposed disciplines and inspired improvisation. When one viewed it from the outside, the organization seemed to verge on chaos. COFO developed its own internal rhythms and somehow the work went ahead.

The work went ahead in an atmosphere of hate and fear that is hard for an outsider to comprehend. Working in Mississippi was probably the first time that a large group of white Americans fully experienced the lonely fear and vulnerability that for centuries has been the lot of Southern Negroes. One felt that vulnerability and fear driving at night down rural roads, through seas of dark countryside. White men lived here who were without pity for anyone who did not think or act as they did. One felt the fear in bright daylight, rolling into small towns where people moved slowly around somnolent courthouse squares with their Confederate statues, boys with shotguns caught in a granite moment of charge, never to triumph, never to fall. I felt the vulnerability every time I crossed a railroad track, each crossing marked with the sign:

MISSISSIPPI
STOP
LAW

The letters were drawn long and thin. The words epitomized, to me, a sparseness of spirit, a meanness and contraction in the life of the state. The volunteers did not dwell on the violence. COFO handled the risks intelligently, exercised reasonable caution and placed great reliance on phone checks whenever the workers moved any distance. COFO did not permit prudence to cripple its work. The best of the workers came to remind me of good combat soldiers, achieving a nice balance between a desire to remain in one piece and the need to get the job done. The job was done from door-to-door on the streets of a hundred "Niggertowns"; in churches where old Negro faith in God and new faith in themselves came together; in the fields of Mississippi, and in the Freedom Houses where children and adults came to learn everything from geometry to pride.

Mrs. Pilcher, an elderly church lady with a mouthful of gold and a heart to match it, sits in her cramped living room in Greenwood in a clutter of religious tracts, battered hymnals and saccharine lithographs of Jesus looking as if they were colored with Easter egg dyes. She is talking sympathetically with COFO staff worker Idell Smith, an eighteen-year-old Mississippi Negro with a beautifully composed head set on a graceful neck. Beside her are a girl and boy, white volunteers. Trying to sign up people for the Freedom Vote but without too much success, they are canvassing that night.

"People sometimes just sit on the porch and look at us and won't say a word," says Idell. " 'Course, lately I've been goofing."

"Yes, I really do get discouraged sometimes tryin' to rouse people," replies Mrs. Pilcher, her black matriarchal face looking discouraged, then brightening. "But then I have to turn around and reconsider. When you look at conditions, you have to reconsider. Because there's something involved. Yes, there's something involved.

"Now just down the block is a man with twelve children was given three days to get off his farm when he tried to register. Peoples here chipped in to rent him a house. And he feels mighty good about it now. He said he wished he had gotten off a long time ago. On that farm, they was tied down like cats."

The white girl, twenty-year-old Susan Spragg of Westfield, New Jersey, has just started work in Greenwood. She is a shy, quiet girl, trying hard to understand everything.

"Everyone is nice to me and seems to agree when I talk about registering," she says. "Do you think that's just because I'm white?"

"That's just it, honey," Mrs. Pilcher says. "You just go down to the courthouse at registration time and see if they show up. We had a Freedom Day in the spring and there was lots of arrests. And then came the excuses. A woman told me: 'My boss lady will fire me.' That's one of the holdbacks."

Idell, the old pro, tells of a local Negro high school principal who will not allow the Free Southern Theater in his school, yet permitted liquor to be served at a dance. Parents want to get a petition against him and Idell is going to encourage it.

"Ain't I evil?" she asks, a beautifully wicked smile on her full lips.

They chat a few minutes more and then leave to resume canvassing. The white boy, twenty-one-year-old David Garson of Springfield, Massachusetts, does not say much as they enter a succession of poor, one-story wooden houses, some not much better than shacks, talking to people who receive them courteously but are noncommital about participating in the vote. Many have small television sets.

"The white man made a mistake when he invented TV," Idell observes. "It lets us see the white man as he is."

The question rises in the mind, Why don't they put the money in food, education, something constructive instead of television? The answer is in their faces. Like most people, they have to have some extravagance to dress up their days. Although their lives would be better if they were disciplined enough to do without for their greater good, life would be better still if they were not poor. After a few hours, the volunteers go down a long dark street to the Negro home where they are staying. The dark streets of Greenwood have seen much violence done by white men. A very lonely feeling pervades late at night, as one mounts the creaking steps of the sagging front porch, lies in the strange bed in the poor room where insects scurry, stares at the dark and listens and thinks. Springfield and Westfield are very far away.

"I went down to the crop board last year and this year to get a little increase on the corn acreage," says William Weatherly, a forty-nine-year-old Negro who has a hundred acres of his own outside Liberty in the southwest and another 350 shared by his family.

"I did get a little. Not much. I wouldn't vote on allotments any more since they won't let me be a first-class citizen. I've made three trips to register and they won't let me. They don't want to give no kind of justice around here."

The volunteers, a white boy and a Negro from the North, know the words "corn" from a supermarket and "acreage" from suburban housing developments. Talking dryly as country men should, they sit on the front porch of Mr. Weatherly's pleasant old white clapboard farmhouse with its gnarled crabapple tree in front and a bright patch of red peppers along the rutted road to the highway. Although it is a federal program, Negroes have long been excluded from the crop allotment boards. The farmers are beginning to stir with the encouragement of the COFO workers, who often could not tell a cotton boll from a boll weevil.

"It's hard to get the Negroes involved," says Mr. Weatherly. He has a family of two boys and five girls. "They say, 'No, I get all my help from the white people, I don't want to fool with it.'"

"I'd like to come out next week to discuss the entire situation in the county," says the Negro volunteer. "Maybe organize a small meeting."

"Uh-huh," replies the farmer with some reservation. The longer they talk the more determined he gets. Old complaints rankle. Although the county paves the roads of white farmers, he cannot get his road paved. A white man has warned him, after a Negro church was bombed, that when the colored try to act like whites they get taken care of. The same man suggested that if he stopped trying to register, his road would get fixed.

"I told him," says Mr. Weatherly, "I'm not tryin' to act white. I just wanna be a first-class citizen an' maybe I can get my road fixed.

"Then the sheriff came up to see if there were any boys in the Move-

ment livin' with me. He acted nice and everything like that. But why
was he coming up here on my property to ask me?"

The sense of property is very strong in the Negro farmers as it is in
all men wedded to the land. Fear is strong that if credit is cut by whites
and notes cannot be met, the land will be lost.

"A friend of mine had a son went into the Movement," Mr. Weatherly
says. "The banker asked him about it and the man told him, 'Yes, my
boy is in it.' So the banker said, 'Well, we're not supposed to loan out
money to anybody connected with it but I can't do that to you. I've
known you too long.'"

Finally, he agrees to the meeting.

"And I will try this fall to vote on the allotments. Yes. I don't see
nothin' wrong with the Movement. It's nobody teaching against nobody.
If I see something wrong with it, then I'd get out."

The volunteers go into his field to pick some souvenir cotton bolls. He
watches tolerantly, but little time is in his life of work for frivolities.

"I don't want to run you off," he says, not unfriendly, not apologetic,
but measuring his words to their task, "but I got work to do. So I'll be
glad to see you when you come out again."

> No church burnings,
> No church burnings,
> No church burnings over me.
> And before I'd be a slave
> I'll be buried in my grave
> And go home to my Lord and be free.

The Negroes singing in the McComb church while white volunteers
tap and swing and clap know about church burnings and bombings.
Burning and bombing have been their lot all summer. In an effort to
break the Movement and force COFO out of town, more than a dozen
homes and churches have been levelled by whites. By now, the whites
have failed. A throb of triumph is in the singing as they light into a
rousing spiritual, "I'm Gonna Sit at the Welcome Table One of These
Days." The song had a special refrain for Mr. Charley, the white
man. . . .

> I'm gonna tell God how you treated me,
> One of these days.

A lanky twenty-two-year-old Negro named Jesse Harris gets up to
speak. He was a Freedom Rider and now directs the COFO project in
McComb. He says:

"A lot of people come here tonight to find out what's goin' on. (That's right, that's right.) I guess you can understand how the mayor, the sheriff, the police chief all get elected. It all boils down to the fact that a minority of the peoples in McComb voted them in there because you didn't vote. (True, true) That's why you don't have street lights or paved roads. That's why *your* kids got arrested the night white men bombed the houses, and they came out to protest. An' that's why us workers came to McComb.

"But we don't do no good cooped up in a corner down there at the Freedom House. (No, sir) We get lonely. (Laughter) We can't make any progress unless you try to vote. You owe it to the sheriff and all those nice officials. (Laughter) As long as they can keep you from the courthouse, you're gonna stay up at night with a shotgun lookin' for bombs. But I don't live here. Someday, we'll be gone. Who's gonna keep the sheriff under control then? Some organization is gonna have to do it. You're gonna have to do it. So you might as well start."

Applause and enthusiasm fill the church, which is new and pretty with white plaster walls and light pine pews. Although the church's insurance does not cover bombings, the board of deacons has permitted a meeting for the first time. People get up to talk of a beer boycott against white suppliers. A year ago such a move would not even have been whispered. A café owner says he will go along and he tells a story.

"You know where the bomb went off over in Beartown? Well, there was a lady across the street with her little girl got woke up by it. She had raised the child to believe God would protect her. An' when the bomb went off, the little girl asked: 'Mama, where's God?'"

In the front pew, a baby slept in his mother's arms. Asleep and unaware, he seemed a living symbol of what all this was for, what all the singing and sacrifice was about. A strapping railroad worker named T. J. Marshall spoke loudly but the baby did not awaken.

"We've talked long enough. We have to stop talkin' *about* Mr. Charley and start talkin' *to* him and start actin'. (Boy, that's right) We sing, 'Before I'd be a slave I'd be buried in my grave, and go home to my Lord and be free.' Now if you don't mean it, don't sing it. (Yes, sir!) Let's get on the bandwagon. Let's ride it till the wheels fall to pieces. And I know one thing—if there's nothin' to COFO there's nothin' to you, me or anything else."

The Freedom Schools, when they weren't being bombed or set on fire, presented an almost idyllic aspect: In makeshift classrooms, sometimes old buildings freshened with paint or new ones smelling of just-sawed wood, or on shady lawns, Negro children gathered around Northern boys and girls to learn things not being taught in their Mississippi schools. The most important lesson, one reiterated in every class, was that Negro children were as good as any other children. Sometimes the lesson was taught directly, more often by example. The teaching always seemed to me a labor of love for the volunteers, a warm ultimate in the summer experience. The teachers had their hands on the fresh clay and all their passionate beliefs in brotherhood could be infused into it. I saw the small dark faces looking into the white ones, sometimes in puzzlement but never with fear and often with love. For the first time in their young lives, white skin was behaving as if it were not better than black. That change was something to think about. Sometimes the volunteers, with their infinite capacity for carrying a good idea to an absurd extreme, would not permit the children to address them as "sir" or "ma'am." Since everyone was equal, youth also was equal to age and no deference should be shown. Parents and deacons had problems reestablishing good Southern manners without bruising principle.

Older children and adults were urged to attend academic classes and to use libraries donated from the North. Some libraries were excellent, particularly the one in Greenwood, which may have been the best library in the state that Negroes could use. Its shelves held everything from *The Bedside Esquire* to *War and Peace,* from Sartre novels to Churchill histories. I did not see much evidence of the books' use. The average Mississippi Negro had a fourth-grade education. Even if enough leisure had been available to read, minds unaccustomed to handling the abstracts of advanced language were not up to the task. COFO claimed its classes were a howling success, but COFO sometimes confused goal and the achievement. In communities where qualified teachers ran the classes, students made strong strides and were encouraged by their advances to aspire toward more education. I don't think there was any "great leap" accomplished. In other communities, classes were haphazard, intermittently attended and unproductive.

I remember one night sitting in the McComb COFO communications office when a volunteer dashed in and cried:

"Anybody here can explain trigonometry? Somebody in class is asking about it."

Told that there were no trigonometry teachers on the premises, he smiled and said:

"Okay. So I'll get a book and look it up."

Off he went into the night, indomitable. Once I drove three Negro kids to their farm home from the McComb School.

"Can you speak French?" a boy about fifteen asked me.

I told him I remembered one sentence from a bout with French in a Brooklyn elementary school: *Le livre est sur le banc.* He repeated it and said (as nearly as I can remember):

"Je ne parle pas français."

His pronunciation sounded pretty good to me and I complimented him.

"I just started learning it," he said. "That's all I got so far. I'm bringin' home the records the COFO's loaned me."

He had a Berlitz beginner's French record. He took me into his house. His father himself had built the stout, comfortable house with big, solid planks in the floor tightly joined. The family was pleased at my visit, a little shy, but not intimidated as they would have been six months before. By now they were used to the white COFO presence. The father was a work-worn farmer, half-asleep with fatigue, but he listened proudly as his son played the record, repeating the sounds of the French instructor. His rich Mississippi Negro drawl squeezed itself with difficulty into the precise patterns of the French. At first the French lesson seemed ludicrous, even wasteful. This black boy, needing a mastery of basics if he were to prosper against the long odds laid down by the system, was fooling around with a foreign language that had all the practical application of a primer on moon travel. The reality of possibility, the limitlessness of aspiration—these concepts were needed by people who did not know how to believe in their intellectual capabilities or to dream of matching the white man's achievements. I don't know whether the boy pursued the French lessons. Perhaps they only lasted a few weeks and then the records were stuck away in some cupboard—consigned to dusty forgottenness. Their absence might have been momentarily noticed by the family, like the disappearance of a brilliant bird who comes to your tree for a day or two and then is gone. I hope not. Before we left, the father gave me half a sack of yams to take back to the Freedom House.

The Freedom House. Certain whites hated these places enough to bomb them. That gift of the yams for the volunteers' table said a lot about how most Negroes felt. I came to know best the McComb house and its people. I think this house was a fair sample of others throughout the state. Actually the McComb house was two houses on a corner in the colored section. The wooden structures were in passable condition except for the patched-up side of one where a bomb had exploded. All civil rights activity radiated from this central place. A constant stream of visitors came in—ministers and visiting firemen from the North, writers from all over the world coming to see the Mississippi phenomena first-hand, COFO staff passing through, local Negroes coming for classes. The only people who never came were white Mississippians. They chose to rely on a few colored spies and their own imaginations and so they never really understood what COFO was all about. One McComb white man named Red Hepner, whose daughter was Miss Mississippi of 1962 (no slight honor in that state vain of its proud beauties), made the mistake of inviting a few white COFO workers to his home to discuss the city's racial problems. Ku Klux Klan harassment forced the family to leave town before the summer was out.

With all the traffic, Freedom House-keeping ranged from adequate to awful. It is my conviction that a majority of girl volunteers were born slovens. Efforts were made to assign kitchen responsibility each day. With people eating at all hours and crises commonplace, the kitchen generally looked like hell. Greasy dishes in the sink, roaches playing leapfrog, vile coffee of questionable age, floors—God, what floors. I think the local matrons who each day brought marvelously cooked variations on a theme of chicken, beans and hamhocks, and deep-dish pies were scandalized. The matrons also must have questioned the sleeping arrangements which generally put boys in one house and girls in the other, but admitted exception existed. The house was no place for persons who conceive of morality only in terms of sexual morality; neither was it, to again quote McComb Mayor Burt, a "screwin' orgy." The McComb house was a much more moral place than the McComb City Hall or most any city hall. The people who stayed inside were continually struggling to grasp moral ideas and to implement them. They were not concerned with making money, or reputations, or any of the other material pursuits that occupy most of our days. If my son Sean had been of age that summer, I would have wished him in a Freedom House more than any other place on earth.

The quality of the people varied wildly. Sometimes at night when there were no meetings or pressing commitments, spontaneous talk sessions would start on "weighty topics." The sessions had sense and nonsense. I don't think adults should monitor such proceedings but occasionally as I listened in my role of senior citizen (I kept reminding them that Jim Forman was thirty-five, too), I would form an image of a composite volunteer from the group who was smart, spirited, probing, brave, selfless, uninhibited and, to boot, able to sing a folksong at the twang of a guitar string. No one person embodied all those qualities; a few lacked all of them. An unfortunate characteristic of McComb was that the local young Negroes enlisted to help mobilize the community were of uneven character. They functioned mainly in the role of hangers-on, not above cadging beers from outsiders passing through. They were committed in a loose, emotional way to the Movement, but not really bestirring themselves to thoughtful attitudes.

One girl in McComb represented many of the best qualities of the volunteers. She happened not to be an American but a girl born in Hitler's Germany. Ursula Junk, twenty-two, came to this country from Darmstadt in the Western Zone to attend Iowa University. She had a strong, not particularly pretty, freckled face, light blue eyes, long straw-colored hair which she braided, and an attractive, big-bosomed body. I detail her physically because McComb citizens singled her out as an example of the dirty and sexually loose girls staying at the Freedom House. She often wore sheer black hose and short skirts which were proof enough of her morals. No one, of course, except a widowed sixty-five-year-old Southern lady from the adjoining town of Magnolia, ever spoke with her to learn what she was like. Because of this defiance of social stricture, the compassionate widow had rotten eggs thrown against her door and tacks sprinkled in her driveway. The inherent tragedy in Mississippi was the social pressure that tried to throttle interchange of speech and ideas.

Ursula's critics had blindly hit on the worst possible example to back their denunciation of COFO girls. She was teutonically tidy and worked valiantly to raise the Freedom House kitchen from its customary position as a model for a board of health horror film. From what I observed over a number of weeks, she was either sexually abstinent or abnormally discreet. She disapproved of the sexual adventuring of some of the white boys who were casually taking fifteen- or sixteen-year-old local girls to bed. She disapproved not necessarily on moral grounds, since lovemaking was endemic among young teen-agers in the community, but because she felt that it might confuse purposes in the minds of the adults and weaken community approval of the COFO presence.

Ursula was dedicated, as many of the girls were, to her rounds of teaching Negro children and encouraging adults in the voter drives. She had a balanced mind, which many volunteers lacked, which could encompass criticism of COFO tactics without losing faith in the cause. She had a reflective mind. I once asked her why American youngsters attracted to civil rights did not seem so bitter against their parents as post-war German children were bitter against theirs for having tolerated Hitler, for not having fought racial prejudice in the twenties and thirties.

"I think there are two things," she said. "First, what happened here was not so graphically bad or so compressed in a little time as it was in Germany with the Jews. That happened in a generation and so a generation could be easily held responsible. And then parental control here is not nearly so strict as in Germany, and children did not feel their parents had been forcing them to accept the immorality of racial prejudice as German children did who had been in Nazi Youth or perhaps had older friends who had been in it. Do you agree?"

I thought she was logical, and agreed. I also thought that she, knowing that her foreignness would single her out for special persecution, was an extraordinary girl to come to a place like McComb. And it did. She was regularly cursed by women in downtown stores, frequently spat on, and always had to bear a weight of hatred in the air around her. The hatred coming from the populace at large was one thing. There were other things. On the night of September 21, Ursula and her co-workers held a prayer meeting at a church that had been destroyed by bombs and fire the night before. Police arrested her and five others on charges of inciting a riot. They had been praying.

"I told a policeman," Ursula recalled, "that I had the right to contact my embassy, and have them provide a lawyer. The officer replied: 'When you come to Mississippi you ain't got no rights, don't you know that?' I said that I had heard this but I did not know personally until now. He then made some remarks to the effect that if I did not like Mississippi I should stay out and that Germany had burned plenty of people also. I replied this was correct and the reason why I was in Mississippi."

The clarity of this logic was lost on her interrogators. They asked whether she had lived in East Germany and belonged to the Communist Party. The jailers listened to her denials with the skepticism of men who lacked adequate knowledge to judge the testimony they elicit. Then they swung to the subject which is an obsession with so many Southern white men. When Ursula said they asked her if she dated "niggers," I thought of Ruth at the Klan rally in Atlanta.

"I told them," she said, "that I dated people. 'Do you mean white people or niggers?' they asked me. I said the word 'people' again and then they asked me if I meant two of the Negro boys arrested with me. Finally, a man who was a plainclothesman asked, 'Do you sleep with niggers?' I didn't answer and he began to insult me in awful language. Other policemen came in and started making remarks about my relationships with Negroes in language I can't repeat.

"They asked me if I had a veneral disease checkup and whether I slept with a different nigger every night. Finally I told them that I was a Catholic and one said, 'Those niggers like to climb on top of Catholics too.'"

The relish that the officers took in questioning her came as no surprise. What came next did. The local police cleared out and two FBI men came in. They asked her a series of questions about where she stayed, about the bombed church, and the bombed home of a Negro resident named Mrs. Quinn who was friendly to Ursula and the other workers.

"Then," she said, "one suddenly asked: 'You said you were a Catholic?' I said, Yes. 'When are the Masses?' I told him seven and nine A.M. 'But you didn't go to church last Sunday?' I told him I had gone with one of the Negro workers. 'But you were late?' Yes, I told him, I was late. I couldn't understand what he was getting at. Then he said: 'If you were late, you didn't go to Mass.'"

When a Catholic reaches Mass after the Transubstantiation (when the wafer is said to be changed into Christ's body and blood), he technically has missed Mass and must confess it. The FBI man followed up this excursion into liturgy by observing:

"But you offended the feelings of the community by being brought there in a COFO car and picked up after Mass. And you offended the community further."

"By what?" Ursula asked.

"Don't you know the proper way a lady dresses for church?"

"Yes, I do."

"But you were not wearing a headdress. The feelings of the community were that you went to church to demonstrate."

Ursula said that she had covered her head with a kerchief because she had no hat. The interview was assuming unreal dimensions. A church had been dynamited. A headdress worn or not worn in a church that still stood was somehow more important. Finally, she told me, the FBI man brought the ends of seeming unreality together.

"Don't you see the connection?" he asked.

"What connection?"

"The connection between your offending the community in church, and the church bombing and the bombing of Mrs. Quinn's home?"

He told her that a short time before it was dynamited she had left the Quinn house. Ursula says she checked this with Mrs. Quinn and found that it was not true.

"He seemed to tell me this to evoke my sympathies and make me feel even more responsible," she said. "I was so amazed I was not able to answer."

What was the answer? The FBI man, living symbol of our judicious federal government, seemed to be asking: "Don't you see it is your presence that is responsible for disorder?"

Ursula was amazed that the agitator was an object to be challenged, but local custom, however careless of constitutional rights, was an object to be tolerated. In COFO generally, amazement had long since given way to cynicism which was finally replaced by contempt—contempt not only for the FBI or the Mississippi white man *but for virtually all of adult white America and for much of adult black America.* This feeling must be understood if the actions and attitudes of these young people are to be understood, and their significance judged rationally. Because no matter how faulty some of their thinking processes, how irritating their look or behavior, they realized through experience the extent of the awful lie adult America was living. Their minds made the necessary exertion to probe behind the facade of democracy to see the wormwood and then went further, trying to understand the cause of the rottenness, and further still to propose repair. What did they think? Let me try to distill a general argument from dozens of conversations with some who were humanists and some who were Marxists and others too vague to be classified.

"What good does it do to get a Negro a seat in a restaurant for a meal he probably can't afford if you don't change the environment that produced him? New federal laws may weaken the apparatus of segregation and discrimination but they don't touch the structure of American society that makes possible a Mississippi or a Harlem, New York. When a society is primarily motivated by desire for profit, any sin can be committed with impunity if it insures profit. Unless the structure of Mississippi and America is completely overhauled, unless poor whites and Negroes who farm the land and work the mills can forge alliances to wrest political power from the exploiters, then all we will be doing is introducing the Negro to his place in a corrupt bourgeois world. Mississippi has to be turned upside-down, and the time to start is now when great upheaval produces a kind of emotional mobility. But if it's deferred, then things will solidify here again and we will witness the slow and painful process of Negroes being corrupted the 'whiter' they become."

They longed for a new populism, coalitions of farm and factory men dedicated to the general welfare of the common man. They dreamed of model communities where interracial bodies plotted, not for political power, but to expand the human spirit. Since nowhere in the state could Negroes enter local government, some projects tried to set up para-governments with colored citizens running mock departments of housing, recreation, and the like. Each individual would be free to think his own thoughts and act unfettered by custom or narrow moralism.

All of this theorizing sounded either utopian or communistic. At any rate the arguments seemed ill-considered, brash, and calculated to inflame white folks who were mad enough as it was. If we suspend judgment on the value of these goals, the fact remains that most of America simply was not up to thinking in such drastic terms. The newsmen who tried to cover the COFO volunteers as a group exemplified this lack on America's part. All but a very few came in wanting to collect stories of violence, police brutality, volunteer heroism, Negro suffering. These stories *were* necessary so that America could see the features of Mississippi, and many newsmen ran great risks to get them. But America had to see that the features of Mississippi were part of its own face, and to a disturbing degree, part of the face of all adult Americans. That characteristic included the men who were getting the news, many other writers and me. We were nicely dressed and fairly well-heeled and mentally satisfied that we were on the side of the angels because we were not rednecks itching to hit a "nigger" with an axe handle. To be treated disdainfully by arrogant kids, regarded with hostility when one was trying to do them a favor by getting their story and taking a chance with one's life in the process, was frustrating and humiliating. "Snotty." That was the word for them.

What was the word for those of us who perhaps saw in them ghosts of our own vital spirits of rebelliousness which had, like stomachs, grown slack with years? If they were right, if adult America had proved itself inadequate, we were part of that inadequacy. They were taking their moment of youth to try to set things right. Had we done much with our own brave years, had we ever even stopped to analyze hard enough what our America was supposed to be about? The conscience is troubled to see someone doing what you know you should have done. So now there was a choice. Either let them prod us into reevaluation, with all its painful imperative to reject long-held and comfortable beliefs, or dismiss them as snotty kids. I have my private vision of this confrontation that led to much misunderstanding between the press and COFO, between America and COFO. I saw the adults, slightly pot-bellied, thoughts corpulent, anxious over sex, bedevilled by health and money, watching the volunteers but disregarded by them, as the workers went their lean, instinctual way, exuding sexual vigor, sure of health, contemptuous of money. We were disregarded. Leaving them in their tight little world, where threat and tension and material lacks somehow produced contentment, we went back to our motels on our expense accounts, puffy and pontificating.

I say "contentment" because that was the emotion I sensed most strongly in them, in the good ones. They regarded their Freedom Houses as enclaves of the genuine in a world of fraud. A Negro girl from Chicago, named only Loren in my notes, once told me:

"The only reality seems to be here. Maybe it's truly reality or maybe it isn't, maybe it's something we've created that will go away. I don't know. We drove to Atlanta a few weeks ago for a big staff meeting and on the way I said, 'It's funny to be in the outside world.' I said it without thinking. I can't stand the thought of going back to Chicago. Here you feel so secure and peaceful. You live together as people, not as white and colored, and I don't ever want to live another way again."

"Secure and peaceful" may seem strange words to apply to a way of life ringed by hate and shot through with fear. This feeling was the secret that made the volunteers strong and impervious. Dennis Sweeney, a twenty-two-year-old, clean-cut, collar-ad youth, was at the same Atlanta meeting where ideological differences were threshed out in interminable discussions.

"It was like some kind of socio-political drama," he said. "Some factions felt that COFO should continue to be structured in a normal way with authority coming down from the top, a staff of leaders who would do the decision-making. Most of us felt decision-making should come from each community because that's the whole essence of why we're here . . . not to tell people. My God, people have been telling Negroes what to do for years, but to feed ideas in and let them think it out and put it together. But this thing in Atlanta, I mean, we were all in the same cause but we were tearing each other apart.

"That's why it was so good to get back to McComb. You feel you're really *doing* something here. And this may sound idealistic but you get such sustenance from the people. The kids especially. They're so eager and—uncorrupted."

To the eager and uncorrupted, COFO was trying to bring a creed laced with the sophisticated thinking of Camus and Sartre. To many who watched and reported, COFO's creed seemed a typical presumption, proof of their unsoundness and radicalness, to belabor with complicated philosophy Negro minds not trained to handle abstract ideas and needing instead simple, straightforward help. Bob Weil once explained to me:

"What's involved is a continual assertion of man's right to make decisions for himself. This implies complete equality of everybody in the Movement. And this means everybody with no exceptions. The drunk counts as much as the preacher. He is part of what everything is about.

He drinks because he is black and oppressed. But no one can be allowed to assert superiority over him or tell him what to do.

"At the Atlanta meeting one session was to be chaired by a seventeen-year-old boy from McComb. But he was anxious about whether he could do it and he got drunk. But we let him go on. Well, he did pretty badly, yelling and letting the meeting get out of hand. And some people there finally got him removed. That broke him. He left crying because he had failed. But he was more important than the meeting and no one should have stopped him. He drinks because he is black and oppressed in the South. Still, he's as good as anybody."

More than Weil would care to admit, this kind of absolute permissiveness probably reflected the personal needs of many volunteers in rebellion against society and their parents. The notion of unencumbered freedom, a howling "Yes" to people beaten down by an eternal "No" may have been beautifully humanistic in theory. The assertion may have helped build confidence in adults who needed massive reassurance that they finally were independent human beings. But the notion often worked mischief with youngsters with little life experience (and all of that warped by race) who came to believe that they were equally equipped as any adult to make decisions.

The experience fostered sullen wise-guyism in some, a suspicion of any adult, a maddening inability to discuss without falling back on the COFO Book of Revelation. If anyone of an older generation were hesitant about committing himself or expressed doubts, he was dismissed as an Uncle Tom. They lumped these people all together as being bent on safeguarding their contemptible material gains. They could not see that youth, with nothing to risk, can easily risk all. To them virtually anyone in the NAACP was an Uncle Tom. Perhaps by 1964 standards they were. Many had joined fifteen or twenty even thirty years before, when it was an act of heroism. The years had worn some of the hard edge off them. For these black kids getting hold of a creed, the only time was now. The only history worth recording was the one they were writing. I think the COFO staff also fostered in them excessive cynicism about. Dr. King. His ministerial mien, to say nothing of his bourgeois orientation, aggravated many staffers. To use Norman Mailer's handy divider for our times, they were hip, he was square. He epitomized to them a galling success of a philosophy they did not share, an incomplete vision, an adult's cautious, modified revolution. They had the sweet, absolute, hard truth of life in their program, in their bodies, in the spiritual web that joined them together. The notion was noble and callow. Youth exercised absolute authority but without absolute wisdom.

Youth had all the answers; age had all the responsibility for generations of failure. Compassion for failure was nonexistent because compassion is only learned through knowing that sometimes you have failed.

Young black Mississippians were being remade in the image of young whites and Negroes, who came to their state to smash idols of authority as they made a revolution. Would the situation have been better if the invaders brought neater hair and minds and deeper tolerance, if they had been uniformly wholesome, if they had been more to the national taste? My questions had flaws that really makes them meaningless. My query does not consider whether they could have met those conditions and still have achieved what they did.

I would sooner take them as they were, babes and sucklings, some psychologically and physically messy, raw with needs and lacks. They could have wallowed in Northern coffee houses dismissing all life values, drowning their manhood and womanhood in talk, or drinking down their insufficiencies, or drugging themselves to impotence. Instead, they chose to work for an ideal. They found somewhere in themselves a kind of mental and physical courage that had disappeared in American young. They packed their guitars and oddball ways, and came to Mississippi to serve. They would have been hated by white Mississippi had they been well-barbered and conformists. Being as they were pitched the hatred higher, and they touched off sometimes murderous fury.

Their leaders had said that the only way to crack Mississippi was to force the issue by bodily presence, inviting retaliation by the politically corrupt and morally bigoted. The volunteers were to force the issue until the national government was moved by national shame and revulsion to rise up against the anomaly in our democracy called Mississippi. Before 1964 was out, the reluctant FBI and the Justice Department began translating legalisms into action, and an awakened federal conscience began contemplating new laws to make all Mississippians citizens. Sparks of determination were struck in black communities. Even the minds of some white men—if not their hearts—were stirred to question, where before they had slavishly accepted anything in the name of white supremacy.

These changes, incomplete but momentous for Mississippi and the nation, were the achievement of the COFO staff and volunteers. Thinking of them now, I know the day will come when the beards come off, work begins, and the blood will not flow so brightly. Age slowly replaces militancy with caution, and compassion sometimes is gained at a loss of commitment. But I think that what they did will always remain with them, no matter how deeply they slip into the pettifogging routines of adult life, no matter how much the inevitable growth of self-interest chokes off idealism. The knowledge that one summer they dared to love their fellow man at risk will be a small, warming flame inside them, a reminder of what they were—and of what man can always be if he will.

DOUBLE-BARRELED
UNIVERSITY TOWN

A writer occasionally gathers physical reminders of stories and later the reminders serve as tangible aids to memory. I have a battered, steel-jacketed rifle bullet. I hold it, and its cool mite of weight summons that beachfront cottage outside Saint Augustine, Florida, riddled by shotgun and rifle fire because the white owner had permitted Dr. Martin Luther King to stay there. I see myself picking the bullet off the sunlit floor again; broken window glass crackles under my feet, an echo resounds with the violence done the night before. Dunes go down to the white level beach that stretches before the surge and fall of small waves that are bonded in the brotherhood of Atlantic waters to other waves falling on Black Africa. The muffled fall of the water on the sand enhances magnitudes of silence, and then the glass crackles again.

This pamphlet in front of me now says:

Presenting
Philadelphia
Mississippi
La Wa Chito
Aickpachi
(Heap Big Welcome)

The Chamber of Commerce pamphlet points out that Philadelphia is the heart of the Choctaw Nation. Photographs are shown of a new hospital, new schools, handsome churches, a golf course.

"The most outstanding attraction of both Philadelphia and Neshoba County," I read, "is the friendly and hospitable people who make the area their home. A visitor to our community finds an old-fashioned welcome and a degree of friendliness that exists in no other place."

I see a bright orange helicopter vivid against the blue, humming over Philadelphia pine woods, looking for the three boys named James Chaney, Michael Schwerner, and Andrew Goodman. The irony is almost too great.

Something as mundane as a yellow garage receipt for car repairs puts me back in touch with the life and death of Lemuel A. Penn. The receipt is from the Guest Garage, 423 East Hancock Avenue, Athens, Georgia. The date is July 21. The biggest item is one Spitfire Axle Assembly at $80.00 and the total is $87.75, a fair enough price. The receipt brought me close to a story in which random death came to a man because he was a Negro traveling a new road. The symbolism is there for the taking.

The date was Saturday, July 11, and Sean and I were playing football in a park across from the house. The grass was springy with summer rain and the ball picked up warm mud when it bounced on bare spots. The smell of grass, mud, and leather pointed me irresistibly back to young days past. Earlier that day, the circle of life that a father and son can make had been broken for another man and boy.

Ruth called me to the phone. A radio news editor from CBS in New York wanted me to go to Athens on a free-lance assignment. A Negro educator from Washington, D. C., Lieutenant Colonel Lemuel P. Penn, had been shotgunned to death near Colbert outside the city of Athens while driving home with two other Negro officers from summer training at Fort Benning, Georgia. Evidence indicated the incident was racial murder with Penn a chance victim of white extremists. The KKK, flaunting guns publicly, had been active in Athens. The Civil Rights Act was just nine days old.

Georgia Governor Carl Sanders was already denouncing the crime on the radio. He had always struck me as a bloodless sort—a handsome All-American boy grown into a predictable young politician. In the past, he had given bland endorsement of moderation in things racial. Political winds were mixed in Georgia. Since the prevailing wind seemed to be in the direction of progress in race relations, I thought his stand took no special courage. Besides, the approaching national Democratic convention could be the setting for the emergence of a new breed of Southern leadership—men who carried moderate credentials. Marking the streams of conviction and expediency in a politician is as hard as is knowing his depth. How well do they know themselves? On that July 11, Governor Sanders found the voice to say what had to be said:

"What's happening is that we are permitting the rabblerousers and extremists to become more and more vocal and influential while the good people—the vast majority—are either not concerned enough or not cou-

rageous enough to speak out as they should. If we want to see our
state destroyed, our citizens demoralized and the very foundations of our
nation undermined, we have only to let this type of individual assume
greater prominence and eventually take over, and this will be the end of
America."

To Penn's wife, he wired:

"On behalf of the people of Georgia, I extend our deepest sympathy
to you and your family in your hour of bereavement."

Three weeks before in Mississippi, faced with the probability of a
similar racial crime, Governor Paul Johnson had said:

"They're probably off in Cuba laughing at us."

That reaction came from a man who had said a few months before in
a campaign speech that the initials NAACP stood for "Niggers, apes,
alligators, coons, and possum." The difference between his reaction and
Sanders' denunciation was the difference between these two Southern
states. One was envenomed with hate, proud of being a pariah, a syn-
onym for the worst that American democracy could produce. The other
was trying to remake itself, crack the shell of tradition, not open-heart-
edly embracing the creed of equality, but at least reaching a hand to
reason and maybe grasping understanding in the process. Something
murderous now had been let loose.

   I did not stop to pack or plan. I pushed the car as hard as it would go
along Highway 85 leading to Athens about seventy miles away. The '61
Triumph convertible was in bad shape. The compression was shot; each
grade became an Alp. A morbid noise was developing around the right
rear wheel. The grinding sound was misery to hear because I felt that
at any minute something would wear through, fly out, fall off. Still, for
as long as the car held together, I had the old sense of elation to be
hurrying toward an important story again. Actually to touch the event
that others will only read about or watch on a television screen is a narcotic that keeps many hooked to the profession. The job livens the
senses while it dehumanizes. Reporting stimulates action and defers reflection, and sometimes cripples the ability to reflect beyond immediacy.
The man, Lemuel Penn, only existed for me and the public because he
had died. About ten hours had gone by since he had passed along the
road I drove. His mind had probably been alive with the hundreds of
trivial and meaningful thoughts that fill our moments when we are well
and feel no intimations that our mortality is limited. Yet up ahead, can-
cellation, one of life's tragic flukes, was waiting. The murder was something for a white-skinned driver to think about. The incident deepened a

little more his knowledge of the dimension of Negroness in the United States. All my thinking was not the news story of Lemuel Penn. I stopped at a gas station near Athens to ask directions to Colbert.

"Where?" said the young attendant.

I told him again, pronouncing it as actress Claudette Colbert's last name. He still didn't understand.

"Where they had that shooting this morning, the other side of Athens," I said.

He gave me the directions, courteously and with that precise knowledge of traffic light locations and road intersections that always impresses me, for I'm dense about such things.

"Yeah," he said. "I heard over the news where they said that nigger got killed."

Lemuel Penn, university educated, holder of a master's degree, lieutenant colonel in the United States Army, or a Negro field hand, illiterate and unskilled, were both the same—"that nigger."

Athens, befitting its name, houses the state university. One sees little of the intellectual side as one enters. An overall impression exists of a clean, well-ordered small city, commonplace and distinctly American. Assuring him by their presence that the primary needs of existence will be satisfied in Athens, the visitor is first received by gas stations and used car lots. The commercial heart of the city is clotted with utilitarian business buildings that could be put down any place in the country and not seem strange. Athens *has* quiet streets with fine old trees and substantial homes, yards for grass, flowers, and children. This best part of the American town tradition is not evident as one rolls in. Another part of the tradition, called "Niggertown," is also not evident.

Driving out the other side on Route 72, I saw red clay fields, plucked corn stalks, virginal green alfalfa, and small herds of fat cows. Night had fallen when Penn passed, and all these sights, the last things he would see on earth, must have slipped into a nighttime blur.

Colbert is the living example of the joke about the town so small that one would miss it if one blinked. I saw the road sign COLBERT, went by a gas station across from a railroad track with a patch of blood-red canna flowers alongside, and I was out of town. When I drove back, I saw a small red-brick building near the station with a sign, CITY HALL.

Police Chief Dewey Carruthers and two townsmen were lounging and talking in a room with a beat-up table, a few chairs, an oil heater gathering spider webs, and a Boy Scout calendar. The chief was a blunt, friendly man, notable only for some fingers missing on his trigger hand.

A .38 was slung on that side. He and the men were not reluctant to talk about the murder. For this day, at least, Colbert would stretch from coast to coast. We are all impressed to be part of the major event.

"I don't believe it was local people," the chief said in a slow, country accent. "I believe it was some outsiders, either that or a mistake of identity. That's the one, that's the only thing I can figger. I don't think it was any local people whatsoever."

The police chief's explanation was one of the two customary reactions when crimes against Negroes were concerned. The Southerners reasoned that local people did not do it or the "niggers" themselves did the killing. This explanation was said of the Birmingham church bombing and, for a time, of Neshoba. The sheriff's night officer, Billy Smith, who had been on duty, gave this account:

Shortly after five that morning, with fog hugging the ground, a motorist drove up to Smith's patrol car parked outside city hall to report some "nigras" in trouble up the road at the intersection of Routes 72 and 172. Officer Smith found a car wrecked in a ditch and the body of a forty-eight-year-old man, identified as Lieutenant Colonel Lemuel A. Penn, a Negro. He had been killed by buckshot fired into the left side of his face. Two other Negro men, a bloodstained Major Charles E. Brown and Lieutenant Colonel John D. Howard, were in the car. They said they had been en route to Washington after completing a tour of duty at Fort Benning. Major Brown had been driving, but in Athens, Colonel Penn took over and the major went to sleep in the front seat beside him. Colonel Howard relaxed in the rear with his eyes shut. They had heard that Route 172 would help them beat early morning truck traffic, so Colonel Penn steered off down the deserted shortcut. Near a bridge across a narrow creek named Broad River, on the boundary of Clarke and Madison Counties, a car overtook them. After two shotgun blasts, Colonel Penn slumped over the wheel, mortally wounded. Major Brown was later to describe the incident on the witness stand:

"You're asleep. And all of a sudden you wake up to something that's out of this world . . . . He slumped over on my arm . . . . I felt something hot on my arm. It turned out to be blood."

In those unbelievable seconds, Brown and Howard managed to stop their car as it scraped against the bridge. Up ahead, the murder car also stopped. They thought it looked like a late model Chevy, yellow or cream in color. The officers turned their car around and raced back to Route 72, the lights of the other vehicle following them through the fog. They missed the turnoff and swerved into a ditch. The lights following them disappeared, leaving them in the pre-dawn darkness and country silence with the body of their friend. The dimension of the nightmare expanded and became fixed. The nightmare was really true. They were standing on a spot of Georgian ground neither had ever seen or thought to see. A man, who had been as warm with the anticipation of family and home as they, was dead. They somehow lived. Major Brown hailed a passing car and soon the word went out to the world.

I asked Chief Carruthers if there had been racial trouble in his town.

"Naw," he said. "None whatsoever. Martin Luther King? I've never even heard his name mentioned. They don't seem to care much for him around here. We got about eight hundred people an' only five or six Nigra families. They're all good, law-abidin' Nigras an' we get along fine."

The Ku Klux Klan had been reactivated throughout Georgia. I asked hadn't there been any night-riding or cross-burnings in the area despite their good relations? No, he did not know of it and if the Klan *were* active, he would know.

"The townspeople is pretty upset," he went on. "It's come right in on us for some reason or another an' we here don't know why. It sorta upsets the people an' they want the guilty party found."

After Philadelphia, Mississippi, his explanation sounded civilized. I hoped he was telling the truth. We said goodbye and I went to the car to edit the tape of our conversation. A man about my age, sallow-faced and nondescript, walked over to the car and started reaching out in my direction. I braced for God knew what, but all his hand held was a picture postcard.

"Howdy," he said, his voice mild, almost apologetic. "I hope you're not fixin' to say anything bad about us. Here, I'd like for you to take this. It's a view of the town."

The postcard showed the city hall, the gas station, and railroad track with its bed of canna flowers. The legend on the back, brainwork of local booster or postcard maker, said: "Colbert—Town of the Canna Flowers."

"People aroun' here wouldn't do nothin' like that killin'," he went on. "We got good people in Colbert, white an' colored, an' we're real shamed it happened here."

His shame was real. I took the postcard and assured him the town would not be mistreated. He had the doubtful look of a man on familiar terms with undelivered promises. I thought of all the glib assurances we swoopers-down-on-news give people to gain their confidence. I wondered if he somehow divined this. He smiled and we shook hands. Had he waited here all day for the reporters, bringing his plea and postcard to each? I called in a preliminary story to CBS. Then I drove to the murder scene. I thought of that man who cared enough for the reputation of his town, that homely speck on a map, a gas station and canna flowers. His feeling was ludicrous and praiseworthy, gauche and touching, and altogether human.

Nothing was on the bridge except a paint scrape and tire marks. Imagination made the place depressing and ominous. I drove back to Athens. The noise in the wheel was now a death rattle. Nothing was happening for the moment at the police station or the FBI headquarters which had been set up in the post office building. The car needed repairs, probably drastic from the sound of things, but I did not want to stop now. I looked for a hotel within walking distance of the FBI. A policeman recommended the Georgian Terrace, two blocks away, as "the best in town."

The hotel was six or seven stories, red-brick, solid, and respectable. Inside, the lobby gave off the musk of age, old tobacco smoke, the stale air of slow time. The place had probably once been the glory of Athens, but instead of growing venerable it had merely grown old. The Georgian Terrace had grown old like the men, who I guessed were pensioners, sitting before a television set showing whatever Athens showed in the late afternoon—in their late afternoon. One wall was banked with half a dozen oversized vending machines offering peanut butter crackers, cookies, milk, and ice cream. Would they taste faintly of oil and metal? The walls were dark with grime and shadows, and the brass spittoons unpolished outside, God knew what inside. The Georgian Terrace still clung to class. A black velour announcement board told when Kiwanis, the Civitans, Rotary, the Insurance Underwriters would arrive for their weekly comradeship and hotel meal. The white plastic letters were removable but many had uniformly yellowed in place. The board read "Tuesday—12:15." The yellowed, lettered board stirred an image of an infinity of meetings, of Tuesdays at 12:15 stretching forward and back, plates of fried chicken or glazed ham, sweet yams with marshmallow, hush puppies, pole beans. Plates were full and empty; faces—white, of course—grew older each Tuesday at 12:15. Next Tuesday, Lemuel Penn might be a topic for discussion in death but never a diner in life.

For $5.50 I got the kind of cheerless room where generations of salesmen had died, night by night, thousands of premature deaths. No Southern hospitality lived in gray-white walls whose grimness was made manifest rather than relieved by the framed magazine cover of some kittens around a vase of flowers. One wanted to get away quickly from those walls, from the rug scuffed down to its dusty threads, the bureau mirror with bile yellow spreading up from silver depths, the loveless bed. The room exuded a commercial meanness typical of an older South and Midwest that is slowly disappearing as motels move in to cater to the new traveling man who does not want the rigors of Fundamentalism at the end of a not-so-hard day and who demands coziness and the cocktail lounge. Modern motels are murdering places like the Georgian Terrace and it is a mercy killing.

The Negro bellhop wanted to sell me a pint of Scotch for seven dollars. Clarke County is dry except for beer. Since bootleggers operate all over, no one who wants to drink liquor is bothered (except financially). The rigid Baptist conscience of the county is not bothered; out of sight, out of mind. Being "dry" is, perhaps, not so hypocritical as the state of Mississippi which each year collects millions in taxes on whiskey brought illegally into the dry state and stamped by Mississippi officials. The bellhop did not want to answer questions about the local race situation or to discuss the murder. He did not shuffle, scratch his head and play Uncle Tom. He shrugged. He wanted to sell a pint of Scotch. He has his role in the corrupt white enterprise, and if some Northern "nigger" named Penn had gotten himself killed, well, that had nothing to do with him or peddling booze. His eyes and his attitude as he waited my order combined suspicion, hostility, and indifference. Martin Luther King and all of the King's men could not put *that* dark spirit together again.

I felt good leaving the hotel. I walked over to the post office. It was twilight, somber and misty. Midway to the post office, on a lawn next to the police station, stood a monument to the Civil War—a double-barreled cannon. The inventor had been a local man who dreamed of a way to beat the Yankees and came up with a cannon whose twin barrels were to eject balls linked by heavy chain. The theory was that the balls would sail into the blue ranks, chain lethally taut between them, mowing down the enemy like a scythe. Unfortunately, according to the marker, no one could ever get both barrels synchronized and one ball would invariably fire first, snapping the chain, and, I imagine, raising hell with the gunners' nerves.

The FBI had appropriated the third floor of the post office. An Air Force recruiter on the floor would find himself dispossessed when he came in Monday morning. My encounter was a typical exercise in frustration with the FBI. The press would get no information and no hope of any until Hoover released what he thought pertinent. This procedure was the only proper way to run any investigation. In the role of reporter, one's pressure to tell something pertinent makes one crowd the agents for information to which one has no right. One makes a show of gnashing teeth at official silence. One haunts halls where investigators enter and leave. The reporter is a dreadful hanger-on, asking and re-asking questions he knows will not be answered—not an edifying way to pass time. As the agents brush past I felt like a whore must feel when those solicited aren't having any.

"Can you tell us if anyone has been picked up for questioning?"

"No comment."

"Well, is there anything promising, at least?"

"No comment. Excuse me, please."

"Well, listen, there's a lot of people in the country would like to know if there's been any headway or it's a stonewall. How would you answer that?"

"I wouldn't. Really, fellows, no comment. I'm sorry."

"Have you been able to trace the car the killers were driving?"

(This from a young local radioman with the hopefulness of the young. He is not even answered with "No comment.")

"This is a helluva situation when you have the whole country in-terested and a federal agency won't give them any information. Will there be a press conference in the morning at least?"

"No comment. Goodnight, boys."

The elevator door closes on exasperated grumbles.

A death watch was kept in the post office against the longshot chance that a suspect might be brought in. During the night, some NAACP officials, led by Leon Cox, a precisely dressed young field secretary, came by. They wanted to find out what the FBI was doing and the FBI told them it was doing what it could. Cox was asked for a statement and he condemned the "dastardly" crime. He used the word "das-tardly" two or three times. He was cool. He kept a distance from the white reporters. Some of the press were irritated by his manner, his clothes, his "dastardly." I thought the cool anger and cockiness of Mr. Cox were understandable. After all, it might have been Mr. Cox instead of Mr. Penn, while it could *not* have been one of the white press who did not appreciate a young "nigger" dropping "dastardlys" all over the place and demanding explanations of the FBI.

Twenty hours before the Penn killing, a car carrying a Negro family had been fired on along the same highway taken by Penn as he left Athens. Clarence Ellington, an insurance manager from Florida, was en route to South Carolina with his wife and two small children when four shots hit the car. One entered the driver's window and narrowly missed

Mr. Ellington. His car, like Penn's, bore an out-of-state license which indicated someone was gunning for "outside niggers." Local Negroes were not immune. A seventeen-year-old boy and his sister were wounded about a month earlier when shots were fired into a colored housing project.

Three white men had been arrested. I saw their names, but they made no impression and I did not dig deeper—a sloppy oversight. Apparently some lethal element, declaring its own racial war, was stirring in the university city.

About noon, I drove the car to a garage recommended by the hotel. The Guest Garage was on Hancock Street a few blocks away from the Georgian Terrace. Small and dark, the garage smelled of damp and grease, and was cluttered with automotive guts and disemboweled cars. A boy about twenty years old rolled out from under a car he was working on and I explained the problem.

"I have to have it as soon as possible," I said. "I'm reporting on the Penn killing and I have to get around town."

He smiled.

"You mean that nigger that committed suicide out on one seventy-two?" he said.

I let his pleasantry pass. He examined the wheel, making non-committal grunts that I interpreted to mean trouble. I tried to pretend that I knew a lot about wheels to head off possible larceny, but it was hard since I know nothing about them. Mechanics have a sixth sense about spotting ignorant car owners. They tolerate his feeble stratagems ("It sounds like a bearing might have flattened out," said in a knowing tone by me because years ago in another wheel on another car a bearing *had* caused a lot of noise. "That's what it sounds like to me.")—aware they have him in their power and can do what they like.

"Somethin's bad with that axle," he said. "I got to finish up with this man's car here first. Then I got to pull the wheel off yours an' take a look at that axle. Come by aroun' four o'clock."

I asked for the garage phone number and he went into a small office for pencil and paper. A rifle of about .30 caliber and a sawed-off shotgun fitted with a curving pistol grip stock hung from pegs on a side wall. There was one set of empty pegs. Finding weapons in such places that were open all night and prey to bandits was common. Sawed-off shotguns, favored by bank robbers of the thirties, were weapons modified primarily for concealment and to facilitate the killings of men. They were not hunting weapons and federal law banned them under twenty-six inches. The mechanic copied down the number. I, prepared for a long Sunday in Athens, walked back to the hotel.

That Sunday *was* long and futile. Reporters gathered, talked over the same ground again and again, watched a drizzle come down, longed for a bar, ate in the hotel, and wondered why so many people from Athens with homes to eat in also ate there. Lemuel Penn would have been spending the day in Washington with his family. Possibly he would be telling his children about army life. At four o'clock, expecting a problem, I returned to the garage. The problem was waiting. The axle assembly was spread over the floor. According to the mechanic, the assembly was hopelessly broken and no place open on Sunday would have the replacement. He thought he might get the part someplace tomorrow. Might meant might not, so I asked if the owner could give me any assurances. No, he couldn't do that, and anyway he was out someplace, the mechanic answered. Could we call him? Didn't know where he was. Would he be back later? Couldn't say, didn't think so. Evasiveness in mechanics being nothing new, I resigned myself to misfortune. The alternative was to tell him to put it all back together and I'd take it somewhere else. This alternative would be a fine idle threat. We agreed that a definitive axle decision would be made in the morning.

Since the first, reportable phase of the story was running out, I planned, if nothing new developed with CBS, to leave on Monday. The story had not received much attention in the national press. I am convinced the lack of attention was because the case was all-black. This fact casts a different aspect on violent death in editorial minds. My pocket money was gone and my clothes could not go another day. I phoned Ruth to bail me out and, as ever, she was ready. Next morning, she and Sean arrived. Their first impression of Athens began in a taxi at the bus depot. A little old lady, a sweet-voiced and fragile little old lady, asked to share their cab into the center of town. And my, said her smile, wasn't Sean a nice little boy, and Lord, said her voice to the driver, I just came back from Atlanta and they've got the meanest "niggers" there I ever saw in my life. That word and the attitudes behind it by now were a probe in a sore wound, metal outraging nerve. Lemuel Penn, father of three, was murdered outside Athens and this sweet goddamn little old lady chirping away about the mean "niggers" of Atlanta.

I had been apprehensive about Sean's exposure to such prejudice when we came to the South from Mexico. It is one thing for a boy to be against bigotry in the abstract when he is in a liberal bastion like

Brooklyn Heights or Mexico City, where poverty, not color, stings the conscience. Sean was in the stage of boyhood—hanging a sign reading "Down with Good Taste" on his bedroom wall and letting his hair grow long like a blond Beatle wig. Could convictions scarcely formed and untested belief in the rightness of white and Negro brotherhood be proof against race feelings all around him? I took him on assignments wherever feasible so that he saw the sign in the window at Leb's, the alligators in Saint Augustine, the burned high school in Notasulga. At home in Atlanta, Deep South prejudice was in our neighborhood but so was considerable enlightenment. A teacher in his public school said during a spelling class:

"The next word is Negro. It is capital N-e-g-r-o. *Not* n-i-g-g-e-r."

At a private school he first attended, an elderly bachelor lady teacher lectured one day about Africa.

"Three-quarters of the people," she said, "are nigger-os."

He laughed at that. In the going vernacular, she was a superhick. She went on to say:

"Now some of the nigger-os are good. But most are lazy. And they are unpleasant to be near when it is hot."

She told about plantation life in her native South Georgia. "Nigger-o" servants were treated well and everybody, black and white, was happy, happy, happy. A debate, pitting Sean and a local boy of liberal outlook against the rest of the class, developed.

"We sorta won, I think," he said. "I mean, they said how good the Negroes got paid and I told them it wasn't true. Negroes got paid less even for the same jobs because they were Negroes. And they couldn't eat in restaurants and go to the movies and all that no matter how much they earned."

I had discouraged him from getting into specifics about figures and finances. I discouraged him not from timidity, but because twelve-year-old boys are not competent to know how much anybody should be getting paid unless their parents have souped them up with statistics and turned them into liberal declaimers. The obvious moral issues inherent in the right to hold any job, go to any school or restaurant seem more within a child's natural compass. One can't be hard and fast about these things or one might jam a spirit seeking to find its way. Sean went on:

"Then this dumb girl said about her colored nursemaid, 'I'd never feel the same if my nurse quit. That's one real good one I know.' I mean, big deal."

His "big deal" said as much as I could preach at him. He was on his way and destined to make it all right. Times would be sticky with play-mates when the jokes came:

"What's hungry, black, and has four legs?"

"Two niggers trying to get into Leb's."

He worked out his plan of turning away from such conversation. The idea gradually got across that he didn't like that kind of talk and his friends laid off when he was around. Many drawling kids' parents had had enough of the eternal bigotry nonsense, and their presence pumped sanity into the atmosphere. But I think that if we had been in Jackson or Birmingham, Sean's life would have been brutal. Most parents are not sane in these cities and the children ape their madness.

Pleasant and unpleasant, the experience was good for him. He was seeing the naked face of prejudice. He might have missed that face behind the Northern mask. He watched the Klan and heard the Negroes sing "I love everybody." He did not have to read or be told which side to be on. I don't mean to say that Sean first viewed race in the South with innocent eyes and sagely weighed all the evidence before choosing the side of the angels. He was preconditioned. One generation accusing a colored kid of stealing Christmas tree lights or sentimentalizing over memories of old Willie is enough in a family. Sean came to his own pri-vate awarenesses, and he came unhandicapped by the tired blood, the tired brains, the tired soul of adulthood. He was not worn down—or out—from trying to determine who he was or why he reacted as he did. He'd try to find out whether he felt wholly from conviction or partly to obtain psychological satisfaction. Belief in brotherhood and disdain for bigotry flowed naturally in his boy's blood as did his love for base-ball and contempt for bullies. All the little, old, mean-mouthed ladies in Athens could never take that away from him.

Sean and I walked over to the garage, and this time Mrs. Guest was on the scene. She was in her early thirties, with frizzly hair, faintly bulging eyes and a shapeless body. A womanliness managed to come through, softening the appearance and the greasy setting. She was sorry, but they still didn't have the part. Hardest thing in the world to find. She used to have an Italian car and that's why she gave it up. No spare parts. Mrs. Guest seemed more concerned about my affiliations than she did about my axle. Who did I say I was with? I told her. Lis-tening as unobtrusively as Ben Turpin used to spy in the silent movies, a skinny teen-age boy with ratty black sideburns came in and stood at the doorway. By now, I was accustomed to suspicion about Yankee re-porters and I gave them full particulars about the work I was doing. Mrs. Guest shook her head.

"Nobody aroun' here would do a killin' like that," she said. "You'll see, somebody followed them up from that camp, I bet. What do you think?"

I told her I didn't know what to think, but had Mr. Guest any hope of getting an axle?

"He's home sleepin' now," she said. "He worked all last night an' he's wore out. You know, I'll tell you, it looks like to me that somebody is trying to cause trouble, stir things up. Why, a month ago here, right here in Athens, they had a shootin' over in Niggertown and they caused us all kinds of trouble."

"Who?"

"The niggers. They came down here an' swore that a boy who was workin' in the garage all night had shot at them."

"Was that where the boy and his sister got shot in their house?"

"Yeah, that's the one. Well, if he was here all night working', he couldn't of shot at them, could he? But they just sat there an' lied their damn heads off."

"Why?"

"I don't know why. Ask them. It looked like they just wanted to get some white people in trouble. Lots of time, you know, you fix their cars an' they won't pay. So they get mad when you go to collect it. I don't know, maybe they did it an' wanted to put the blame off. An' it cost the boys that got arrested seven hundred and fifty dollars for a lawyer. Now that ain't right, is it?"

A small curiosity was stirring and I did not want to spook her by seeming to be impartial which is immediately taken by such people to mean you are hostile. So I said that maybe the "boys" could sue for false arrest.

"What good would that do? The niggers don't have any money."

Yes. Well, it was a hell of a note. What were people saying about the Penn murder, by the way?

"'Course, I don't know nothin' about it. Except it's like I said, folks just know it wasn't nobody from around here. You just can *know* that. Now I wouldn't be surprised if maybe they bad-mouthed somebody who followed them here. Or maybe those two in the car shot him. You never can tell what a nigger will cook up."

Sean's expression rarely covers what he feels. I did not want what I saw he was feeling to break into words and I got back on the subject of car repairs. Ben Turpin eased out. Mrs. Guest said that since I surely didn't want to go to the expense of a new one which they probably couldn't get anyway, they would certainly keep trying to find a second-hand axle assembly. I surely didn't. They were going to put out a call on an interstate teletype that went to junkyards in eight states specializing in used parts. I was impressed. Junkyards now had their own teletype network which was proof, if any were needed, that the free enterprise system was viable. I was to call each day from Atlanta and live in hope. We parted amicably. I noted one set of gun pegs still was empty.

We were hardly out the door when Sean exploded. I see his face now, blue eyes intense, soft mouth indignant.

"Papa, did you see that shotgun on the wall, the small one?"

"The sawed-off shotgun. Yes. And don't talk so loud."

Turpin and some inevitable garage hangers-on were watching us leave.

"I know this might sound crazy," Sean whispered, "but I'll bet anything that gun has something to do with the murder."

"Now listen," I said, "that's the wildest, most unfair kind of thing anybody could say. Can you imagine the harm you could do somebody by starting a rumor like that with nothing to go on?"

"But you heard the way she was talking about—'niggers.' Trying to blame them. And some boys, she said, who worked there got arrested that other time Negroes were shot."

"Sean, you just can't jump to conclusions because somebody uses those words or has those ideas. Probably ninety percent of the people in town do. I admit it's an exciting coincidence. I bring the car to a place where somebody was mixed up in another shooting, they've got guns all over the wall, they talk the way they do."

"And you saw that guy come in and listen."

"Sure I saw him. But for God's sake . . ."

I proceeded to lecture on objectivity, the danger of loose talk, the natural suspiciousness of people in small towns. I felt old and logical, crushing the boy detective in him.

"I know, I know," he said, striving to comply with parental logic, but hating the effort, "but there just was something about the way that gun looked to me. I know it sounds crazy."

"Now if you wanted to speculate, Sean, what about those empty gun pegs? What had they held? And why should they be empty?"

"You mean you think—"

"That's just it. You can't let yourself think too much. Unless you have something solid to back it up. There could be a dozen reasons why the pegs were empty. Maybe a gun is being repaired. Or loaned out. Or maybe was never there in the first place."

I did not have to talk him out of sanguinary conclusions about gun pegs. He had *his* clue, the tangible sawed-off shotgun. He was damned if he would give that one up for logic, fair play or anything. The Guest Garage was undeniably an interesting place and destined to become more so. We returned to Atlanta and after ten days, Mrs. Guest called with the good news that the teletype had located an axle in Virginia or someplace. I returned to Athens the next day. Mr. Guest, who had taken on a fictional quality since I had never seen or talked to him, still was absent. His wife was on the job and there was my car, whole again. On those wall pegs that had been empty the day after the murder of Lemuel Penn was a double-barreled shotgun.

Possibilities now arose which coincidence could not easily turn aside. Mrs. Guest was sorry the bill was higher than she had anticipated, but then, no one could figure on having to get an axle all the way from Virginia. No one, I agreed, could. I paid and drove to the post office. The FBI was still operating at the old stand. Reporters were no longer hanging around but the Air Force recruiter remained dispossessed. Apparently the Bureau had come to stay. I explained that I had some information and an agent took me into an empty room. He was a quietly natty young man, typical of many agents met in the field. The agents gave the general impression that Mr. Hoover had a factory somewhere turning out Brooks Brothers suits, shirts, and faces. I cautioned him that the information might very well mean nothing, and his lack of reaction to what I related indicated he agreed. As I was about to leave, he asked:

"Did you vacuum yourself before you came over?"

The question sounded like television detective talk and he added:

"Did you come right over here from the garage?"

As a matter of fact, I had characteristically taken a wrong turn en route, which possibly had "vacuumed" or cleaned the trail.

"It doesn't pay to take chances around here," he said.

Did that mean that the solution might be in Athens, somewhere down a vacuumed street, maybe in a garage?

"We'll evaluate all the information," he said coolly. "And we appreciate your coming in."

The agent's role was one Walter Mitty would have loved. I drove back to Atlanta, thinking that the information probably did not amount to much but also thinking how satisfying it would be if it did have value and could help get those who killed Lemuel Penn. Almost two weeks passed and the case stayed dormant.

On August 6, I went to Jackson to cover the convention of the Mississippi Freedom Democratic Party. The delegation would try to unseat the regular all-white Mississippi delegation and, on the grounds that Negroes were barred from participating in either the political life of the regular Democratic Party or of the state, have itself seated. The three workers who had disappeared in Philadelphia still were missing and now even Governor Johnson did not think they were drinking beer in Cuba. At 6:30 that morning in the COFO headquarters, I watched a lone white boy in a typically last-minute COFO effort to prepare for a convention due to start in a few hours. He was lettering county signs for the delegates. The signs were stacked all over the office—Sunflower, Bolivar, Rankin, Panola, Neshoba. My eye kept returning again and again to the word "Neshoba." Later, across the street in the Masonic Temple, limp, bleached-out orange streamers hung from basketball backboards raised to the ceiling above the auditorium floor. Bunches of delegates, sandwich bags in their laps, sat on folding chairs. The signs above them read—Sunflower, Bolivar, Rankin, Panola, Neshoba.

The speakers rostrum stood on a platform just above the spot where Medgar Evers had lain on his bier. The scene looked ragtag—the delegates and their leaders did not have much money for trappings. Some had arrived that morning after long bus rides from remote towns. At day's end they would ride the buses back. They would be marked in the eyes of white townspeople as troublemakers with all the physical and economic reprisal inspired by that stigma. The delegates hoped their project might succeed but were not confident. The atmosphere lacked the buoyancy of the usual political convention—with the throb of pugnacious enthusiasm and fevered visions of political gain. These people were realists who knew the ultimate realities of American life. They were campaigning, in a real sense, for the right to live as Americans. They knew from experience that the kind of white Americans they would encounter in Atlantic City for the most part had almost unlimited tolerance for their black status as servitors. A white lawyer from Washington named Joseph Rauh, who once headed Americans for Democratic Action, was the link to politicians in the capital—a capital which, while lecturing mankind on the wonders of democracy, had countenanced Mississippi over the years. He was a happy liberal, an optimist who looked like Dave Garroway and sounded almost like Jackie Robinson.

"We're a real, not a paper party," he said. "When you have two parties that claim to represent the regular party, you take the loyal one. There's not a Goldwater fan in the house."

Rauh meant that Mississippi Democrats were officially going to back Barry Goldwater. Would the Freedom Party stand a chance as it tried to make the Democratic high command translate its protestations of concern for Deep South Negroes into the drastic action proscribed by national, if not party, law when states turned potential voters into something less than citizens?

"LBJ is the single most important factor," he said. "I would be very happy with his benevolent neutrality."

Aaron Henry, a Negro druggist from Clarksdale, was leader of the Freedom Party and president of the state NAACP. He was having internecine problems along with the old black-and-white ones. Medgar Evers' brother Charles now was field secretary of the Mississippi NAACP as Medgar had been. Evers was annoyed at certain SNCC arrogancies and he did not believe in mock Freedom Party elections but in court offensives against Mississippi intransigence.

"As native Mississippians we know the most practical way to do this," Evers once told me. "Sure, the SNCC people came here to help but, for God's sake, if you come to my house to help me then don't turn around and do what I don't want you to do. It's going by way of Tokyo to get to New York."

Evers' office was on the second floor of the Temple but he would not come down, even to watch.

Henry, a very sober-faced man who from the rostrum pronounced a party principle with the same gravity he announced that a missing suitcase had been found, listened gravely as the Rev. Merill Lindsay opened the convention with a prayer. The prayer contained the observation, "We readily admit, Lord, that it is by far easier to go to heaven than to bring heaven here." Black Mississippians uttered a fervent "Amen" in full agreement. Henry had trouble bringing earthly understanding to the delegates. Their road to representation lay at the end of a labyrinth starting with the Democratic Party convention credentials subcommittee, then the credentials committee, minority reports, and a minimum of eight states sending word to the Atlantic City podium they wanted a roll call vote on seating the Freedom delegation, on and on. A man from Sunflower County stood to ask:

"Exactly what are we going to do at Atlantic City?"

"As we stand right now," Henry conceded, "we don't know what the hell we're going to do when we get to Atlantic City."

The convention would have been easy to burlesque but unfair. People with scant or no experience at voting were trying to grasp the workings of political machinery deliberately made complicated in this democracy by men who did not want any but predictable party professionals aspiring to the controls. Ella Baker, a Negro who began civil rights work in the thirties, had to bring cohesiveness to the meeting. She would reveal to a white listener by her words, by the contrast of her thought and demeanor to the bombastic behavior of speakers of past major party conventions, just how far America had slipped away from the democratic concept. She wore a neat, businesslike suit; her graying hair was simply combed; she was a lady in charge of herself. I had first seen her in the COFO office when the signs were being painted. She had come in, weary from a plane trip, looking for a chair to go to sleep in. She spoke to simple people from the complex political knowledge she had gained during three decades. Her experience began with the Young Negro Cooperative League in 1932 and extended to her present job as field secretary for the NAACP. She spoke almost as a schoolmarm to pupils, as she denounced Southern states for using the "big lie" that they were sovereign and so could deal with the Negro as they chose.

"The truth is," she said, "that there has been no sovereign state in the United States since the Confederation of States decided to become a United States of America." The audience applauded but she silenced them with a peremptory wave of her hand—the lesson would continue. "But the rest of the country tacitly agreed. What does that mean? It simply means that the rest of the country went along with it. They did little, very, very little to change the situation in the South. At no point were the Southern states denied their representation on the basis of the fact that they had denied other people the right to participate in the election of those who govern them."

A simple history lesson and unemotionally stated.

"The rest of the country accepted the old slogan that the Negro people of the South were happy and satisfied. And this, of course, was never true, it was never true in the darkest days of slavery. It hadn't ever been true."

She risked stamping on a few toes in the auditorium with a warning against black demagogues:

"We must be careful lest we elect to represent us people who, for the first time, feel their sense of importance and will represent themselves before they represent you. Now, this is not the kind of a keynote speech, perhaps, you like. But I'm not trying to make you feel good. We have to know what we're dealing with and we can't deal with things just because we feel we ought to have our rights. We deal with them on the basis of knowledge that we gain through using people that have the knowledge . . . through sending our children through certain kinds of courses, through sitting down reading at night instead of spending our time at the television and radio just listening to what's on. But we must spend our time reading some of the things that help us to understand this South we live in. Read Cash, read his book, *The Mind of the South*."

I thought of a Dirksen or a Pastore urging a convention to become wise, not merely partisan, or saying as Miss Baker did:

"Young men and women want some meaning in their lives. Big cars do not give meaning. Place in the power structure does not give meaning."

She knew enough not to be wholly abstract. She told of a sharecropper who was always forced to settle accounts with the wife of a plantation owner who was cheating him. If he challenged the figures on the bales he picked, he could be charged by the woman with insult and rape. But the audience roared at that. That example was something they knew. Whether they learned from Miss Baker some of the things they did not know, some of the essentials of citizenship that much of white America did not know or care about, was a question that would be a long time in the answering. They gave Miss Baker, the party, themselves a traditional placard-waving march, the first in American political history that stepped off to the tune "Go Tell It on the Mountain," and "This Little Light of Mine, Boys, I'm Gonna Let It Shine."

At almost eight o'clock I got to the Jackson Airport for the flight back to Atlanta. I called Ruth and she told me that CBS had been urgently on the phone. With only a few minutes to plane time I called New York and an editor said that the FBI had made four arrests in the Penn killing. I was to head straight to Athens. By any chance, I asked him, did any of the suspects have anything to do with a garage because I had given the FBI information on a garage that might be involved in the murder? The Guest Garage.

"Wait a minute, lemme check," the editor said, some casual interest in his voice.

When he came back on, he was not casual.

"Listen, it looks like you got something," he said. "One of them is Herbert Guest, thirty-eight, owner of a garage on Hancock Street. And, let's see, he'd been arrested before in another racial shooting. Listen, if you can take credit for this, great. So check with the FBI and get to Athens as soon as you can."

I felt a nice rush of satisfaction and excitement. How good, how satisfyingly good to have played a part in getting them. The credit would not be bad either. To my discredit, I dwelt on the satisfaction and the credit all the hours the plane flew through the night to Atlanta. I did not think of Lemuel Penn, dead because he was a Negro traveling a new road, but of the satisfaction and the credit. I would learn that neither was mine, that I had touched accidentally the edge of the FBI solution but had not been instrumental in it. In fact, Sean had come much closer with his intuitive stab of youth.

GEORGIA JUSTICE

When I saw him on August 6 in the U. S. Commissioner's office in Athens, Herbert Guest turned out to be a blubbery thirty-seven-year-old illiterate. He and three friends—members of Clarke County Klavern 244, United Klans of America, Inc., Knights of the Ku Klux Klan—were being arraigned and charged with conspiracy under the 1964 Civil Rights Law to "injure, oppress, threaten and intimidate members of the Negro race." Since murder comes under the purview of the states, this charge was the strongest federal charge that could be brought. The FBI had a confession that all had played a role in the murder of Lemuel Penn from Klansman James Lackey, twenty-nine, a dull-witted gas station manager. The remaining two were Joseph Howard Sims, forty-one, and Cecil William Myers, twenty-five. They had been standing up for God and country at the Klan rally in Atlanta a few months earlier.

The small hearing room was jammed with relatives, lawyers, and newsmen. In the crowd I saw Mrs. Guest. She smiled. Her husband looked a good deal like Oliver Hardy except for a vacuity in his eyes and no moustache. Sims, a machinist by trade and veteran of the Normandy invasion with a reputation for a bad temper, was a heavy man with drooping beagle eyes and big forearms. Sitting alongside him was Myers whose profile was a series of prognathic juttings—brow, nose, and jaw—under a cap of black crew-cut hair. His eyes, behind glasses, were flat and the corners of his mouth turned down. The crime they were charged with carried a maximum penalty of ten years in prison and a $5,000 fine. The state was preparing murder charges based on the FBI evidence. At the time, Georgia had capital punishment and put to

175

death more persons proportionately than any other state in the union. The vast majority of those sent to the electric chair were Negroes.

After trying to have the press barred from the hearing, defense attorneys waived examination. The waiver meant that the federal government did not have to present any of its evidence and the defense tactic was a common one—to prevent publication of unfavorable evidence which might prejudice potential jurors. The hearing was undramatic and most of the legal chatter among the contending attorneys was clearly over the heads of the defendants who bore expressions ranging from Sims's haughty ignorance to Guest's bug-eyed fear. As the hearing broke up, Mrs. Guest beckoned to me. Did she want to resume her tale of persecution begun in the garage? No.

"How's that axle holdin' up?" she asked.

"Pretty good," I replied.

"That's good," she said. "I'm awful sorry we had to take so long sendin' all the way up to Virginia. That's why I wouldn't have a foreign car."

A relative drew her off before I could turn the conversation to something of greater moment than my axle.

The state shortly charged all four with murder, and indictments were quickly returned against Lackey, Sims, and Myers. A grand jury chose not to indict Guest. Since Lackey had confessed, the prosecution moved first to try Sims and Myers. No one could remember the last time, if indeed there had been a first time, an avowed Klansman accused of killing a Negro faced a Southern jury. The trial was to be held in the small town of Danielsville (population 362), slumbrous seat of Madison County. The murder had occurred just inside the county line which began at the bridge on Route 172. Madison County residents were greatly annoyed that their tax money had to pay for the trial, when neither the accused nor the victim came from there. If that expenditure wasn't bad enough, Negroes were being considered for jury duty.

"We read in the papers," said Sheriff Dewey Seagraves, "where the Supreme Court said you had to have both colored and white in the jury box. Up to this term of court, there's never been a nigger in that box."

The brick courthouse of Georgian architecture sits beside great old water oaks on a small island in the middle of Highway 29. Lemuel Penn would have passed the courthouse, which was about twenty miles away when he died on his shortcut. Night and day, diesel trucks roar by bruising the silence of a rather typical Southern farm town. Around the perimeter of the highway as it encircles the courthouse are a few modest homes and stores, a colored general store on one side, white on the other. I counted twenty-three separate Coca-Cola signs on the various

buildings; some locals still call it "dope." Danielsville's only prior claim
to fame was an operation. An historical marker by the courthouse ad-
vises that a local man, Dr. Crawford Long, first used ether as an anes-
thetic in a surgical operation on March 30, 1842. The patient, coincidentally, was James Venable, the same name as the present Imperial
Wizard of a Georgia Klan.

To speculate on how Georgia would have pursued the prosecution had
Penn been some field hand, black and expendable, is idle. His promin-
ence in Washington insured interest from newspapers in the capital.
Normally, the case would have been handled solely by Northern Circuit
Solicitor General Clete Johnson, an easy-going, almost diffident man
with a respectable record. Governor Sanders sent in Jeff Wayne, the
solicitor general (or district attorney) from the neighboring circuit.
Wayne, spare and leathery as a mummy, in his fifteenth year on the
job, was an old pro at murder prosecutions. Presiding was Judge Carey
Skelton, an aristocratic-looking man with a folksy Georgia drawl who
would have been equally at home in the Union Club or on a possum
hunt. Judge Skelton, soon to retire, had been a friend and booster of the
late President Kennedy. Before the trial began, he issued stern rules of
behavior which included no conversation in the courtroom or tobacco
chewing. He had told the grand jury that handed up the indictments:

"We in Georgia do not condone 'taking the law into one's hands' by
any individual, group or mob. Any American . . . who sanctions, con-
dones, or encourages defiance of duly constituted legal authority or who
advocates or participates in violence . . . does his country and its citizens
pernicious disservice."

The defense was headed by thirty-five-year-old Jim Hudson, a young
man on his way up. He was the Republican candidate for the State
Legislature from Clarke County. He had a country boy twang, pale, unsmiling blue eyes, and a face that easily screwed up into anger or contempt, depending on the way testimony was going. At his side were
John Darsey, sixty, a lawyer of the florid old school and a prosecutor in the
Japanese war crime trials, and Harold Boggs, who practiced in Danielsville and knew everybody in town.

On August 31, the trial began. At this point in time, America was
nearing the end of the long, hot summer. The bodies of the civil rights
workers had been taken from their grave in Philadelphia. Bombs still
were going off in McComb, Mississippi. While they chafed inwardly
at his refusal to lace his oratory with the blood-and-fire phrases that
matched their mood, right-wing extremists were telling each other
Barry Goldwater was going to win. Although Southern justice was on

trial as much as the defendants, these things tended to overshadow the Danielsville courtroom.

Sims and Myers brought their families. Sims's wife was slender and fair-haired. She had given him eight fresh-faced children ranging from a two-year-old girl to a sixteen-year-old boy. Myers, a textile mill worker when he was not running with the Klan, had three children. His wife was about to have a fourth child. The wives and children swarmed to the railing behind the defense table at every opportunity. The courtroom watched familial kisses and embraces.

About two hundred whites, mostly country people and a sprinkling from the university in Athens, filled the downstairs benches. Upstairs, in a dark, segregated balcony, twenty-five Negroes watched. Judge Skelton sat before a wall clock, which was always wrong, that advertised Coca-Cola. Paint flaked from the pale green walls, and the embossed tin ceiling was patched in places with what looked like strips of adhesive tape. Two bricked-in fireplaces recalled the unsteamheated justice of an earlier day. Sepia photos of the men who had dispensed that justice looked out at Judge Skelton with fading judicial mien. Even if the setting resembled an argument for a courthouse rebuilding fund, the judge invested the room with sensible decorum that suited the God-fearing temper of the community and the gravity of the crime.

A jury was quickly chosen. Two available Negro jurors, nervous to the point of incoherence under questioning, were dismissed by the defense. Most of the jurors were farmers. Sitting in the box were a construction worker, a cotton gin company employee, clerks, and merchants. Throughout the trial Klansmen were rumored in the jury box. One searched the faces for a clue. The jurors were expressionless, rarely even glancing at the defendants, unsmiling, sun-darkened faces, whitish borders showing in back at the hairline freshly clipped for the big day. The state had tried to guard against racists or Klansmen. In a small rural county, uniformity of thinking on racial matters was unavoidable. The prosecutors had not much maneuvering space in challenges. As Clete Johnson confided:

"If you can't get first best, sometimes you have to settle for second best. And then you just don't know."

The first two witnesses were Major Brown and Colonel Howard, both in uniform and neither about to play humble in deference to local folkways. Major Brown told of his awakening to murder and seeing lights speeding down the road.

"And you assumed they were car lights," Mr. Hudson asked in cross-examination.

"I don't assume anything," Major Brown snapped back.

The officers set the time at about five A.M. Colonel Howard said the other car was cream-colored, a 1961 or 1962 Chevy. Before he left the stand, Mr. Hudson apologized for bringing up the question, but by any chance did the three men have any kind of racial trouble when they stopped for gas at an Atlanta service station before reaching Athens?

Colonel Howard: No.

Mr. Hudson: Did you ask to use the restroom?

Colonel Howard: Yes.

Mr. Hudson: The regular [white] restroom?

Colonel Howard: Yes.

Mr. Hudson: Nobody objected?

Colonel Howard: No.

The implication was that someone might have trailed the car from Atlanta. Later, in light of Mr. Hudson's summation technique, this line of defense would be interesting to recall.

Suspicions were already forming among the spectators. An elderly red-faced farmer in overalls whispered:

"Maybe them niggers was so rough on the boys in camp that *they* did it to him. Damn New York niggers, county payin' their expenses every day an' they don't tell nothin'."

Outside during the lunch break, there was only one topic of conversation. A spectator said to a gas station attendant who had been working and missed the session:

"They put two on today."

"Two what?"

"Two niggers."

The consensus was that the Negroes either knew who did it or had done it themselves. The local people seemed unable or unwilling to concede, publicly at least, that night-riding and racial murder requiring punishment of whoever was guilty had been done. Negroes were somehow guilty of *everything*—the bad publicity, the upset, the expense. The sight of Colonel Penn as an innocent victim was entirely lost.

The state now began its attempt to link Myers and Sims to the crime. At the same time, the state wanted to establish that a conspiracy existed among the four—not a conspiracy to kill Penn but to harass Negroes generally. This route was the tortuous legal path that had to be followed. The reasons became clearer as the trial progressed. For now, the prosecutor explained that the murder of Penn was only an incidental occurrence. If the statements of Lackey and Guest were eventually to be admitted, proof of conspiracy was vital groundwork that had to be laid. Skillful work by the solicitors general and accommodating rulings by the court were needed. Judge Skelton had to rule on the admissability of evidence which ranged far afield from the actual murder charge. Time and time again, when witnesses referred to the defendants carrying weapons in the city of Athens, Mr. Hudson would be on his feet to object. "Irrelevant . . . immaterial . . . prejudicial to character." Time and time again, the judge overruled on the prosecution promise to tie the evidence all up eventually. Once the defense counsel challenged the testimony of a witness as hearsay and Judge Skelton asked him to cite a case substantiating the objection.

"I never looked up a case of hearsay in my life," the young lawyer said. "But when I hear it I recognize it."

The judge grimaced while spectators nodded approval of the attorney's horse sense. A university type behind the press row said to his friend:

"I guess Penn was killed by hearsay."

A Negro dishwasherwoman from Athens, Mrs. Landys Miriam Moore, worked at the Open House Restaurant near the Guest garage-Klavern. She testified that she often saw the alleged conspirators drinking coffee late at night and carrying guns. She said specifically that she saw them enter wearing pistols around midnight on the date of the murder, that they left and returned twenty or thirty minutes after 5 A.M. The state had fixed the murder at about five; the restaurant was twenty-four miles from the scene. Mrs. Moore, a handsome woman with high cheekbones and bright, wide eyes, was not treated by the defense with the deference it had shown to the Washington Negroes. Bulldozed until the judge had to caution Mr. Hudson, she stuck coolly to her story.

The prosecution next produced an eighteen-year-old Klan neophyte named Thomas ("Horsefly") Folendore. He liked to hang around the garage. He was in the garage shortly after 5 A.M. on July 11. A nervous and reluctant witness, he said he saw Sims and Myers enter carrying sawed-off shotguns which they cleaned. Folendore said he told them:

"I got me one tonight. How did you-all do?"

Sims told him "none of your business," said Folendore. Off the stand, Folendore explained to newsmen that his morbid greeting to the men had been just a little joke.

Three Negro teen-agers testified that on July 4 men armed with pistols and shotguns chased their car from in front of Guest's garage on a terror-filled ride through the streets of Athens. This evidence was part of the state's pattern of conspiracy.

The conspiracy was given striking reinforcement by Athens city policeman Joe Marvin Flanagan. That same night, one week before the murder, Flanagan said he was giving highway directions to a Negro couple in a New Jersey car. Flanagan stated that Myers and Sims came up, pistols slung on their hips, and inspected the car. Then, according to the officer, Myers leaned inside and said:

"Hit 29, you black son of a bitch. Go back to New Jersey where you come from."

At one point in his testimony, the officer said he saw "members of the Ku Klux Klan" standing on a street corner. Calling for a mistrial, defense lawyers flew up as flushed quail. The jury was ordered from the courtroom and lawyer Darsey shouted:

"This court will take judicial notice of the fact the Ku Klux Klan is on the subversive list of the United States Government.

"I called attention to the court if this matter were brought out directly or indirectly I would make such a motion . . . in the light of that clear-cut understanding that the answer of this witness is not a normal answer but a planted answer—"

"Just a minute, wait a minute," Judge Skelton said sharply to the almost apoplectic Darsey. "I'm going to ask you not to speak in such a tone that the jury might hear you."

"I did not anticipate the answer," said Prosecutor Wayne.

Since everyone in the courtroom, jurors included, knew from countless newspaper stories that the defendants belonged to the Klan, the uproar seemed excessive—particularly since Officer Flanagan had not mentioned Sims or Myers among the Klansmen he saw. The judge denied the motion for mistrial but asked the jurors to "eradicate" the reference from their minds. Lost in the shuffle was the import of the testimony. Pistoleros could harass and curse an American couple on a well-traveled street in a city that houses the educational center of the most progressive state in the South, and an officer of the law did nothing about it.

Moments later, Assistant Police Chief James Hansen testified that he had been called to a colored drive-in where the Negro teen-agers took refuge after being chased from Guest's garage. Sims, armed, was present, but Chief Hansen did nothing either. He said instead *he* gave *Sims* information about an Athens car with expired license tags that for some reason had piqued Sims's curiosity.

The night ride was no isolated occurrence. Denver Phillips, a scrawny teen-age worker in Guest's garage, testified that he had driven frequently with Guest, Lackey, Sims, and Myers. Pistols and sawed-off shotguns were in the car. Phillips himself was under a warrant for assault with intent to murder in connection with that shooting at the

Negro housing project which cost a teen-age colored boy his eye. When Prosecutor Wayne sought to question him about that incident, Mr. Hudson cut in to advise Phillips of his rights under the Fifth Amendment. Spectators laughed. The Fifth Amendment, in their minds, was the resource of radicals and Communists. Now the shoe was on the other foot. When Phillips finally said:

"I refuse to answer on the grounds it might incriminate me," soft applause was gaveled down by Judge Skelton.

The prosecution was at its make-or-break point—the already repudiated statement of James S. Lackey. The statement was in uncertain legal waters. Georgia permits testimony of co-conspirators in a continuing conspiracy but state law recognizes no conspiratorial crime except conspiracy against the state. The prosecution was in the position of using a federally oriented conspiracy to prove a state charge of murder.

Mr. Hudson candidly commented, "There's no crime in Georgia against intimidatin' colored people. And they haven't shown any conspiracy even to do that. If cursin' out a colored man is a conspiracy, I suppose we're all guilty of that."

Citation and counter-citation were produced and argued. The spectators grew restive. Judge Skelton broke in to announce:

"I've just been reminded to tell you that the Women's Club of Bond Community will be serving lunch at the American Legion Clubhouse . . . just a stone's throw from the courthouse. I understand they're gonna have Southern fried chicken, pole beans, slaw, ice tea and lemonade. I ate there yesterday and it's a mighty good place to eat."

Half of the state's case would have to be thrown out unless it could be connected to the murder through Lackey's statement. Lackey's statement was given to the defense table for inspection. With a sick fascination in their eyes, Sims and Myers watched their lawyers read it. With the judge's ruling in abeyance, the architect of the statement, FBI agent Jack Simpson, was called to the stand.

Simpson was dark, handsome, and quietly self-assured—a Hollywood concept of the complete FBI man. He described in detail how the questioning of Lackey was handled, reading off notations from his records: ". . . 7:22 he had a hamburger and a pint of milk . . . 7:42 we started to take a statement . . . 8:54 bathroom and cigarettes."

"Was he afraid?" asked Hudson. "What's your opinion?"

"We deal in facts," Simpson said dryly, "not opinion."

The agent stressed that Lackey came to the temporary FBI headquarters in the Athens post office of his own free will.

"He was very friendly," Simpson recalled. "There was an atmosphere of friendship and cordiality. . . ."

To which Hudson snapped:

"Did you let him blow the siren on the way to the post office?"

Judge Skelton finally allowed the statement, signed on August 6, to be read into the record. Lackey said that during the early morning of July 11, he was driving Myers' 1964 cream-colored Chevy Two station wagon with Myers beside him and Sims in the back.

"At some time between 4 A.M. and 4:30 A.M.," the statement said in part, "we spotted a 1959 Chevy occupied by several colored men. We trailed the car and noticed the Washington, D.C., plates. I believe Mr. Sims said, 'That must be some of President Johnson's boys.'

"Sims told me to fall back and follow the Negroes. I asked the others what they were going to do and Sims said, 'I'm going to kill me a nigger.'

"When I came alongside the Negroes' car, both Myers and Sims fired shotguns into the Negroes' car.

"We didn't stop anywhere but drove straight back to Guest's garage in Athens. Herbert Guest and a boy named Horsefly were at the garage when we arrived. Both Myers and Sims cleaned the shotguns. Guest asked what had happened and Sims said, 'We shot one but we don't know if we killed him or not.'

"The original reason for our following the colored men was because we had heard that Martin Luther King might make Georgia a testing ground for the Civil Rights Bill. We thought some out-of-town niggers might stir up some trouble in Athens.

"I was surprised when I learned that the colored man had been killed. I didn't think Sims and Myers had actually killed the man. I said to myself, 'Those sonsofabitches killed that man.' "

Myers' wife burst into tears when the statement was read. He remained stoic; Sims flushed, blinked his pouched eyes. Additional Lackey statements, later introduced, dovetailed with the testimony of Horsefly Folendore, the Negro teen-agers, Chief Hansen, and Phillips. The prosecution case that had appeared disorganized and episodic suddenly seemed to tell a full and terrible story. The alleged murder weapon was offered in evidence, a sawed-off, double-barreled shotgun. I learned from the FBI that the gun was the same one that Sean and I had seen hanging on the wall in Guest's garage—the same one that had excited Sean's suspicions.

Ballistic proof is virtually impossible with shotguns, which do not leave the same telltale groove markings on shells as rifles do on bullets. Prosecution experts could not say definitely that it had been used to kill Penn. The weapon was one of the two that Horsefly Folendore had seen Sims and Myers wiping off. An agent told me that the shotgun which I later saw on those wall pegs had nothing to do with the case. My son was generous in his moment of triumph, but a flickering smile of superiority betrayed the long, long thoughts that youth was thinking.

The appearance of Herbert Guest, whose garage was such a hub of Athenian activity, was anticlimactic. He looked like an overaged fat boy scared to death of a whipping. To such simple questions as his age, he sometimes delayed half a minute in answering while his small eyes rolled in pitiable uncertainty that always verged on the comic when you thought of Oliver Hardy. He could not read or write, but he had signed a statement saying that Sims and Myers told him they shot at Penn's car. He insisted he had "blacked out" the day he was questioned.

"I definitely don't remember nothin' about signin' that statement," he said.

The state's case was completed. In the quiet outside the courthouse (Judge Skelton had ordered state troopers to reroute all trucks when their passing clatter drowned out testimony), townspeople grouped and talked. Had the evidence made any impression? I heard one farmer say,

"I wouldn't believe nothin' that I couldn't see."

With my Yankee accent, drawing people out was impossible. One man was the exception. He was about forty-five years old and worked in a clothing factory. He was curious about what would happen in a similar case in New York. All those riots, what did people think about them?

" 'Course, it ain't right no how to kill a man in cold blood what hasn't done nothin' to you," he said.

"Is that what most of the people around here think?" I asked.

He lowered his voice.

"Well, I don't come from aroun' here so I don't know. An' I wouldn't ask. You know, people are funny, an' you never know who you're talkin' to. A stranger like me comes up an' asks somebody somethin', why I just might get a punch in the nose."

I was surprised to hear he was a stranger, I told him, because his accent seemed local.

"No," he smiled. "I'm from Commerce in Jackson County."

Jackson was the next county. The town of Commerce was twenty miles away.

The defense took less than two hours to present its case. Two respectable Athens residents, a man and a woman, swore they saw the defendants in the Open House Restaurant at the time the murder was taking place twenty-four miles away. A psychiatrist, Dr. J. A. Jordan, testified that he had examined Lackey in jail and found his IQ on the borderline of normalcy. The defense, naturally, was readying an attack on Lackey's statement. Dr. Jordan said the gas station manager was "an individual whose pattern of living is marked by suspicion and supreme mistrust of others." He called him a "paranoid personality" who thought he had a misshapen head that made people laugh at him. Most tellingly, Dr. Jordan said that Lackey told him the FBI investigators "tried money" on him during questioning and said his friends were "putting his neck in a noose."

Outside the courtroom, Lackey's wife stopped the doctor. She was a scrawny, lank-haired young woman, her face full of fright and ignorance.

"Doctor," she said, "does that mean my husband is crazy?"

I could not hear his answer but he spoke to her reassuringly. In Mrs. Lackey's dull young eyes and slatternly body could be read a white tragedy of the South as poignant as the black tragedy of Lemuel Penn. The poor white, physically and spiritually impoverished, was manipulated by his leaders to take sustenance from hatred for the Negro. He was denied a decent portion of education and income, a rational climate in which potential, however slight, could develop fully.

Georgia law permits defendants to enter the witness box and make unsworn statements without opening themselves to cross-examination. Sims and Myers availed themselves of the opportunity.

"I am innocent of this," said Sims in a level voice, looking straight at the jurors. "I had nothing to do with the killing of Lemuel Penn. I believe I was in Athens at the time."

Myers made a similar, bare statement and that was the defense save for the introduction of Lackey's repudiation. In the repudiation, he said that all statements made to the FBI were inspired by "fears and threats."

"I was told by federal investigator Simpson that if I gave information helping to arrest or convict the 'killer' of William Penn [sic] that the federal government would see that I was well taken care of at all times. He told me that in cases such as this the government has started with a three-thousand-dollar reward and gone higher.

"I am making this statement within my own power. I am under no threat or duress. I am doing this to clear my conscience for the harm I've done my co-defendants."

FBI man Simpson was recalled as a prosecution rebuttal witness. He gave additional details that had been omitted from his earlier, precise account of the Lackey "interviews."

"In general conversation," said Simpson, "I made a remark that in complicated cases when the government spends a large amount of money, utilizes a lot of men, it is not unheard of that the government pays money for information. In some cases, as much as three thousand dollars."

Attorney Hudson observed sarcastically:

"You just told him, 'James, come on and confess and we'll electrocute you.' "

Prosecutor Johnson observed that $3,000 was not much inducement for a confession that could put the confessor in the electric chair. Through the phenomenon of courtroom telepathy, one sensed the conviction the FBI had bought its evidence.

Summations came on the fifth day. A subtle change came in the courtroom atmosphere. More men identified as Klansmen were filling the seats and swarming up to Sims and Myers during recesses. Ruth had come with me for the final day, and she recognized one of the men around the defendants. He was a very tall boy in his early twenties and the only Klansman I've ever encountered who wore a goatee—perhaps the better to spy on beatniks. He had been in the pack that surrounded Ruth in Hurt Park during the March rally. He recognized her.

I was up front and unaware when the harassment started. He spread the word, apparently, that she was a civil rights worker and/or "nigger" lover. Persons began turning around, pointing at her and whispering. Spreading from row to row, hostile or smirking faces stared. She told me at the next recess and pointed out a man who had been involved in it. Let me put in that Ruth is a composed, non-paranoid woman with an aversion to scenes. She did not want to do anything but leave. I confronted the man, undersized and lout-faced. He denied doing anything in a deep country drawl.

"I waren't lookin' at your wife," he said. "I don't know who your wife is even. What you talkin' about?"

A rudimentary slyness in his dumb eyes, he was on safe ground among friends. His posture of innocence was proof against a smart-aleck Yankee with a crazy wife thinking people were looking at her. His face contained a sum of ignorance and prejudice that was both lamentable and infuriating. I did not trust my temper and sought out Sheriff Seagraves to advise him what was happening and to warn that the responsibility for provocation was not mine.

"We certainly don't want nothin' happenin' here," he said. "An' I ain't goin' to let nothin' happen. I'll keep an eye out, don't you worry."

Twenty minutes later I saw him walking outside the building with the goateed Klansman who had one arm draped over the sheriff's shoulder.

They were laughing together. In the courtroom the pressure on Ruth increased until, unbelievably enough, word was passed to Sims who nudged Myers and both raised up a fraction in their chairs to turn and glare. She was thoroughly spooked by now. Since darkness was approaching, she left and drove back to Atlanta. She was not a coward. She realized, for the first time, what it was like being at the mercy of hate in a small Southern town where sheriffs fraternize with Klansmen, where men on trial for murder feel free to intimidate a woman in a courtroom. The feeling was one that local Negroes knew well. By late afternoon, all were gone from the balcony, even the hardy civil rights Negroes from Atlanta.

Prosecutor Johnson was not renowned for impassioned oratory, but this day he found a voice as he described the state's version of the killing.

"They were a-looking and a-hunting and trying to regulate things, trying to take the law into their own hands. They followed this car some twenty-four miles away and then they passed them and Bam! Bam! Colonel Penn's life was snuffed out by a person he had never seen. Now, gentlemen, that is not right. I don't care if it's a white man, red man, yellow man, or black man. Something has got to be done to stop this kind of night-riding."

Johnson hit at Sims and Myers for not having explained exactly where they were that murder morning. He attacked Lackey's repudiation which was made in a jailhouse and witnessed by eight other prisoners.

"You get a bunch of thugs together in the jailhouse," he said, "and they think they are lawyers. He didn't dream of repudiating his statement until he got down there with them."

Johnson and everyone else in the courtroom knew that any argument, all the thousands of words of testimony on the facts of the crime, paled before its inescapable essence. He kept returning to that essence, looking down at the defendants.

". . . the only thing they knew was that he was born a Negro. And could he help that? He came in here with black skin. Now is that a crime and does it justify someone taking a shotgun and shooting off his head?"

He focused on the latent issue of the trial in his closing words:

"I feel that the honor of the great state of Georgia is on trial here today. We are practically testing the strength and efficiency of the state government. . . . Gentlemen, have the courage to do what's right."

He asked for the death penalty.

Young Hudson's summation was generally restrained, all things considered, although his country accent broadened considerably and his universal use of "ain't" suggested he had gone through grade school, high school, college and law school without learning to conjugate "to be."

Like any good defense attorney with provincial jurors, he sneered at the outside world ("Don't you care what people in New York City, or Washington, D. C., or London think about it") and extolled his local alibi witness ("Thank God for God-fearin' country folk"). He called Lackey a person with a proved mental illness and stressed Guest's illiteracy. Both deficiencies were unwitting commentary on the types attracted to Ku Klux Klan membership.

"The solicitor general tries to convince me," he said, "that this Brown and Howard and Colonel Penn hadn't any trouble with anybody. I don't understand why he would try to convince me of that. Who in the world said they did? The only thing I think is maybe they know something I don't know. I wonder how come they said it? It looks funny to me. . . ."

The sly innuendo was perfectly tailored to local suspicions. Mr. Hudson apparently forgot that he himself had raised the point of possible racial trouble at the Atlanta gas stop. He noted that the Negroes were officers and mentioned his military service.

"I wasn't no officer," he said. "Officers have a pretty good deal, we all know that."

The connection to the case was not apparent. Mr. Hudson went on to point out, accurately enough, that there would have been no case without the Lackey statement.

"There's no question about it, this man was killed and it's wrong," he said. "And I'll tell you one thing, I'm a citizen of the state of Georgia, I stand for law and order, too. But that don't mean I got to convict an innocent boy." He drummed on Agent Simpson's mention of $3,000. Effectively, he attacked the testimony of each state witness as failing to place the defendants at the murder scene. Over and over, down the list . . . "that don't place them boys out there. Not one bit in this world." And he ridiculed evidence of conspiracy as proof of murder.

"They're tryin' to show you," he said, "that these boys was tryin' to intimidate colored people. If you ever cussed one, hit one, abused one of them, I suspect you're guilty of murder, too."

For the second time during the trial, Mr. Hudson had conceded white mistreatment of Negroes. If the jurors felt any tweaks of memory or conscience, their expressionless faces hid them. Mr. Hudson's summation was spirited and convincing, marred by a few lapses from taste and reason. His final "stone cold walls, lights getting dim" reference to execution seemed to embarrass even him. The summation of Defense Counsel Darsey truly had to be heard to be believed. Darsey, jowly and carrying his excess weight like an overstuffed sausage ready to burst, contrived to place the federal government of the United States on trial.

He began by thundering that he was not afraid to stand up against the "untold resources of the federal government."

"Gentlemen," he shouted, teetering up and down, arms flailing, "I'm not afraid for the most part because I am standing in the presence of the symbol of the greatest tradition mankind has ever known . . . the jury system . . . twelve good men and true, a jury of peers through whose veins flow the rich Anglo-Saxon blood and the milk of human kindness."

Plunging on from this fluid metaphor, Mr. Darsey recalled the assassination of President Kennedy. Then he jumped to "that fateful morning of July 11 [when] there rang out over this nation the message that a murder, a gruesome murder had occurred in Madison County. We stood indignant that such could happen in our midst."

Mr. Darsey was also indignant that a "horde" of FBI agents had come to the area. He pointed out the agents were under the supervision of Attorney General Robert Kennedy. He argued that while an army of federal outsiders had done the bulk of the work in the Penn case, the arrests in the president's assassination had been handled by the officials of Dallas County. Mr. Darsey did not let the fact that circumstances differed wildly in the two cases interfere. He hopped up and down, thumping the jury rail and causing one juror to blink and start back in alarm. He demanded to know why there was a difference in the administration of justice.

"I will tell you what it is and mark you well, gentlemen," he cried, his voice beginning to wear down. "Mark you well, that difference is the key to this case, the key that will unlock the door to this mystery.

"In the interim between the assassination of our president and the slaying of Penn, there was in progress in this great nation, the land of the free and the home of the brave, what has been designated as a social revolution. Sit-outs, sit-ins, walk-outs, walk-ins, lay-outs, lay-ins, insurrection, riots, police dogs, fire hoses, United States marshals, federal troops.

"On the morning of July 11 there was heard throughout this land a murmur in growing intensity . . . an outrage has been committed against a member of our race, the administration of justice is on trial . . . . Fe, Fi, Fo, Fum, I smell the blood of an Englishman."

What Mr. Darsey intended by the nursery rhyme was soon indicated when he said the FBI had been sent down from Washington with the order:

"Go down to Madison County and don't come back, stay for the duration, don't come back until you bring us white meat!"

He was red in the face, choking and losing his voice, but the phrases rang on. "Now is the time for all good jurors to come to the aid of their country . . . within the name of all that is holy they will never, until the ruins of this nation fall in ashes around our feet, destroy the jury system which is the heart and soul of Anglo-Saxon jurisprudence . . ."

He apologized for overzealousness because "my mind is boiling." The overzealousness simmered down to deliver this icy threat:

"If they don't leave to us the administration of justice and punishment of crime in our midst, leave to the local level to handle law enforcement as it has been doing through the years and is doing now, a different kind of revolution will be a-loose in the land. Let's let 'em know before any momentum gets into any carpetbagger administration of justice."

Night riders versus carpetbaggers. A foreign student of United States history might have found it hard to believe the year was 1964, not 1865. In his charge, Judge Skelton did not refer to any specific evidence. He had stayed up most of the previous night writing out the law on conspiracy, and the possible verdicts on the murder charge. He read and sometimes reread the intricate legal wording; the jurors gave him their polite attention and perhaps followed him. The spectators downstairs made no sound. They seemed fascinated with the formalities of justice. Upstairs, the segregated balcony was silent and deserted.

Ten minutes after the jury retired, some members were seen lounging on the window sills of the jury room, deliberating on the view of twilight Danielsville. They had a choice of three verdicts: Guilty, which automatically meant the electric chair; guilty with a recommendation for mercy which meant life; or acquittal. About the courthouse little of the tension usually felt while waiting for a murder verdict existed. Acquittal was in the air, on the constant smile of Mrs. Sims as she chatted with friends, about the shadows of the empty balcony. The jury's going to supper without reaching a verdict caused a momentary stir.

After a little more than three hours actual deliberation, the jury was ready. While court was being reassembled, an Atlanta newspaper reporter tried to talk to Sims. Sims used the few minutes before he would hear the life-or-death verdict to denounce the reporter, but not for his trial coverage. Four years earlier, the reporter had written a story about illegal slot machines in the American Legion post to which Sims belonged. With his wife within earshot, he cursed the reporter in foul barnyard language for costing the Legion money. A few minutes later, when the acquittal decision was read, Sims bowed his head and said to himself—or so he later reported —"Thank the Lord."

Governor Sanders had vowed to leave no stone unturned in solving the case and a weary Prosecutor Johnson unconsciously returned to that phrase as he wearily packed his briefcase.

"I'm disappointed," he said. "We left no stones unturned but the jury had the last say."

Jury foreman C. S. Logan, a sixty-four-year-old retired merchant, denied the jurors ever were split.

"One feller," he said, "was just a little slow about what he wanted to say."

What did the jury want to say by its verdict? Prosecutor Johnson had told them that they were testing "the strength and efficiency of state government." Defense Counsel Darsey warned it must be left to the local level to "handle law enforcement." Both men would seem to be speaking on the side of justice. The jurors' private interpretation of justice and right remained their secret.

The next night near the base of Stone Mountain, a massive granite outcropping just outside Atlanta, the National Ku Klux Klan Association held a cross-burning rally. The area was hallowed ground for the KKK. On a chill and gusty Thanksgiving night in 1915, the Klan had been revived up on the mountain by a salesman named William Simmons who once sold ladies' garters. The group, gathered in an open field the night following the verdict, was one of the seven or eight splinter Klans that did not owe allegiance to Imperial Wizard Shelton of Tuscaloosa. This Klan had its own Wizard, James Venable, an Atlanta lawyer in his sixties who spoke piously to reporters of his nonviolent beliefs. About two hundred robed Klansmen were present with a sprinkling of their women and children. A great wooden cross wrapped with kerosene-soaked burlap bags was fired and blazed while a scratchy record (Klan records are always scratchy) blared "The Old Rugged Cross." The soft light from the flames played on the creased face of a middle-aged Klansman next to me as he gazed on the cross.

"Ain't that purty?" said a friend next to him.

"It's the most beautiful sight in the world," he said, his voice tight with soulful emotion.

The voice of the Klan chaplain, or Kludd, was also tight with emotion as he opened the rally with a prayer to God to "put grace and grit in the hearts of our Caucasian people that they might destroy this black ape race." The "amen" from the lips of young men was fervent. The response came mumbled and dry from an ancient Klansman whose conical hood drooped down limply over one ear, an old man's phallic symbol. Venable said these words:

"You'll never be able to convict a white man that kills a nigger what encroaches on the white race of the South. They tried it in Philadelphia and over in Danielsville. You see a jury there last night turn 'em scot free. Now, Mr. Hoover and Mr. Johnson, what do you say about that?"

The crowd cheered. The Klansmen wanted action, not words, and within an hour they had a report that Negroes were trying to crash the gate. The implausibility was no impediment. Young and old went whooping off, pulling pistols from under their robes. Some loaded as they ran. Of course, no Negroes were crashing the gate. The rally shortly petered out for lack of alarms. Venable's words remained in the mind: "You'll never be able to convict a white man that kills a nigger what encroaches on the white race of the South." Was that what the Danielsville jury had been trying to say?

Lynching, in the old form, is a thing of the past. Yet, white men got away with murder against Negroes. I safely assumed they were going to continue to get away with murder in the foreseeable future. Even if state authorities were anxious to get convictions, verdicts were in the hands of twelve men from the community where the crime occurred. So, for the most part, are the investigations. Ironically, the federal government, for all its civil rights legislation, was unable to guarantee to Southern Negroes the prime right, the indispensable one—the right to live.

The defense in the Penn trial inveighed against the intrusion of federal authorities in a murder case that properly lies within state jurisdiction. The theme of the complaint is familiar. Whether the issue is a murder or a school system to be integrated or jobs to be filled in a factory, the South and the right wing have been repeating the complaint for years. The Washington people had no right coming in, trampling constitutional precedent in the process, carrying the government irresistibly to a point of centralization. The noble experiment of a truly federal government is just about over. The fiction of a sacrosanct Constitution can no longer be maintained. We are sliding toward national control in the hands of a power elite, the only kind of apparatus that presumably can handle the super-bigness of modern America. Stupendous growth probably would have made this transformation inevitable.

They made a fiction of the dream that democracy and the fair administration of justice could flourish equally in this America. In forcing Washington to intervene in Little Rock and Oxford and ultimately and howsoever reluctantly, in hundreds of hamlets throughout the South, the extremists throttled free thinking at a critical moment. The various civil rights acts, stretching the concept of the original Constitution beyond any elastic ability to resume its inherent shape, should have been widely and deeply discussed. The years from World

War II on should have been years of great debate in America, as citizens drew from themselves the distillation of the experience of their years in this country, deciding how much traditions meant, how far the simple and comforting ideal of the town meeting could be altered in a world of increasingly inhuman technocracy, how we could change and yet remain. To speak against Washington intervention gave comfort to the enemies of humanity. The American liberal (whatever that means) might suspect the political science practiced by J. Edgar Hoover and his FBI. Yet, the liberal wanted Hoover to send his agents swarming over Mississippi to protect the Negro. He wanted the thinking of a handful of men on the Supreme Court to cut great channels for the future course of American life, because, for the moment, that thinking agreed with his.

With barely a word, we watched the form of our government begin to change. Once set on this way, there was no returning. To every abstract objection rose a pragmatic example of need. The Penn case seemed to suggest that another eventual alteration in our system of states' rights might be necessary. Georgia had tried hard to convict the men it thought guilty of the crime. Powerless to intervene juridically in the slaying, the federal government, while turning over its evidence of homicide to a receptive state prosecution, sought to prosecute for a milder legal affront to civil rights. Someone still got away with murder. Any Negro driving in the Deep South at night must tense as a car behind him sped up, drew abreast, and passed on a lonely highway. Could we pass a law permitting the federal government to prosecute the murder of a Negro? No. Such a move would obviously be a class law, odious to our concept of universal equality, terrible in precedent-setting implications. If whites continued murdering blacks South or North, if extremists continued to indulge their hate and expanded their means, how could the sane, the responsible, the humane of America or the politically vulnerable power elite, permit it?

To the Southern rural Negro, these philosophical, constitutional and juridical involvements were of small moment. They know of the ministerial mentality that can ask God—ask God—for the grace and grit to destroy the "black ape race." They believed, on the basis of the history they have lived, the boast spoken by Imperial Wizard Venable while the ashes of the cross glowed below Stone Mountain: "You will never be able to convict a white man that kills a nigger what encroaches on the white race of the South." They knew, with an old knowledge of violent death, that Lemuel Penn was killed on a Georgia road because he was black. And all the civil rights acts, and all the Anglo-Saxon jury systems, and all the fine points of constitutional legalisms or philosophies would never breathe life into *him* again.

AMERICAN
CURRENTS

It was a summer of seeming contradictions. By mid-August, Mayor Allen Thompson's anti-riot tank had run up no mileage and gathered dust in the Jackson police garage. The Movement, born in Montgomery and come to manhood in Birmingham, was moribund in both those cities—a victim of faltering Negro leadership and skillful white manipulations. The North suffered the race riots, while Southern whites, some gloating and the more refined, bearing the noble air of one, long unjustly accused and at last vindicated, took this as proof of their immemorial claim, "We really understand them, we know how to get along."

The public accommodations section of the Civil Rights Act had received such surprising compliance in certain large cities that *Time* magazine headlined its story, "And the Walls Came Tumbling Down." Administration spokesmen and even civil rights leaders like Dr. King were moved to extortionate praise. Lester Maddox, whom we left shivering on an Atlanta street in January, had, on the steaming third of July, pulled a gun on some Negroes trying to enter his Pickrick Restaurant. Heart of Atlanta motel owner Morton Rolleston, a more sophisticated man, was turning away Negro guests with a word. He was not depending on violence but on a legal test of the new law.

An uncritical assumption gained currency, particularly in the North which did not know any better, that Southern Negroes no longer had to worry where their next cup of coffee was coming from. The South, which knew better, was pleased to foster this belief.

Then, too, Barry Goldwater had become the Republican presidential nominee only to confound some critics by demonstrating moderation had virtue after all. In August, he spurned Ku Klux Klan support, which the Klan persisted in giving him anyway. Eventually a pamphlet from the Goldwater-Miller campaign headquarters in Washington began appearing down South. The pamphlet's intent was to prove to Washington Negroes that Senator Goldwater was stronger on civil rights than President Johnson, and it said in part: "Opponents, friends and neutrals agree . . . Goldwater is personally dedicated to the cause of civil rights." Democrats cynically distributed the pamphlet in Atlanta. Goldwater's behavior became so circumspect that persons who warned that his candidacy might start a race war were beginning to look like extremists. Mississippi, of course, was still mired in violence. Mississippi was a dark star in the Southern firmament, and proponents of the Southern reformation argued, with some logic, that that state should no more be considered typical of Dixie's atmosphere than riotous Harlem be judged the Northern norm. The trouble with these optimistic appraisals of the Southern scene was that realities and illusions and hopes were mixed together into a vague picture of progress that promoted confusion, when clarity was needed to gauge precisely what had been achieved and what remained to be done.

Thompson's tank did not roll because Negro leadership had decided not to march in the South with elections in the offing. They opted to play it cool lest colored militancy frighten white votes away from President Johnson. For every big-city restaurant that served a Negro, there were ten or fifty—no one knew—where asking for service would be worth a Negro's life, or at least his physical well-being. A colored family driving through the South still had to plan its itinerary with attention to details the AAA did not supply its members. Would there be a gas station available where the kids could use the bathroom when they had to? Did the town reached at midday have a restaurant where they could safely stop for lunch? If at nightfall the big chain motels, ordered desegregated from their home offices, were filled, would there be any place to sleep? If these problems faced the mobile Negro with a buffer of cash in his wallet, what of the plantation Negro whose tenancy was at the whim of the plantation owner, or the black man living in unnumbered cotton gin towns among rednecks who didn't give a damn about a progressive image, or even the majority of colored city dwellers locked tight as ever in the vise of white economic and political supremacy?

A professional pessimist might deny the South was changing; but only the naïve or deceitful would pronounce the area changed. Gracious

concessions were few, fewer purging acknowledgments of past un-
fairness and open-hearted pledges to build a humane and rational future. Most of the South retreated just so far as it was pushed by federal law and no further. In many areas that went untested by the
Movement no retreat at all was found. As this opportunity for racial
cooperation went untaken by the white man, seeds of discord were
planted that later would send up rank blooms in places such as Selma
and Greensboro, Alabama, Bogalusa, Louisiana, Americus, Georgia,
and hundreds of other communities which did not make headlines,
but where white let black know no racial millenium was forthcoming
if he, by God, had anything to do with it.

Do I malign the South? Where were the reasonable men ready to
speak out and say, "The past is dead; let's cooperate equally to make a
meaningful life for the present"? A few existed—a principled, stubborn,
and often brave few. Most could be found in Atlanta, the home of the
Southern Regional Council, which was a beacon of sanity in a sea of
racial madness; home also of the *Atlanta Constitution,* a mediocre newspaper with a vital editorial heart named Ralph McGill. Much self-
interest was inherent in Atlanta's racial climate and considerable hypocrisy. Yet the city was a place where Hamilton Douglas, chairman of
the Mayor's Committee on Racial Matters, could tell a group of
Jaycees:

"If a right means anything, the person guaranteed it is entitled to it
in his lifetime, not in the next generation.

"People keep asking how long is it going on, saying, 'Every time we
yield there's another demand.' These demands are entirely logical if
you put yourself in the position of a citizen of the United States who, a
century ago, was guaranteed certain rights. He isn't going to ask for
half a right and stop.

"Don't kid yourself that this is a Communist-inspired movement. It
is a movement from the bottom of the people to achieve things promised
since slavery . . . . I don't know if any of the leaders I talked with were
Communists, but you can't kill it by calling it Communist. I've never
cared about a man's motives if he's conveying a truth I have to hear."

Whether this tough-minded wisdom got through the button-downed
prejudice of the Jaycees, a group which, North or South, is distinguished by atrophied social consciences and buccaneer materiality, is
debatable. But at least, a voice was not tyrannized into silence. In other
parts of Georgia, however, and west in Alabama and Mississippi,
certain words could not be spoken. Birmingham had already driven
lawyer Charles Morgan into exile in Atlanta because he espoused racial

justice. A group of women in Mobile was trying to save that Gulf city from turmoil, and another group of citizens in Huntsville was trying to achieve racial accord before Washington decided to remove its multi-million-dollar rocket research to a place where black and white workers did not feel so overcome. The city of Auburn had a newspaper owner named Neil Davis who didn't worry about the reading preference of bigots. When whites and Negroes, trying to work together in nearby Tuskegee, were stymied by the venomous little local paper, Davis bought the paper and opened a window on reason.

Once these groups and individuals were enumerated, the number of Alabamians publicly declaring for a new Southern vision dropped off to virtually nothing. Mississippi, of course, was worse. One could spread out the map of the state and put pins in places where even one person was standing to buck the midsummer tide of hate and know-nothingism. The dissidents would include a gentle old priest in Yazoo City, whose congregation would not listen to him . . . a widow lady in Magnolia, who had garbage and tacks thrown in her driveway because she asked a white girl civil rights worker into her home for tea . . . a handful of men and women at interracial Tougaloo College in Jackson. The vast majority of newspapers either condoned racism or were afraid to offer truth to their inflamed readership. The *Jackson Clarion-Ledger*, in a column by Charles M. Hills, could print the following letter:

> I am here in Rochester (N.Y.), attending a technical school representing Ladd Photocolor Pictures of Jackson. Everyone I've talked to seems to have a special interest in Mississippi and high respect for Governor Paul Johnson.
>
> The white people in Mississippi and most of the colored people are fortunate that they should enjoy better health . . . that is, they do not have to witness so many sickening sights as here.
>
> Tonight we were amazed and disgusted as we saw a blacker than tar Negro man walking along a main street with a white girl. My personal thoughts were, should it be best to knock the dickens out of the Negro man or kick the white girl. . . .
>
> All you have to do to appreciate Mississippi is visit New York.
>
> (signed) D. L. Perkins

These violent speculations appearing in the state's leading newspaper give some idea of the editorial sense of responsibility. Of course, a few exceptions were found in the state. Pulitzer Prize winner Hodding Carter in his Greenville *Delta-Democrat-Times*, and Jackson weekly publisher Hazel Brannon Smith preached gospels of understanding and decent behavior. In McComb, an editor named Oliver Emmerich and his readers were playing out a Southern tragedy. The attitudes and behavior involved were not limited to McComb. I felt they were reflected in happenings involving Goldwaterites in Atlanta and Democrats in Atlantic City. As this story enters the political dog days of the summer, I would like first to tell about the *McComb Enterprise Journal,* the man who wrote it, and the people who read it.

Oliver Emmerich is a moderate, if that word has any meaning left. At the age of sixty-six, he had owned his newspaper for forty years. In that time he had tried to make the paper responsive to a changing South.

"We've had this racial problem all along." he told me, pale blue eyes unblinking and righteous behind rimless spectacles. "If you keep one part of your population in the ditch, it's not reality."

One son, a graduate of Ole Miss who went to the University of Paris, is an editor of the *Baltimore Sun.* A daughter is married to an Austin, Texas, neurosurgeon. The family is an intellectual world removed from the Snopeses. Emmerich loved to travel, and in his office in the modern *Enterprise* plant on McComb's Main Street was a map tracing a Far East tour he and his wife had taken early that year. He related that when he was in India in February, he picked up the *Times of Bombay* to find his picture in it. His mother had died unexpectedly back in McComb and the same day the Ku Klux Klan had burned a cross on his lawn. When he returned from India, the head of the Klan in McComb, a farmer who struck oil and became wealthy, came to him and said:

"Mr. Emmerich, I'm sorry. The boys hadn't known your mother died."

The Klan had burned the cross because of Emmerich's moderate ways and his reputation as a friend to Negroes at a time when many regarded the Negro as an enemy. Emmerich proudly told me that fifteen years before, he had begun awarding a gold cup from the *Enterprise Journal* to the Negro community making the greatest progress in farm and home improvements. The award smacked of paternalism, yet in a society characterized by white indifference to Negro needs or aspirations the award was, at least, constructive. But, he said sadly, in 1962 worsening race relations made attending the Negro get-together at which he had always presented the cup impossible for him. He had to leave the cup at the door. The following year, Emmerich said, a Negro man had to come to the office to get it.

"He had tears in his eyes," Emmerich recalled. "This year, we discontinued it altogether. Just too much pressure."

Since 1961 when the Freedom Riders came to McComb, pressure had been mounting on him. He helped to avert mob violence through careful planning with police and he befriended out-of-state newsmen. Whites broke windows at the paper and a few days later . . .

"I was in a store and a feller came up and said, 'Are you the feller who runs this paper? Why do you have all these out-of-town newspapermen around?' All of a sudden he slugged me without warning. Broke my glasses and cut me. Turned out he was an oilfield roughneck who had been put up to it by others. He came around later and apologized. Cried when he did it, too. He was a decent man but like so many others he got led astray by all the emotionalism."

Emmerich and everyone else in McComb saw trouble coming when COFO would establish its Freedom House. He alone tried to do something about the impending violence. Beginning on May 25, he wrote five editorials trying to allay fears about the "invasion" and head off violence. He even convinced a reluctant Governor Johnson to announce a ten-point policy which included the statement: "The law will apply to all people alike. To everyone—to whites, Negroes, Chinese, everyone; even to my own brother."

Pike County Sheriff R. R. Warren had a ten-point program, too, which on May 27 was carried in the *Enterprise Journal*. The program included the declaration: "We cannot tolerate anyone taking the law into his own hands. If this should happen, mob law would prevail and under mob rule anything could happen." Finally, the city had a ten-point program which ran the next day. Mayor Gordon Burt promised effective law enforcement and he hoped publicly that tear gas supplies on hand would go bad sooner than be used. "So long as demonstrators are not violating the law nor interfering with the rights of other people," he said, "we will exercise restraint. But if anyone interferes with the rights of others he will be arrested."

With thirty points neatly assembled, Emmerich wound up the editorials this way:

"Our conclusion is that we should all try to relax. Let the law enforcement officers handle the situation for us. They are willing. They stand committed. They insist that they are prepared. What more could we ask?

"May we on September 1, look back on the summer of 1964 and be able to truthfully say, 'We met a crisis with maturity. We did not panic. We exercised restraint. We upheld the dignity of the law. We met the challenge intelligently.'

"If we can say this on September 1, then we will know that we successfully stood the test; that we proved ourselves to be smart and that we were not outsmarted."

The good people of McComb did not have to wait until September 1 to learn how the test would go. On June 21 before the summer volunteers reached town, the homes of two Negroes planning to house them

were bombed. Before the summer was out, sixteen homes and churches
in the county would be bombed or burned. Beatings and harassment
of civil rights workers became commonplace. All those reassuring editorial points added up to zero ability to cope with violence. The failure
was not surprising when the thinking of Mayor Burt, who also served
as head of the Citizens Council, was probed. Three white roadhouses
also were burned or blown up in Pike County during 1964. I once asked
the mayor what he thought about that.

"They were places where drunks and troublemakers hung out," he
replied. "Now you know, people here in Mississippi believe in doin'
things the direct way. You got a place like that an' you burn it down,
then you don't have any more trouble there, right?"

Emmerich was sadly disappointed with the failure of his efforts to
promote reason and inclined to rationalize by placing the onus on the
rights workers.

"What I'm saying first is that their program started with bad timing,"
he told me. "It came at a time when we needed a moratorium. The second thing is the terrible advance billing it received. Stories like that one
in the *Harvard Crimson* predicting a blood bath. They got photostated
and distributed around here. The effect was like it was a hostile army
coming in which called for a patriotic local response even if that response
was contrary to law. Third, too many volunteers were like beatnik
types . . . even though I concede many were sincere. But that's why
people have been inflamed. They came in—untidy, don't you know—expecting, almost courting, hostility. These things developed a climate
among a segment that would bomb and burn."

Had he done any stories on the volunteers, what they consisted of
and how they lived?

"No," said Emmerich, characteristically edgy when even a whiff of
criticism arose. "Your voice was almost extinguished. My God, here
were white girls and colored men living in the same house. That just
doesn't go down here. I don't know where it does go."

What "went" in McComb were three months of terrorist activity. An
insurance broker, one of McComb's leading citizens, told me:

"You didn't know if the man next door was doing the bombings. The
Klan's influence was everywhere. And the higher-ups never were caught.
Some are probably officials of the city. People kept thinking city officials would do something but they didn't. Of course, we almost all are
segregationists, that never was the issue."

Emmerich explained why the *Enterprise Journal* did not print a single editorial on the racial situation from May 29 until October 15. The editorial would not have been effective, he said. He convinced me that he believed this reasoning and was not deterred by anything so simple as physical or economic fear. The majority of his six thousand readers were civilized, law-abiding churchgoers, not Klansmen or rednecks. Yet, they and he did not move against terrorism even when the object was not a Negro but one of their own. Parallels between white behavior in McComb and Saint Augustine are obvious, except that in Saint Augustine the newspaper editor did not give a damn about being effective. But in both cases, respectable whites tolerated—and I believe condoned—intimidation of Negroes until the violence got out of hand and began to hurt the community's reputation, ergo the town's economy. Little or no moral concern came from these people because they believed basically that Negroes lay outside their moral obligations.

They could not admit this belief. The concept ran against Christian logic and prevailing national opinion. An elaborate hypocrisy was developed, both personal and political, as McComb and the rest of the South prepared for the national elections. The phrase "states' rights" meant all the old beliefs about white supremacy and all the old determination to keep the black in his place. References to "crime in the streets" stood for Negroes raping white women, the ancient Southern sex obsession. "Sacred property rights" invoked divine sanction against having to eat with Negroes in restaurants, and much of the wrath vented on the "welfare state" was loosed with Negroes getting relief in mind. How much Barry Goldwater believed in the attitudes behind this code only he could tell; his thought processes, as revealed by his printed words, were so muddled and contradictory that maybe he himself didn't know.

The "nice people" supporting him in the name of states' rights placed a mask of principle over their face of prejudice. The mask often slipped. A good place to view the face and observe the mind was at the Pickrick Restaurant in Atlanta. After having chased Negroes away at gunpoint on July 3, Lester Maddox continued with business as usual, which meant white customers only. Forty-four Negro workers, paid good salaries and well-treated by Maddox, kept dishing out the Southern fried chicken, turnip greens and ice tea that, together with Maddox' Southern fried prejudice, had built a half-million-dollar business. He wrote his own ads for the *Atlanta Constitution* combining corn pone polemics with self-promotion. The food was inexpensive and undistinguished but people liked the atmosphere. Newspaper clippings of Congo atrocities festooned the walls along with accounts of rapes and murders committed by Negroes in the United States. One table by the door was covered with right-wing pamphlets and newspapers inveighing against everything from urban renewal to Chief Justice Earl Warren. Advertisements included such items as:

"Kiss of Death is a graphic illustration of beautiful white maidenhood clasped in the arms of an African savage . . . 10-50 for $1100."

His ads, which always carried an explanation of the restaurant's name (*Pick*, to select, to fastidiously eat; *Rick*, to pile up or to heap, to amass,—You pick it out, we'll rick it up), contained examples of Maddox' logic. On August 1, he wrote:

> And then if it is all right for Negroes to discriminate against Negroes (which is what they do every time they eat in a white restaurant when they could have eaten in a Negro restaurant—which brings up the question, "Why is it that some Negroes insist on eating with White people, rather than with Negroes, what do they have against Negroes?") and it is all right for Whites to discriminate against Whites, but it is always wrong for Whites to discriminate against Negroes. . . .
>
> Soon the President will start rolling off some strong talk about his stand for America and will start openly opposing Communism. Wouldn't be surprised to hear him speaking in favor of segregation and against race mixing in early fall. One last question that the race mixers should answer: "If racial integration is right, and all people are equal . . . then why not integrate the White race into the Negro race, rather than the Negro race into the White race?" None of you can properly answer that question from the White House on down to the Black House.

By the time Maddox was putting his unanswerable question, a federal court had ordered him—along with the Heart of Atlanta Motel—to desegregate by August 11 or face contempt charges. More whites than ever were coming to his restaurant to demonstrate solidarity with their Lester. Many bought his Pickrick "drumsticks." These so-called souvenir ax handles were engraved with his signature. Ax handles are an historic Southern white weapon used to intimidate rural Negroes, and I wrote in a *Washington Post* article:

" 'You can keep 'em as souvenirs,' Maddox told customers, 'or use 'em for something else.'

"The drumsticks sold like hotcakes. Maddox has been accused of catering politically and gastronomically to the redneck or poor white element. But the bulk of his clientele has always been solidly middle-class. The customer purchasing a drumstick and making a smiling show of feeling its heft to friends would usually be a businessman or occasionally a student from Georgia Tech a few blocks away."

Maddox liked this appraisal so much he later ran it in one of his ads.

I think that his bourgeois patrons got a delicious thrill from being part of the violent implications in the drumstick, from feeling allied with Maddox as members of a doughty band of true patriots who were willing to risk all to repulse the forces of evil. They were, from my observations, persons who ordinarily led bland lives, buffered by material well-being from disturbing realities of American life, convinced by their membership in church or Rotary that they were acting decently, if not dramatically, in the cause of God and country. Their fear of Communism was real because Communism threatened the house nearly paid off, the annual new car, the church that gave them comfort, the social system that gave them privilege over the blacks. The emergence of the Negro cast a dark shadow over all their social scene and implied that if he could come on then everything else that once was fixed forever might go.

On August 12, Negroes came to test Maddox' reaction to the court order. A wildly emotional day was underway. The whites who gathered were not the customary genteel patrons. Customarily, they stayed away when the dirty business of violence was threatened. Maddox met two colored students at his door and said:

"You sorry no-good devils. You're Communists. You've stolen my job. You've stolen my business."

He called out a moon-faced Negro baker named O. Z. Bruce who had worked at the Pickrick for fifteen years. The baker, pressed by the whites who brandished drumsticks, looked like a man standing in hot tar and unable to get out. Sweat streaming down his face, he quoted Matthew 20:15 to the students:

"Is it not lawful for me to do what I will with mine own?"

Bruce pleaded with the integrationists to give Maddox more time.

"No," said one of the students, "we've been down that road before."

A white employee whispered to Maddox that he was going after the Negroes.

"No," Maddox whispered back, "let the others do it."

A few harmless punches were thrown, but quick police work prevented a major clash. Police began diverting traffic to side streets to hold down the crowds in front of the restaurant. Maddox screeched off in his automobile to blockade the side streets. When police called a wrecker, driven by a Negro, to remove the car, Maddox leaped into the wrecker and removed the keys. Five minutes later he gave the shaken Negro a five-dollar tip—an arcane gesture. He was off to the restaurant on a commandeered bicycle, pedaling past cheering supporters (That old

Lester, they don't put nothin' over on him.) Next he halted a city bus, ironically filled with Negro passengers, and rode back to where another wrecker, driven by a white man, had come to remove his automobile. This time Maddox staged a sit-down on the tow hook while the crowd whooped. The driver radioed his garage that he was damned if he was going to move Mr. Maddox' car. The scene was Keystone Kops. But the funny pie-in-the-face contained a brick.

Next day, the show was over—temporarily. Maddox closed his doors rather than risk contempt proceedings should he continue turning away Negroes. A few days later he was back, not selling food but his drumsticks and carbonated drink called Gold Water. "Daddysize" drumsticks cost two dollars, child's size one dollar. Entrepreneur Maddox sold his Gold Water warm at twenty-one cents a can, chilled for twenty-six cents. Later, after an Alabama court ruled that a restaurant not in interstate commerce could escape the Civil Rights Act, Maddox reopened his place as the Lester Maddox Cafeteria. He stood at the door, telling customers he would not serve interstate travelers or integrationists. On and on went this travesty, complete with a coffin containing a mannequin that Maddox said was the corpse of free enterprise. The story was absurd; Maddox, an anachronistic buffoon. Yet, the point that escaped a North anxious to believe in progress and a South preening itself on its coming of moral age, was this:

Although the Pickrick in Atlanta made the headlines with its defiance of law, hundreds, probably thousands of restaurants throughout the Southland echoed defiance, perpetuated segregation, and undermined the spirit of the Civil Rights Act. This host of Pickricks, invisible to the Northern eye and winked at by the Southern, loomed starkly before the Negro. He would have to keep pressing, insisting, risking. A lot of people were getting tired of militancy, and they were not all Goldwaterites.

The Mississippi Freedom Democratic Party, technically open to whites but practically all-black, went to the Democratic Convention in Atlantic City in August, hoping to replace the regular Democratic delegation by virtue of emotional and legalistic appeals. The emotional appeals would be based on myriad stories from Negroes disenfranchised by the state and disregarded by the state's white democrats. Legalistically, damning facts and figures were presented. Negro voter registration in Mississippi had dropped from nearly 190,000 in 1890 to about 23,000 in 1964, representing about six percent of the Negro voting-age population. The dropoff had been the direct result of repressive action by the state's judicial, executive and legislative branches—all of which were controlled by the state Democratic Party. The convention, which chose Paul Johnson as gubernatorial candidate, was held in a segregated hotel. Johnson's campaign literature stated: "Our Mississippi Democratic Party is entirely independent and free of the influence or domination of any national party." Another statement began, "The Mississippi Democratic Party, which long ago separated itself from the National Democratic Party, and which has fought consistently everything both national parties stand for. . . ." These words were not political bluster. In the 1960 Kennedy campaign, Mississippi Democrats reneged on a pledge to support convention nominees and supported unpledged electors. In June, 1964, when Democratic precinct meetings were held throughout the state, registered Negroes got the old runaround when they tried to attend. In eight precincts, no trace of a meeting was held at the appointed time. In three precincts, Negroes located the meeting but were refused entry. The Negroes were allowed into ten other meetings but were prevented in many ways from full participation. Their efforts to get resolutions of party loyalty passed were defeated universally except for one precinct in moderate Greenville. Mississippi's un-Democratic record could not be seriously questioned.

Politics, however, is not basically responsive to morality or even legality. The political system is moved by power. Joseph Rauh, FDP adviser and chairman of the District of Columbia Democrats, was aware that if the regulars were illegal, the sixty-eight delegates were extralegal. He knew if he could get the question of their seating decided in the open on the convention floor, the FDP delegates would have a very good chance. Voting against white Mississippi, that murderous summer, would be highly popular. However, Rauh knew that despite strong support in the credentials committee for at least a minority report that could send the question to the floor, the final decision would come from the White House.

"I would be very happy with Johnson's benevolent neutrality," he had said in July. He did not get it.

I was not in Atlantic City and so the convention unfolded for me through television. In a way, seeing the convention on television was even more revealing than if I had been there. By the time the convention opened, the president, acting through Hubert Humphrey, had evolved a so-called compromise and had applied sufficient political pressure to dissuade credentials committee members from filing the minority report, which would have dragged the party's dirty linen all over the floor. The "compromise" would seat all regular white Mississippi Democrats signing party loyalty oaths. Aaron Henry and the white Rev. Edwin King, leaders of the FDP delegation, would be seated as delegates-at-large with voting privileges. They would not be seated with the regular delegation. The rest of the FDP delegates were to be invited in as "honored guests." Finally, at the 1968 convention and thereafter, states sending delegations would have to assure equal opportunity to all who wished to participate in party affairs. The most unusual feature of this compromise is that neither side in the dispute wanted it.

"I did the best I could," said Joe Rauh. "I got the most I could get 'em. I hope they like it. God bless 'em."

The FDP delegation formally voted a unanimous rejection. Most white Mississippi delegates started packing to go home. Some civil rights leaders such as Dr. King were urging FDP acceptance. SNCC members demonstrated on the Boardwalk and were likely to hold sit-ins. The convention was, in short, a lively, complicated, many-sided story which television, given the glut of air time available, could have laid out objectively before the American people. Instead, exhibiting an egocentric arrogance increasingly evident in a medium—half reportorial and half show biz—and reflecting subjective identification with the White House Establishment, television commentators often behaved before the Mississippi Negroes as proctors charged with keeping order rather than seekers after the roots of disorder.

On opening day, Chet Huntley of NBC allowed that the Mississippi Democratic Party was "entirely open to Negroes." The Huntley-Brinkley axis, whose habitual posture was that of a crusty moderate, occasionally was guilty of flagrant editorializing. More often, the commentators subjectively made the point through attitude. The tone came down from Olympian height of supposed objectivity. One sensed impatience with the refusal of the FDP to accept the compromise and distaste for the SNCC demonstrations on the Boardwalk. The viewer was made to feel that the FDP Negroes damn well had an obligation to accept and stop jamming up the works. On the floor, carrying portable receivers and transmitters with antennae bristling, the television newsmen struggled through the mob scenes created when FDP members sat in the seats of the Mississippi delegation. ABC's John Scali, his antenna bent in the uproar and scuttling like a wounded bug, said to one of the Negro women:

"Ma'am, now that you've made your point, don't you think it would be best to leave? We don't mean to advise you. . . ."

"I intend to stay here as long as I can," replied the woman, who did not mean to be advised. "Till someone comes in to carry me out."

A few moments later Scali asked another demonstrator:

"Do you think that by sitting here in this manner you will be dramatizing your case?"

Bill Downs of the same network observed:

"The educational factors of sitdowns are, I suppose, questionable. But they get a lot of attention."

What that gratuitous remark was supposed to indicate (except faint contempt) eludes me. NBC's John Chancellor had a more pertinent exchange with Bob Moses of SNCC.

"Would you compromise?" Chancellor asked as persons thronging the aisle bumped them and something just short of pandemonium reigned on the floor.

"What is the compromise?" Moses replied angrily. "We are here for the people and the people want to represent themselves. They don't want symbolic token votes. They want to vote themselves."

Chancellor correctly reminded him that Dr. King said that what had begun as a demonstration now was in the realm of politics where compromise was needed. One sensed that Moses at that moment cared as little for Dr. King's opinion as he would for Ross Barnett's. He avoided conflict.

"This convention hasn't made one vote," he said. "It's a convention by acclamation. What we intend to do is to stand here with our signs, One Man—One Vote, telling our story."

As the clamor of demonstrations on the Boardwalk mounted (Lester Maddox even left his skillet to come and picket briefly for states' rights) and the clamor inside alternated with bloodless recitals of political deals and pressures, the reality of Mississippi was lost. I remember once in the midst of uproar a camera swinging over the crowd caught a dark blur, then focused on the face of a Negro woman, a somber, determined face from Mississippi. Then the image was gone and the circus came back. I know that in the frenetic atmosphere of a political convention, the excitement of the moment often takes precedence over real meaning. In the convention coverage that I saw, the newsmen had a tendency (with CBS an exception) to patronize the Mississippi Negro insurgents, to assume that commentators' judgments carried a certain sophisticated superiority over the judgments of these well-meaning, morally motivated, but rather childishly stubborn Negroes. These people had something vital to say about the American democracy, its philosophy, and practice; but power and hoopla carried the day.

When the shouting and tumult died, the FDP published a twelve-page brochure explaining its behavior at the convention. The brochure was intended for the semi-literate understanding of the majority of

Mississippi Negroes. Sometimes, the brochure read like a first-grade primer. In the book's basic English was basic truth. It began: "The Democratic National Convention was a big meeting held by the National Democratic Party at Atlantic City in August. . . ."

> At Atlantic City the delegates from the Freedom Democratic Party went to a Committee that decided who could sit and vote in the convention. The regular Democratic Party asked the Committee to let them sit and vote in the seats for Mississippi. But the Freedom Democratic Party said that they should be allowed to sit and vote for Mississippi. People like Mrs. Fannie Lou Hamer and Dr. Aaron Henry told about the things that happened to them in Mississippi, how they had been arrested and beaten and how their homes had been shot into. They told how badly [sometimes the brochure writer's grammatical sophistication broke through] all the Negro people in Mississippi are treated. And they told how they had tried to go to the meetings of the Regular Democratic Party. . . . They were on television and many people everywhere in America saw them. Many people in Mississippi saw them too.
>
> Many members of the Committee were afraid. Many of them wanted to support the Freedom Democratic Party. But they were afraid they would lose their jobs in Washington or back home in the state where they lived. In other parts of the United States it is often just like in Mississippi. You can lose your job if you stand up and say what you believe in.
>
> President Johnson supported the all-white Regular Democratic Party. He wanted the Regular Party to be the only official party back here in Mississippi. President Johnson was afraid too. Freedom Democratic Party delegate Hartman Turnbow of Holmes County said the President was afraid he would lose his job too if he stood up and said what he believed in. Lyndon Johnson wants to be elected President again this November. He wants to get as many votes as possible in as many states as possible. President Johnson was afraid that if he supported the Freedom Democratic Party, the Republican candidate Barry Goldwater would get most of the votes in the Southern states and then President Johnson would lose his job as President.
>
> President Johnson knows that the white politicians from Mississippi are very strong in the national government in Washington. He knows that they do not like Civil Rights, or Aid to Education, or more Medical Care. He is afraid that the white politicians from Mississippi like James Eastland, Jamie Whitten and John Bell Williams will stop these programs in Washington. So President Johnson is afraid of these men.
>
> But President Johnson had a lot of power at the Convention. He could tell many of the members of that Committee how to vote. The President can make many people judges or put them in important positions. Since many members of the Committee want to be judges or important officials, when the President told them to vote against the Freedom Democratic Party, that is what they did.

James Reston could not have summarized the convention more succinctly. The brochure went on to explain the terms of the compromise, pointing out correctly that the president did not want the issue brought to the convention floor:

He knew that if all the delegates voted he might lose. . . . He wanted to tell the delegates what to do.

. . . So the Freedom Democratic Party delegation said "no!" President Johnson and Hubert Humphrey could not understand why the Freedom Democratic Party would not give in. And many of our Negro and white friends could not understand either. Very few people in the country understand what it means to say "no!" to what is wrong and to say "yes!" to what you believe in.

Most people think that you have to give in at some point so that other people will not be mad. They think that you are supposed to accept what you are offered by powerful people because that is the way things are done in this country. That is the way things have been done in Mississippi too, for a long time.

It takes courage to stand up for what you believe in. That is why the Freedom Democratic Party was started. But because the Freedom Democratic Party stood up for what it believed in in Mississippi, it knew it had to do this everywhere. So when the President and the Committee said "no!" to the Freedom Democratic Party in Atlantic City, the Freedom Democratic Party continued to say "yes" to what it believed in.

That brochure was not a declaration likely to echo through the corridors of American history. But at a time when men like Barry Goldwater were bemoaning the passage of morality from American political life, and his opposites were revealed in the half-light of political compromise, the FDP statement was as a clear draft in a smoke-filled room. Judged by Oliver Emmerich's standard of "effectiveness," the statement failed as an instrument of progress. FDP's position lost the party many friends more amenable to practicality than principle. The position weakened the FDP bargaining stand in the fast-approaching future when political accommodations would be made in Mississippi. The move sharpened differences within the Civil Rights Movement. Even some ambitious men inside the FDP took long thoughts about their future—should they remain tied to moralists?

As the campaign developed and the mainstream swelled behind Johnson, the Freedom Party (running its own mock election in Mississippi) and SNCC became more and more alienated from those Negro and liberal white forces who wanted to ride on the good side of a sure winner. If Goldwater had not frightened the wits from the electorate with his Neanderthal pronouncements on atomic war and the dangers of social progress, the election would have been different. The outcome—though not the margin—probably would have been the same. Most Northerners and Westerners, happy to guzzle a Gold Water and uphold states' (whites') rights, knew that in the interest of self-preservation they had to stop their self-indulgence at the ballot box. A *New York Times* poll from August 26 until September 10 may be instructive. A majority of white New Yorkers—particularly those over forty-five years old—thought that the Civil Rights Movement was going too far, too fast. This evidence of the widely heralded white backlash carried a corollary which showed an overwhelming majority prepared, with a negligible amount of party-line vote switching, to vote for Johnson.

The Deep South was different because the specter of atomic war was not as bad as that other specter three and one-half centuries older than Hiroshima. To support Goldwater was to support a holy cause. In many sections of Alabama and Mississippi, a white resident, even if he liked Johnson, would no more put a Johnson bumper sticker on his car than he would take a Negro to lunch. In Atlanta, where socialism and creeping bureaucracy were the genteel name of the game, a lady wrote the *Atlanta Constitution* with a new version of the Pledge of Allegiance: "I pledge allegiance to the flag," ran her composition, "of the 'Great Society' which is America, and to the Socialism for which it stands, one nation, under government, with food and shelter for all."

The terrible consequences of a Johnson victory envisioned in those final lines perhaps bothered some who crowded Atlanta's sun-filled Hurt Park on September 15 to hear candidate Goldwater speak. Hurt Park was the same park where the Klan had held its March rally, but no known Klan officials were present. Although former Georgia Republican national committeeman Robert Snodgrass, pushed out by right-wing extremists, had said the night before:

"I see little difference between the Ku Kluxers and the John Birchites. Someone said the only difference is that a Birchite has a net worth of fifty thousand dollars."

The net worth of the crowd must have been impressive. Nice looking, well-dressed, well-mannered people. I heard one man say to his friend:

"Isn't it good to see so many good people in a good place?"

Not a single Negro was in the crowd of about twenty thousand. Across the street where a building was going up some colored construction workers lounged on girders, watching, They were too far away to read the coded signs:

"How safe is it to be out on the streets at night?"

"Does owning property mean anything any more?"

"If you don't like Barry, get a mob."

An exciting feeling of happy purpose animated the crowd. Like some wonderful country club gathering, good things were going to happen to people who deserved and could afford them. The Goldwater young people especially shone with the burnish of the good life. The boys seemed uniformly handsome, the girls tanned and lithe—a new breed of conservative swingers. One group would shout "Viva!" across the park where another answered with "Ole!" Nothing was stodgy about them. Their elders smiled the proud, indulgent smiles of parents on television shows delightfully bewildered by the children's teen-age slang. Then—Goldwater.

The senator looked vital and like the "mature" male model who always posed with younger women. His silver hair shone in the sunlight; his wave was jaunty. When he began speaking, his effect on the crowd was something like a beloved teacher coming into a room of high-spirited students and bringing everybody down to earth with some level-voiced—if not always level-headed—observations. He had a few mild jokes.

"I'm glad to be back where you can hear a real Southern accent," he said. "You hear one once in a while in the White House but that doesn't fool anybody. No matter how you say 'Bobby Baker' it sounds the same."

The crowd whooped politely. Someone waved a placard reading "Dixie Digs Barry," but they truly did not dig him. The senator made some standard passes at foreign policy, the need for peace with honor and against Americans for Democratic Action (but not as that group related to civil rights). He dwelled on the important issue of reapportionment but no one seemed to care. He referred to Senator Humphrey's upcoming visit to Georgia and a few people booed and he admonished them.

"I think," he said, "it's perfectly fair that he should be allowed to state his position here."

I was reminded of Grand Dragon Calvin Craig's endorsement of adequate police and sanitary services for Negroes and of the crowd's sullen silence. Goldwater's listeners were the antithesis of Klansmen. Yet, both groups had come to hear scripture thundered on the issue, to respond to a moral battle cry and to release those racial emotions ordinarily blocked by the niceties of a social class that frowned on the word "nigger." They never heard this harangue. Barry Goldwater left behind in Hurt Park and throughout Georgia a disappointed host who knew whom they had to vote for, but who were emotionally shortchanged by a man on whom they had banked everything. Goldwater's restraint may have been cold-blooded political calculation designed to change his Rough Rider image. Leaving Hurt Park, hearing a middle-aged man ask a photographer, "How come our nigger-lovin' mayor wasn't here?" I had the feeling that Barry Goldwater was elementally a better human than many of his supporters.

Fall

THE UNCLOSED CIRCLE

The front page of the *Jackson Clarion-Ledger* for Saturday, December 5, is a journalistic microcosm of the Deep South as 1964 drew to a close. A four-column headline reads: "FBI Arrests 21 in CR Slayings." Equally prominent, perhaps more so, is a deep four-column photograph of former Miss America Mary Ann Mobley, a Mississippi girl beginning to make a career in Hollywood. She is pictured in a scene from a movie with her arms protectively around the waist of a fat man whose pants have just fallen to the floor. Miss Mobley and two girls watching are scantily clad, and the picture looks pornographic at first glance. Next to the photograph is a box announcing that a $15,800 expense fund needed to send the (Negro) Mississippi Valley State College marching band to the Rose Bowl parade has been oversubscribed.

> Chairman White, who took the task at the request of Gov. Johnson, said that between $4,000 and $5,000 of the money sent to the college at Itta Bena had come from Negroes.
>
> (He) expressed his keen pleasure that all sections of Mississippi had responded to the call for money to send the band West. Valley Staters scored a big hit in Indianapolis at the Memorial Day parade last May.

Under the photo of Mary Ann and the fallen pants, is a long story describing how the federal government was moving on a wide front to implement the 1964 Civil Rights Law. Below the story, readers were told how Mississippi Negro farmers in appreciable numbers voted and ran for the first time in federal farm elections that eventually determined how much acreage a farmer can plant for his cash crops, such as

215

corn and cotton. Agriculture Secretary Orville Freeman was reported pleased at the results.

Finally, above a photo of Neshoba County Sheriff Lawrence Rainey being taken into custody by an FBI man, is a story about Governor Paul Johnson denying the state will borrow 4 million dollars to pay teachers' salaries.

"What loan or bond issue?" the governor is said to have replied to an inquiring reporter, "I don't intend to borrow or float loans. We don't need the money."

The governor of the state with the lowest per capita income in the union, and one which receives four federal dollars back for each tax dollar it pays, concluded:

"In fact, there hasn't been a teacher salary payroll missed since the Conner administration at the height of the Great Depression."

All these stories are related by the Mississippi character and attitude which, by the end of 1964, was a magnification of the Deep South character and attitude. Some elements were distorted in the blowing-up but none unfaithful to the prevailing personality. A sheriff named Rainey was accused by the federal government of complicity in the racial murders of Goodman, Chaney and Schwerner, but the South had never known racial justice. The South sometimes regarded black men with hatred and never convicted white men of murdering them. More often the South liked to treat blacks as racial pets to be sent off to display their inherent musicianship in the passing parade. So, if no justice existed, the Negroes would have largess. Shadows were over the fair land. The despoilers came from Washington with laws that tried to worm into a man's very heart. A certain class "nigger" had been misled into taking advantage of the carpetbaggers and power-hungry Northern politicians and communists to disrupt a well-ordered plan of existence where white and black had a mutually respected place. Where would their contemptible assertiveness end, now that they were voting in elections to determine what should be done with the land?

On a day when the tyranny of change ranged everywhere, a front page, showing an idealized vision of what the Southern white man could be, clashed with the murderous reality of what he sometimes was. That day I drove back to Philadelphia on a journey of recapitulation. Neshoba County was a dark symbol of the whole convulsive year. Gray husks stood in cold cornfields that were green when murder was done in steaming summer. The visitor still received a Heap Big Welcome—*La Wa Chito Aickpaphi.*

Christmas decorations were out on Main Street and so were crowds of holiday shoppers—many of them Indians, Choctaw girls in long red and yellow skirts with their thick black hair braided, the men in white Levis and windbreakers but their faces Indian masks. I drove around the courthouse three times before I could find a parking space. Traffic had not been that heavy since back in June. Sheriff Rainey was his customary self; that is, a hulking mixture of fat and muscle, jaw bulging with tobacco like a stage hick, round little eyes wide with innocence when talking to someone from the outside world.

"There's no tension here," he said. "I'm certainly not under any tension. Because I haven't done anything wrong. I tried to give the FBI some leads on the case but they won't accept. I just can't understand it.

"But you look aroun' and see that everything is calm and orderly. Folks just Christmas shoppin', nigras not afraid. You can go about town any place you like without any problems."

No problems in Philadelphia. The sheriff would not discuss his arrest or the case, except to say that from time to time he still was trying to "run down" leads on the killing. The little eyes did not blink, looked easily into mine. When they looked inward, was the gaze ever troubled? What difference did it make? Rainey's was the face of the enemy, the anti-human factor in man.

Other, more interesting people were in Philadelphia. At the cozy jail-house, a Christmas wreath was on the door to Mr. and Mrs. Herrin's quarters. No Christmas spirit hung in the room where Goodman, Schwerner, and Chaney had signed out on their way to martyrdom. Mr. Herrin was sparse and deaf as ever. Mrs. Herrin had lost her robustness; her flesh sagged like a wax figure melting and her eyes were haggard.

"The arrests have just stirred me up again," she said. "I been in and out of the hospital since last June. I wake up crying when I think about it. Because we didn't have anything to do with it. We did everything just like we were supposed to."

"If I'd of known that was going to happen," piped her husband, "I never would've let 'em out. No, I wouldn't have."

Mrs. Herrin looked like someone badly in need of absolution. She went over the details, how the boys had been well treated, what they ate. Unless my notes from June were wrong, squash was now on their final supper. In her insistence on each detail, Mrs. Herrin seemed to be saying that if all these small material items I tell you are true, then you must believe this greater item, our innocence.

"I'm sick about it," she said. "If whoever did that thought he was helping Philadelphia, he made an awful mistake. People here don't want killin' people. That's just wrong."

Thinking that if only she could believe herself she would not have to wake up crying, I believed her.

In late afternoon, by the remains of the Mount Zion Church, the smoke from T. C. Cole's farmhouse chimney puffed into a pale, cold sky. He and his wife were dubious when I knocked, but they were not the kind to turn anybody away. The room was warm with the dusty-dry smell of pinewood burning in a big iron stove. We sat around the stove. I recalled to them my visit with Dr. King in August and reassured them of my intentions. A wordless little six-year-old girl, too young to be theirs since they were close to sixty, hung about the knees of Mrs. Cole. I asked about her.

"That's Matilda," Mrs. Cole said. Her face relaxed with love. "You say hello to Mr. Goods, honey. She's shy now. You know when we got this little girl she was ten months old and weighed ten pounds. That's right. And look at her now."

Matilda's hand clutching Mrs. Cole's dress was plump. The Coles told me that they had ten other children—most of them grown and up North. The girl's mother had been in some kind of trouble, and they had taken the baby—a late and last chance to raise another child. Matilda had been in the farmhouse the June night white men were slugging Mr. Cole unconscious and burning the Mount Zion Church.

"Our children up North want us to leave," he said. "They worry about us. But I say to them, 'I been here all my life. I can't start a new life up there.' When it first happened, though, we sure did want to leave."

"I still have a notion sometimes," his wife said, "but now we feel like we wanna stick to the puddin'."

They had heard about the arrests the day before and thought it was a "good thing." Either from caution or lifelong detachment from the processes of white man's law, their reaction was mild, as if they were made aware of some development in a remote place that did not concern them. They had never met the boys whose deaths were linked with their lives.

"I believe things are changing a little," he said, "but it's hard. People here don't hold any more meetings. And they won't even talk. White and black, people who knew me all my life won't even speak."

"Now you take one thing," his wife said. "In the stores some of the young white people will call you 'Mister' and 'Missus.' But the older ones say by the first name, or just 'You' or 'Boy.'"

Her husband rubbed his graying head and smiled.

"When anybody's head begins to bloom like mine," he said, "I guess it's a compliment to call you 'Boy.' "

"Still," said his wife, "we don't have no voice. We just have to do what they say. If we don't dance to the music, that's all."

I was satisfied to sit in that warm room with the Coles. A fitness and truth was in their words, a sure dignity in their bearing that had survived humiliations and would endure. In a society where guile and hate were part of the very atmosphere of existence, they were not contaminated. They pieced out life on 121 acres, made room in that life for Matilda, and could welcome me, looking past my skin and their experience with it, trusting to my words that I came as a friend.

I stopped briefly by the Philadelphia COFO house where white and Negro workers also were surviving. Tom Foner, an eighteen-year-old white worker, said that white harassment had decreased as the FBI presence made itself felt. At the beginning of the summer, COFO had reasoned that this result would happen and had called for the presence. Washington had moved belatedly as always in civil rights. Only murder and public outrage convinced Washington to move at all.

At dusk, I drove to Meridian where James Chaney had lived in a neighborhood of cheap frame houses, which were neat enough but dreary, especially in winter. The animation of summer was gone and the chipped paint, the hanging screen doors more desolate for its absence. Two children were on the sidewalk and one of them playing with a single roller skate was Ben Chaney. He was the same twelve-year-old stoic I had last seen in June, the day after his brother disappeared. He didn't remember me. Many white faces had been poking into his life since then. He took me inside to see his mother. Mrs. Chaney was a widow getting on by domestic work and some kind of welfare. She was solemn but dry-eyed returning over the grounds of tragedy. She was bitter at the law that found all the accused out of prison already. The device of bail made no balance to murder in her scales.

"Why do they keep arresting people and then just let them out?" she asked. "I couldn't sleep last night knowing they all had been set free. A few months ago somebody threw a fire bomb at the house, only it hit next door.

"Then yesterday I sent Benji to the cleaners to get a sweater out because it was gettin' cold. As he was carryin' it out of the shop the white man what run it said, 'Look here, ain't that for the mother of that big-shot nigger that got shot and then died a natural death?'

"An' Benjie, he said, 'I don't know anything about that but she's my mother and the mother of James Chaney what was killed.' "

Ben listened with no expression. If any weakness was in the tough little fibers that made up his emotions, it did not show. The brutality of the dry cleaner required, in the name of humanity, its opposite.

Had any white people. . . ?

"One," she said, "no, two. A woman in a dry goods store near here said she was sorry. And that night her son-in-law came and brought a carton of soft drinks and a cake to me.

" 'I have to come by,' he said. 'I'm hurt worse than you are because my people did it. I know nothin' I say can bring your son back but that's how I feel.'

"An then he told me: 'But I can only say it to you because if I said it elsewhere my family would get blown up tonight.'

"He was a good man," Mrs. Chaney concluded, folding her hands in her lap. "But most white folks—what can I say about them—the way I feel with Christmas comin' now without James?"

What was to be said beyond pathos or outrage? Only two from that city, from the state, had been moved to condole a mother. Yet, the majority of white Mississipians were church-going Christians committed by their religion against murder, even if in their reading of the New Testament they somehow overlooked the message of brotherhood. The churches had stood mute out of conviction or fear—the fear produced by racial tyranny that inevitably tyrannized the dominant along with the dominated. The next day was Sunday and I was curious to see if any Philadelphia pulpit would find a voice, now that the crime had openly been charged to some of its citizens.

Next morning I first called the Catholic church and talked to Father Canisius Hayes.

"The attitude of my parishioners seems to be thoroughly Christian," he said. "They are quite disturbed by the picture of the community now abroad in the nation and they hope something will be done to clear it up. We want to see justice done. But we're such a minority here that I don't think we could develop a nucleus that could be heard."

For this reason, explained the priest, there would be no sermon on the crime. Rev. Roy Collum of the First Baptist Church was direct.

"Naturally we're shocked," he said. "We know a lot of the people. And some of them we're not surprised about. The feeling is that justice should be done. We're not dealing with a matter of prejudice separate, apart and distinct. We're dealing with murder and I've expressed this feeling in prayer meetings and my people have responded.

"Mr. Good, we would like to change the climate, to take the leadership away from the extreme element. If I knew how to put the right kind of leadership in the mill, I'd stake my life on it. But we don't know how to do it."

There would not be a sermon in the First Baptist Church, he said.

One of the men arrested, Roy Killen, was a minister in a backwoods Baptist church and when I called and started to explain what I wanted, the phone was slammed down.

Rev. Clay Lee of the First Methodist Church was decided. Yes, he would speak out and I would be welcome to hear him. I drove to his church, a modern building of light brick of no particular style. The church seemed to express in its clean lines and airiness a spirit of progress, a new, more open religious look. He fit the church, clean-cut, purposeful in conversation, frank. He had come to Philadelphia from Atlanta only a few weeks before the murders and had been feeling his way since with a new congregation. He had never preached on the killings.

"Six months ago, three weeks ago," he said in his office, " a sermon wouldn't have been possible. Even today, it may not be popular because there still are people talking about what kind of evidence the FBI has and so forth. That's not the kind of talk needed now. Now we need responsibly to examine what has been done and judge it."

The phone rang, and after a few minutes of conversation Rev. Lee said to his caller:

"I'm a little gun-shy too, Roy. But it's an attitude of conscience I have to take. I'm not going to wave a red flag but just put out a few ideas. You know, Roy, misery loves company and I'd rather we all hang together than hang separately. Good. Well, good luck."

Rev. Collum had apparently changed his mind. Rev. Lee let me read his sermon, which was based on Herod's survey of the land to search out and kill all first-born males in an effort to slay the new-born Christ.

"The Herod spirit is the spirit of bigotry," it said. "There is nothing which provokes the temper of a bigot more than a spirit like that of Jesus himself. If there is one thing that will keep us from knowing real joy and peace during this magnificent season, it will be that the enigma of the Herod spirit still exists and that we are doing nothing about it."

The sermon went on in intellectual style to quote Sartre and a German general, Henning von Tresckow, who wrote, before his execution for being involved in the plot to kill Hitler:

"God once promised Abraham to spare the city of Sodom if only ten just men could be found. He will, I hope, spare Germany because of what we have done and not destroy her."

Rev. Lee's writing style and organization were admirable but the sermon seemed too allusive—a creation of the mind speaking generally in favor of truth and love, but did not go to the heart of the matter in stark terms from which no one in the congregation could escape. I decided to hear Rev. Collum in his traditional, four-square church of unfashionable red brick. He gave permission over the phone to take notes of his sermon. The church was filled with sober-faced, nicely dressed people. As I entered I was handed a program with a Christmas cover, a file of light and dark-skinned people walking across a desert toward the Star. Inside the program was a ballot so the parishioners could vote on a $125,000 loan to build a new church. At the bottom was noted that the land to be purchased consisted of Block 20 and half of Block 21 contained in ". . . Herrod's survey of the city of Philadelphia, Mississippi."

Rev. Collum was built, in face and body, as four-square as his church. He was a rugged, functional man who looked as if he could carry hods, lay brick, and build the new church himself. When he spoke, neither style nor pretension was in his words or voice. After disposing of the ballot, he said:

"My heart has been sick during these days. Crushed, embarrassed and ashamed. My temptation was to preach a Christmas sermon. But there is a burden on my heart."

Rev. Collum read from Ephesians 6:10: "Put on the whole armor of God that ye may be able to stand against the wiles of the devil." Then he spoke of the "brutal murder of three young men" and said that the congregation as Christians "must think in terms of love, not hate, or right, not foolish rationalization." I had never seen such communion between speaker and audience. The minister spoke slowly, reaching into himself with obvious effort to seek each word fit for its purpose, and the words moved through the perfect quiet of the church almost tangibly to become part of each listener—as blood is transfused from donor to recipient.

"We must take our stand," he said. "The nation's eyes are on us. I'm concerned about the nation, all right. But I'm primarily concerned with us and our relationship to the Lord and our responsibility to the Lord. . . . We must take a stand against hatred and violence and for law and order and preserve peace with honor."

I suppose his declaring the brotherhood of man would have been a miracle. He didn't and he cautioned that he was not proposing social integration of the races. Without bringing a whiff of brimstone into the church, he said with calm Calvinism:

"There is a question as to the validity of the Civil Rights Law. There is no question of the law against murder. Whoever is guilty should suffer the penalties prescribed by law. I sincerely hope and pray they are not guilty."

And then he concluded:

"Here I take my stand. I ask that we pray for one another. For if ever people needed to pray, we need to pray."

One year and ten days before, Dr. King's Thanksgiving sermon had touched a nerve of hope in me. Words affirmed that an American soul still lived and might prevail. That same emotion was present now, as the church emptied into warm morning sunshine. Suddenly, a hand gripped my arm hard. The hand belonged to a boy about seventeen; his face was tight with fear and anger. What had I been doing taking notes in their church, trying to stir up trouble? I explained that Rev. Collum had given permission and gradually he relaxed. A group of men began forming around me. Their looks were more unhappy than hostile. The hour must have been long for them as Rev. Collum made his peace with God and tried to make the congregation's peace with Him, too. I asked them if they agreed with what he had preached, and no one answered, until a man who turned out to be president of the local bank said:

" 'Course we do. We always have. The whole congregation agrees with Rev. Collum. We don't hold with killin' here. But you Yankee reporters come down and try to make us out to be a bunch of swamp babies runnin' around without shoes an' wrestlin' alligators. We're law-abiding people in Mississippi except for a few you have anywhere. Where do you come from? New York? Why, you kill more people there in a night than we do in a year."

He was off on the theme I had heard so often that I could anticipate all he said. Television only showed the bad side of Mississippi. Why didn't Yankee papers print things about conditions of the "nigra" up North? Had I heard about the rape-murder by a "nigra" in Philadelphia, Pennsylvania, two days before? If outsiders hadn't interfered, we could have handled things ourselves. As he spoke, the humble plea by Rev. Collum with its hope for spiritual regeneration—"I ask that we pray for one another"—drifted away before a draft of petty sectionalism and self-rationalization. The bank president was all bristling defense. Philadelphia was a nice clean town fighting to survive in a new era, to bring in plants, to make life better for all its people. Publicity like this murder trial could wreck everything. (Let me see, says the plant manager. According to Herrod's survey of Block 20 and half of Block 21, Christ has not been located but it is suitable for industrial development if they don't build a church there first. . . .) We talked for about twenty minutes, or rather I listened to the bank president. All the others deferred to him. I can't remember one of them saying a word. I do remember that when I asked questions about the possibility of Negroes worshiping in their church or taking part in city government, the questions went unanswered. They hung in the air for a moment before our faces and then evaporated as the president resurrected the Harlem riots or Dr. King's communist affiliations. We parted with stiff handshakes. My disappointment and their distrust blighted the blooming morning.

Of course, emotion had tricked me into expecting too much. After a year steeped in hate, Rev. Collum's words stirred extortionate visions of a new Jerusalem. The whites of Philadelphia would rush to rebuild with their own hands the Mount Zion Church. Perhaps a popular subscription to erect a plaque in memory of the dead boys would begin.* Rev. Collum had waited nine months, nine years too long to deliver his sermon. If ever a people needed to pray, they needed to pray. The burden of grace was on the sinner. The quality of his salvation was determined by a self-struggle to cast out demons of prejudice. The vice of racial pride had settled in too long, and the people sought justification instead of penance.

Reading a story about former Mississippi Governor Ross Barnett's address that Sunday to the Citizens Council of Greater New Orleans, I took a melancholy plane ride the next day back to Atlanta.

"People keep asking me," Barnett said, "about improving the image of Mississippi. I ask you people of the state of Louisiana, Is there anything wrong with Mississippi's image?"

From the particular of Mississippi to the general, North and South, what was image and what reality as 1964 came full turn? The year had started for me with a sign in the window of Leb's Atlanta restaurant, "If you was white, you could eat here too." That sign had disappeared, along with pickets and guards to keep out Negroes, as federal edict prevailed. Mr. Lebedin now had two other signs. One told how science had proved that eating oysters prevented cancer. Mr. Lebedin was selling oysters. He was also peddling his disillusion—vowing in another, larger sign never to vote Democratic again because civil rights invaders had once urinated in his ashtrays. A few blocks away from the restaurant, Dr. King was resting in Saint Joseph's Catholic Hospital. He had just gone through two weeks of personal crisis that were to be capped by triumph on December 9. The personal crisis, which had shaken him, was compounded by FBI Director Hoover's charge that he was a "notorious liar."

---

*After a story on the sermons appeared in the *Washington Post*, a reader wrote me suggesting that Rev. Lee might want to initiate a rebuilding fund. I wrote Rev. Lee passing the idea along but he never answered.

They met in Washington and, if I am to believe a man close to Dr. King, Hoover intruded into his private life in shocking and irresponsible fashion. Spiritually low, Dr. King on December 9 received the news that he had won the Nobel Peace Prize. We talked privately in his hospital room which, ironically, looked down on the Heart of Atlanta Motel, defeated challenger of the 1964 Civil Rights Act.

Dr. King said the expected things in the American team spirit: The award was not so much for him as for all Negroes who had sacrificed for the Movement. In triumph, his reserve remained as impenetrable as that day in Saint Augustine when he rode off under arrest with a panting police dog as seat companion. He wore a flashy black silk dressing gown. I said that if the Nobel Committee had ever seen him in *that* he might not have won the prize.

"You couldn't have blamed them, could you?" he said, and laughed.

The laugh was the only concession to the excitement, the wonder that must fill a man when the sum of his days suddenly adds up to the moment when he is acknowledged by the world as something rare among its millions. A few days later, Dr. King and a jubilant entourage were off to Oslo from the Atlanta Airport. Students from Morehouse College, his alma mater, crowded the corridor, singing the school hymn, chanting: "Who's our leader? Martin Luther King!" To one side, excluded from things as I had seen him excluded at the Atlanta summit meeting the previous January, was Martin Luther King, Sr., leaning on his cane, heavy with patriarchal dignity.

"Well, I'm proud, naturally, like any father would be," he said. "Do I feel overshadowed?" He smiled. "Well, I'm glad somebody finally asked me that. Martin has reached heights I never did, that's true. But he had the benefit of a fine education, the advantage of learning in the atmosphere of a dedicated Christian home, and the best schools. But remember, when he was going to those schools it was Daddy who paid the freight."

Lester Maddox must have wondered what had happened to justice in the world. Martin Luther King had a Nobel Prize and he didn't even have a restaurant. In November, Maddox had closed his Pickrick Restaurant, scene of so many wild alarms, and bid another of his tearful farewells to the private enterprise system. The Pickrick later was to reopen under another name after Maddox purportedly sold the half-million-dollar establishment to two former employees who would have been lucky if they were making $20,000 a year between them. Maddox continued roaming Georgia and other racially troubled places in the South—a bald-headed Ancient Mariner telling his tale of woe to whatever Rotary or Citizens Council that paid to hear him.

Other Southern places and persons visited in this book had fared unevenly as Christmas, 1964, approached. In Saint Augustine, the Catholic school was desegregated and Mayor Shelley's children actually sat in class with Negroes. America's oldest city was enjoying its best December tourist season in history. The sun sparkled off Matanzas Bay onto quiet streets, and visitors could snap pictures of the Slave Market and Old Jail to their Kodochromed heart's content, certain that no jarhead would bop them.

"I think the fact we're having such a fine tourist season," Mayor Shelley said, "is proof that most Americans favor the way we handled things."

At the Monson Motor Lodge, where deputies had provided alligators for the swimming pool should Negroes try to reenter, owner Jimmy Brock was on the verge of bankruptcy. Local white bankers were foreclosing, he told me, blinking back tears, because they accused him of helping the moderates. The Negro Movement in Saint Augustine was also close to bankruptcy. Young and old who had marched so bravely at such grave risk wondered where their steps had carried them. White merchants still would not hire them. Millionaire banker H. E. Wolfe still loved patience but not colored bank clerks. A destitute county would not join the Poverty Program because Negroes would have to have a voice in its administration. The long-suffering Dr. Hayling had moved out, and he confessed to feeling that Dr. King and the SCLC had left their pledges to Saint Augustine Negroes unredeemed. Leaving a residue of bitterness and scant progress, the city's "moment of truth" had come and gone.

There were dramatic changes in Tuskegee's Macon County, where hate had burned a high school, and Governor Wallace had done his best to set white citizens against blacks. Fall elections brought a city council of three whites and two Negroes, the first mixed council in the Deep South since Reconstruction. Its election resulted from behind-the-scenes agreement by moderates on both sides which left racist whites and militant Negroes restive and unhappy. Still, Tuskegee High School reopened with mixed PTA meetings. Some of those dusty, muddy colored streets were going to get paved. Even Tuskegee, with a Negro elite unique in the South outside Atlanta, had a long way to go before normal commerce would begin between races that had been too long estranged for a full and natural reconciliation.

Unexpectedly, McComb, Mississippi, was looking better than during the explosive summer. Eleven Klansmen and Klan sympathizers had been caught and pleaded guilty to the dozen or more bombings. In late November, an understanding judge gave them suspended sentences although dynamiting homes was punishable by death in the state. He allowed as how people had been provoked by "unhygienic" civil rights workers and said he was giving the light sentences because the defendants were so young. Four were in their thirties, one in his forties. Apologists claimed that no jury would have convicted them. Since the judge warned that jail terms could be imposed if they resumed bombing, the judicial deal was said to be a shrewd deterrent.

In McComb, where hypocrisy left off and responsibility began was hard to tell. Newspaper publisher Emmerich approved the sentences. He radiated civic pride after the NAACP tested restaurant desegregation before Thanksgiving without incident. A Citizens Committee of 650 helped prepare the way by speaking out against violence and for just race relations, thereby heading off Mayor Burt from attempting a Wallace-type intervention. Mr. Emmerich, who had swallowed his editorial tongue when the bombings were going on, was also working to destroy the militant SNCC-COFO organization. He and the committee created a colored leadership group composed of older ministerial and NAACP people, who were willing to settle for far less than the new egalitarian society preached so passionately by the white and black invaders during the summer. Not so much passion was in the churches now, not so many people in the Freedom House, not so much hope that black and white together *would* create something better than each had been able to manage separately.

Not only in McComb was the bittersweet glory of the summer over for the workers of SNCC and CORE. Throughout the South, many of the best people had gone back to school in the fall and many of the dedicated ones who remained behind saw the same hard facts of the Negroes' lives scarcely altered—despite the exciting activity of July and August. SNCC's philosophy— or one of its philosophies—was that its role should be transitory, that SNCC involvement should phase itself from existence as local Negroes came to the fore to lead the struggle. That philosophy was why the Mississippi Freedom Democratic Party had been organized and an attempt made to form a network of local leaders. A brave volunteer coming to town, defying custom, proclaiming a new dawn of reason, was one thing. A black townsman, trying to find a voice of leadership in a body that has been chattel and trying to continue that same defiance at the same pitch, particularly when the people he is supposed to lead find themselves still going nowhere, is another thing. Some local men and women were asserting themselves, helping in the immediate challenge to the seating of white Mississippi congressmen. Their numbers were few, the difficulties great, their means small.

Many of the volunteers were not helping by their behavior that winter. I felt that many of those who stayed were the worst of the "sordid, bizarre and stupid" glimpsed earlier. Black and white were at loose ends. Odd-balls were more in evidence; sex and drinking were more a preoccupation than an adjunct. COFO habitually complained about the American press being unsympathetic. But many of those same writers who came, saw, and wrote shallow or unperceptive articles could have done worse. By mid-winter, much that was unsavory could have been exploited by a writer and none had to do with the supposed Communist infiltration that caused editorial handwringing. Communists in number and influence were small, I believe. Larger was the group of joyless Bohemians, corrupted beyond their years—not producing results in the Negro communities, wasting days striking bitter or cynical attitudes, and spending nights playing sexual games. They were not up to the challenge of trying to remake a system (admittedly, the challenge was overwhelming). They diluted their purpose by inveighing against Dr. King because he did not match their private concept of what a leader or a man should be, because he prospered and they languished, because he would not be stampeded by their demands.

This anti-King attitude, almost a vendetta, was not limited to the beatnik fringe. Decent workers sniped at him continually—the kind of lethal sniping usually reserved for sheriffs or Bobby Kennedy. This sniping caused dissent and confusion inside Negro communities and in the coming year would complicate the entire Southern Movement. Dr. King continued to give moral and financial backing to COFO despite the attacks, and tried publicly to gloss over the differences. He was less than honest in his pose of solidarity. No reason really existed to insist on harmony, since all great movements have their internal dissensions. In fact, some healthy debate and open criticism of the Movement in general was needed. Most Northern liberals were so mesmerized by the grand rightness of the Negro cause that they considered criticism heresy. What little criticism got into print was usually doctrinaire, almost always from the SNCC end of the spectrum. The result of this generally worshipful attitude was that the Movement went careening along without check. Leaders were holier-than-thou and answerable only to those inside the tight little cliques of the initiated.

If SNCC criticism had been on a more rational plane, accenting inquiry and not inquisition, I think the Movement and the American understanding of it would have benefited. The criticism was snappish, extreme, often personal. Dr. King's position had become so elevated that he could have ignored the criticism. I think he was truly moved by Christian sympathy and appreciation for their sacrifices to try from time to time to smooth down SNCC's raised fur. Dr. King himself was badly in need of stern friends offering judgment on his actions. He made many mistakes in judging people and situations. He abandoned cities like Saint Augustine and Albany after milking them, not of money, but of their pathetic state as a goad to the American conscience. He sometimes chose badly in gathering helpers around him, picking men who were uninspired and erratic, who misled Negro communities—and the public at large—through lies and exaggerations. He left himself open to criticism of his private life, providing ammunition for those men—agents of the FBI prominent among them—who wanted not only to destroy Dr. King but to embarrass the nation's liberals and wreck the Negro Movement. Dr. King was a man, not a god, but he permitted a godlike myth to surround him. The aura did a disservice to him and to the Movement. By the end of 1964, to criticize either was to risk being challenged in the words of another hymn: "Which side are you on, boy, which side are you on?" To the white critic, the words carried the insidious overtone that, no matter how much he swore allegiance to the Movement or demonstrated it, at the root of his criticism was the old white supremist's conceit that he knew best.

So Christmas came to a South still needing gifts of Christian love and understanding for black and white. I was warmed to receive a letter from a woman who had read my story about Mrs. Chaney and wrote to me:

"As I put my two little boys to bed tonight I thought of another mother who had two sons whom she loved as I love mine.

"But then she lost one because somebody didn't like the color of his skin. I wonder if she realizes how very many people share her loss, how many hearts go out to her this Christmas time.

"Could you by any means forward to her this shamefully small gift as a token of love at this season of peace and good will?

"To Mrs. Chaney and her son, Benjamin, from a white mother in Kentucky."

A dollar bill was enclosed.

In Athens, Georgia, two Klansmen, named Sims and Myers, were sitting down to Christmas dinner, but in Washington, D. C., Lemuel Penn's place at the Christmas table was empty. In the North, bitter fights were developing over school integration in New York, Chicago, and Boston. If one scratched under the surface of most white opposition, one found prejudice. Admittedly, carrying white children in buses miles from their homes to Negro schools to create artificial racial balance seemed mad. We had permitted racial madness to become part of our way of life. Knowing how to act rationally any more was difficult for us. The South gloated over Northern difficulties, felt itself prophet at Negro riots and the rise of the Black Muslims. The North tried to reform, read James Baldwin, considered Negro models in the Sunday *New York Times Magazine* as proof of equal job opportunity. The North's collective heart often was not in it. The word "nigger" might be heard less but one did not have to strain to hear the word. Northern watchers of pendulum swings thought the South barbaric, yet were convinced that the racial pendulum *had* swung too far, viewing a race riot, a Negro rape, and the Civil Rights Act all of one piece.

Looking back at the year, I felt we were not rational and had never been, and that the racial crisis had become a hot light that bore into the American body politic and social soul, revealing truths not only about America's relation to the Negro but about its relation to itself. The American mind had always been afflicted with a schizophrenic flaw which has worsened over the years. John Jay Chapman wrote:

> During the decade that followed the Missouri Compromise (1820) everyone in America fell sick. It was not a sickness that kept men in bed. They went about their business—the lawyer to court, the lady to pay calls, the merchant to his wharf. The amusements, and the religious, literary and educational occupations of mankind went forward as usual. But they all went forward under the gradually descending fringe of a mist, an unwholesome feeling cloud of oppression. No one could say why it was that his food did not nourish him quite as it used to, nor his unspoken philosophy of life no longer cover the needs of his nature. This was especially strange because everybody ought to have been perfectly happy. Had not the country emerged from the War of Revolution in the shape of a new and glorious birth of Time—a sample to all mankind?
>
> At the bottom of this nervous concern there was not, as is generally supposed, merely the bumptious pride and ignorance of a new nation. There was something more complex and more honorable: there was the inner knowledge that none of these things were true. . . . There was a chasm between the agreeable statement that all men are created equal and the horrible fact of human slavery. The thought of this incongruity troubled every American.

The flaw troubled them—or should have—from the day the Declaration of Independence was published. The *Pennsylvania Gazette,* which appeared on July 10, 1776, carried the Declaration in its first column: "We hold these Truths to be self-evident, that all men are created equal, that they are endowed by their Creator with certain unalienable Rights, that among these are Life, Liberty and the Pursuit of Happiness." In column three:

> Ten Dollars reward
> Run from the subscriber, living near Talbot
> Court-house the 15th of last April, a dark
> Mulatto Slave, named Harry, about 26 years old;
> he is about 5 feet 8 or 9 inches high;
> stout and strong made; he is of mild temper,
> plausible in speech and deceptive in conversation.
> It is supposed that he will endeavor to pass for a freeman. . . .

Here was one root of the schizophrenia, the lie between the word and the reality. We began by extolling a democracy we did not practice. We preached an equality that always has been a myth in a society devoted to material gain. Devices from country clubs to Cadillacs were each designed to put distance between the man who has made money and one who has not. The well-to-do could easily rationalize that he was the natural example of the fittest democratically rising to the top. This rationalization, like most, did not bear scrutiny. An average mind, given an environment of money, education, and position, could rise to the top with ease. An average mind in average surroundings usually would not exceed its natural level. An average mind in a black body, hoeing cotton on an Alabama plantation, would not rise at all.

We developed unspeakable conceits as we prospered materially, assuming success as proof of talent democratically exercised. Generally, success was only our great dumb luck to have been born on the right side of the national tracks.

Chapman says at another point:

> I confess that a certain hard-eyed, cold-hearted look in the American sometimes causes me to remember that Slavery was always commerce and that commerce is to some extent always Slavery. Such great wealth as has been created in America since 1865 would have hardened the eyes of any generation that looked on it. We have indeed been born to calamity in America, and our miseries have come thickly upon us.

The blooming tree of democracy, flourishing in the American soil, seemed to grow each day before our eyes. How was one to measure the phenomenon? A yardstick was developed early and used still to measure the American man and his country—enterprise in the amassing of wealth and power. An old measure, the oldest in the world probably, on these new shores produced an intensely competitive people, brainy rather than wise, strong on improvisation but weak on principle—a perennial prodigy. At our best we have been dynamic, courageous, audacious, and generous as a nation. These qualities are essentially youthful, attractive in a Prince Hal, but not enough for a man who would be a true king. America could never decide. We remained torn between the American word and the American reality, and these contradictions multiplied over the years. Our concepts made us a tense and quarrelsome people, alternately unsure and bombastically certain. A nation or a person cannot speak one way and live another without suffering psychic wounds. We were a nation that lynched, yet taught our children to venerate justice. We were the Brave New World that kept those same children working in factories and mills, after the Old World had outlawed child labor. We made heroes of our Western pioneers, while relentlessly continuing the slow crucifixion of the Indian that the Pilgrims had begun.

With wealth waiting to be exploited on and below our limitless earth, we permitted millions of foreigners entry to our shores, and while we boasted we were a melting pot, we were segregating, exploiting, and ridiculing each new wave of migrants. By 1900, the American Dream was 125 years old and the fresh pages of history given us to write in were already stained with greed and folly and the blood of a civil war. Still we persisted in our inhumanities to ourselves and others. Bankers squeezed the farmer. The land that pioneers had stolen from Indians at gunpoint was stolen back by the banks, armed with mortgage foreclosures. The noble workingman, a democracy's pride, was savaged by industrial goons and governors alike, as he sought to organize his way into decent existence. The greatest slums in the Western world grew in the richest city in all the world. Until some journalists pricked the national conscience, the anomaly did not attract the concern of our presidents or senators. Our predatory inclinations extended outside our borders. To build a canal, we stole Panama from Colombia. We establish ourselves as tyrants and exploiters in Latin America—a role we have maintained throughout this century with the dictatorships of the Somozas, Trujillos and Batistas standing as indictments against America's Manifest Destiny in action.

Yes, but. . . . This interjection (plaintive when coming from an American kept in ignorance by his histories or newspapers of the dark side of American life, calculating when uttered by those who knew better but sought camouflage for their guilts) would dismiss our sins in the light of our graces. No modern white nation was ever faced with absorbing such a massive black inheritance as we. Far older countries had never resolved the clash of skins, the physical opposition of colors with their hovering spiritual mysteries of distinction. We failed, too. A country with a lusty, extroverted spirit pays a price for dynamism in blunders and inconsistencies between word and act. Still, we had survived with speech still free, the vote generally available and justice that might not always be impartial but at least was not moribund. Prosperity abounded (exceptions noted) despite our early mistreatment of the farmer and laborer. We were paying a price of conformity for our creature comforts, our rows of ranch houses and lines of cars and racks of clothing were what most of the world's people wanted and what a majority of Americans had. The Negro had been treated shamefully, but even for him a new day was dawning, white America's conscience was awakening from a long sleep of prejudice and ignorance. Yet was it?

White had held Black down with few compunctions for three and a half centuries. The idea that this injustice was wrong was not something new in the world or in America. Our "reform" curiously coincided with that moment in our history when the Negro at home was gaining political power and abroad was becoming a political liability. How long could we keep pontificating on democracy to Russia or China, when an African ambassador to Washington might be insulted in a restaurant fifteen minutes drive from the Capitol? How long could political parties disregard the Negro, when his votes in a bloc could win an election in New York or Chicago or even help carry a man to the presidency? Twenty million Negroes lived in the United States by 1964. I wondered how many reforms we would have seen had the population been ten million or five, or if the majority had concentrated in the few Southern states, far from the North, where windows were open on the world and a rough-and-ready political equality had been partly established. The moral faith and fervor in Southern Negroes dramatized the black man's plight and the white man's failure as never before. The response that brought victories like the Civil Rights Act of 1964 were based on politics, not morality. As the Abolitionists had been in a small minority, so were the white and black Americans morally involved in the Movement. The majority of Americans held no thoughtful convictions on the subject. This failure does not mean that injustice did not press on them or that subconsciously it did not affect their most intimate judgments. They could be swayed in one direction by some Southern atrocity as the Neshoba murders, in the other by a Negro riot. They heard and repeated words like democracy, freedom of opportunity, equal rights, but did not bother themselves to see if word and fact were of one piece.

What were we? We didn't know, partly because we were too proud, too ignorant, or too lazy to ask ourselves, and partly because the words a people use to define itself had been sapped of vitality over the years through chronic misuse. "Democracy," once a robust giant of a concept, now could be pulled monkey-on-a-string to serve Southern racist, Northern demagogue, industrial advertising writer, union organizer, Vietnam peace marcher, or our ambassador in Saigon. We were paying the price for generations of anti-intellectual education, for a free press, which dissented politically but rarely questioned American man and his institutions. Suddenly our Alexandrian pride was being challenged, not only by weapons of other countries but by external and internal ideas. We were sadly equipped to meet the challenge.

All this being true, then how did 1964 see some Negro advance begin? I think that politicians, particularly those of the Democratic Party (outside the South), had leadership forced on them by those urgent considerations of the Negro vote and the need to turn a more acceptable face to the world. Always a few in both parties responded to understanding and principle. Politicians decided for the mass. I think the ultimate failure of Jeffersonian democracy was that the people had to be presented with laws they should have demanded. At all compass points, the sluggard American public mind vacillated on the race question, with evidence abounding that dramatic action was needed for justice's sake. Even as the point was starkly brought home by the police dogs and killings, many, not convinced, felt challenged by black intrusion and sought to compromise the uncompromisable. Even the Democratic political leadership might not have been enough had a Republican god-figure come along to reassure those minds and soothe those consciences with a go-slow philosophy. Barry Goldwater alarmed too many whites with his rash words on foreign policy. He alienated virtually every Negro and he insured that President Johnson's manipulation of the electorate would be successful, by and large the same electorate that from 1952 to 1960 had overwhelmingly favored the champion of the American status quo, Dwight D. Eisenhower. The same electorate four years earlier had almost chosen Richard Nixon over John F. Kennedy. The national character does not change in twelve years. When that character is schizophrenic, anything can happen at a given moment under the urge of leadership.

What was the quality of our recent leadership? The late President Kennedy, lionized after his death as a man of exceptional moral courage, throws a small shadow in the light from the most brightly burning question in the country's history. No wonder. He was the end product of intense materialism—the same materialism that mocked our hymns to equality and drove a wedge between man and his noblest impulses. Whether John Kennedy would have made it without the family millions, it is fruitless to speculate. We know he made it with them. We know that to the millions he added charm, personal bravery, and that flaming will-to-win so often publicized in tales of those touch football games with his brothers. Money bought for him an environment of possibility. His mode of existence, his education, and his contacts were produced by an American system that kept the human slag heaps of the white and black exploited well from sight of Newport, Washington, or New York City. No wonder he thought in terms of the rightness of the system whatever its imperfections. In his campaign, he spoke often of the gross national product to the precise decimal, fastening our eye on it, enlisting our belief that a six or seven percent GNP was truly tied to human betterment. Our history showed that whether the GNP jumped a few points in a decade or dropped, the inexorable growth of poverty and exploitation of the least continued. Kennedy was not a man indifferent to human suffering, to the irrationality of bigotry. He had humanitarian impulses—those stirrings of conscience long misnamed charity. He was capable of the bold gesture that many took for a sign of deep commitment. In the closing days of his campaign, when Dr. Martin Luther King was jailed in Atlanta on a traffic charge, Kennedy intervened to have him released. The colored votes he thereby gained may have won him the election. The move certainly helped to solidify his liberal support. Where had Kennedy been in those years before he ordered the call put through to Atlanta? His concern for equal rights, his dedication to a new vision of America do not stand out in the *Congressional Record* during those years he served in House and Senate.

He was adroit with our American words. He invested the abused ones like "democracy" and "national purpose" with apparent new meaning. They momentarily seemed like granite chips from the bedrock on which the America of our best dreams was based. They shaped no grand concept. They amounted to plans for some renovations—at most a new wing on a sagging structure instead of renewal from the ground up. He was quixotic instead of visionary. He could order Cuba invaded on the one hand (lying to the American public all the while), and with the other hand promote a Peace Corps in Latin America and the rest of the world, trusting to the Corps publicity to convince that our humanitarian intentions outweighed any unilateral belligerencies. The Peace Corps itself and its sister in spurious benevolence, the Alliance for Progress, were designed to alleviate an inch of misery in nations where misery was measured by the mile.

I saw him once dedicating some Costa Rican workers' houses, partially built with Alliance funds and partly local money. The bumptious and vastly ignorant White House press corps trailing him dutifully ground out stories on the new lease on life the housing would bring to

Costa Ricans. The Costa Rican in charge of the project told me that if all available funds from his country and Alliance were used until the end of the century, they still would be a hundred thousand units behind the estimated need. This was greater than the need in 1963 at the dedication. The Alliance, which functioned at its optimum in Costa Rica, was grossly inadequate. President Kennedy, like his predecessor, kept this truth from the American people while building progress from words.

Concerning the Negro question, John F. Kennedy was failing, and failing in a dangerous way, until the day he was assassinated. He did not comprehend either the depth of the problem, its reach into our national vitals, or the urgency of satisfying Negro longings for an immediate place. Getting a colored assistant press secretary in the White House, inviting Dr. King and Roy Wilkins in for tea, speaking vaguely, if earnestly, of the need for racial accord were not enough. Kennedy had severe problems with weak congressional support. He had once written a book called *Profiles in Courage*. The time had come for him to make a gallant—if losing—effort to convince America that quasi-slavery had to end, and since Americans, North and South, would not respond to reason, the slavery had to be legislatively abolished.

In all these things—race, the nation's have-nots, poverty abroad sometimes tied to United States business policies—President Kennedy was too remote from the hapless of the earth to truly understand them. He was too absorbed in the good life the American system had given him to question rigorously. His theme was excellence—a predictable theme from a man whose personal gifts of intelligence and courage had acquired a kind of superficial excellence in an environment made to order for these gifts. He would encourage the bright, the beautiful of American youth to go and do likewise, sponsoring government scholarships for them, preaching education, opening educational doors that in turn opened onto larger and more opulent rooms providing all that education (transformed into money) can buy. The mass, black or white, is not bright or beautiful. In a large, unwieldy country like the United States, this mass does not have access to sources or seats of power. The vote is available but choices are not. Although the unbeautiful mass can help to elect people, it is generally unsuccessful in persuading them to act (short of a crisis situation) once they are in office. The failure places great responsibility on our moneyed leaders—who increasingly rise to positions of great power—to force themselves to see life as the mass does, to break out of their protective shells and get down into the dirt where the hard questions lay: Why is a rich nation poor, why is equality unequal?

At his inauguration, President Kennedy had said:

"Ask not what your country can do for you but what you can do for your country."

The challenge sounded fine on that cold, snowy day that recalled a Pilgrim climate. An inelegant rejoinder to the president from some cold and crack-walled colored tenement or shack might have been:

"Shit, man, what we ain't done already? We chopped all your cotton, washed all your laundry, waited your tables, cleaned your men's rooms, got our ass shot off in your wars, an' watched you fuck our women. When we gonna get some of the 'can do' shit back?"

The president seemed to be consecrating his administration to Spartan years of national soul-searching and fulfillment. The new administration did not work out that way. The White House became the shining symbol of the new style in Washington. The president's words, often witty, usually direct, sometimes seemed profound. Mrs. Kennedy's soirees for gorgeous ladies and distinguished men (distinguished black men, too, or especially) were brilliant. An estimated 30 or 35 million countrymen were looking on from poverty, discrimination, or both, as the White House was refurbished. No one was dusting off philosophies of government. The nation needed a reformation and received a feeble renaissance.

From the beginning of President Johnson's administration, there was a whiff of bread and circuses about his rush to promise everything to everyone. While his platitudinous air might have irritated, and the lines between his convictions and political expediency been hopelessly blurred, accomplishment was noted. Washington roused itself in 1964 to pass the Civil Rights Law, however inadequate. By the end of the year the FBI was starting to do its duty in the South. That December a voting rights bill seemed a possibility and so did a poverty program for hapless whites and blacks. Like President Kennedy, Mr. Johnson did not penetrate to the heart of the paradox to ask why a democracy should require a voting rights bill, why the wealthiest of nations needed a poverty program. He caught the public's eye with bills designed to alleviate. However only Medicare suggested a long-range sense of fundamental responsibility to the citizenry. While the Republican Party became a haven for Birchites, Southern racists, and West Coast movie stars, the Johnsonian Democrats, with Barnum and Bailey showmanship, were inviting everybody inside the administration's big tent where everything was going to be bigger and better, although (this was not said) nothing much would change essentially. A power elite seemed to be taking shape in Washington. Militarists and civilians controlled the

awesome power of atoms and billions of dollars, capable of destroying
or buying their way to ultimate power. Broad popular support purchased
through bread and circuses would enable the power structure to operate
internally and externally as it pleased. We were continually being
lied to about our foreign affairs. Statements on our national purpose
were pronounced in Fourth of July oration phrases designed to cloak
rather than reveal. The nature of our democracy and the world in which
it existed had turned upside down since Yorktown. Only a minority of
Americans seemed to care.

We were used to being lied to, used to speaking and listening to meaningless words. From astronauts grown rich through *Life* magazine to the
common man in his punched-out, pasteboard castle, life was obviously
good, so why question it? Turn on the television set and the hi-fi, collect
the trophies from the bowling league and Little League, seek manhood's
power in a power mower or a Ford Mustang, woman's grace in a frozen
dinner or den motherhood. No one had to apologize for material comforts,
and only an anarchist (not even a Communist any more) would claim
that gain was always misbegotten. Sometimes the question intruded,
brought home by news on the television: Why did so many not have comfortable, secure living rooms? Did nice houses have to exist at the expense
of poor ones? Was poverty the cause of plenty or the other way around?
The question was so hard; the answer might be frightening; it was better
to put the question off and concentrate on "Bonanza." Many more undis-
turbing, even fascinating things, could fill the average mind in an age
where atoms and other kinds of electronic toys made the miraculous
commonplace. Once a provincial Babbitt, Mr. America now was an
astral go-getter, bent on the moon. He could not be worrying about every
landlocked Tom, Dick, and Rastus who didn't have the stuff to soar. Did
nothing penetrate? Well, Americans were cracking up, drinking down,
divorcing apart in record numbers. Personal catastrophe was the result
of a stressful age, not the mark of personal or national guilt. One only
had to remember President Eisenhower's sage observation that the
welfare state of Sweden had the highest suicide rate in the world. That
proved something, didn't it?

One man saw an entirely different picture.

The American Negro expectedly would become an acute observer,
perhaps *the* most knowledgeable observer of the American scene. He
was an expert on the gap between word and reality. He had the experience of his own life, which he knew to be true, and the testimony
of television, the movies, and magazines of what American life was
supposed to be. The judgments he made were the raw judgments of a

man who is nothing, and knows it, and so, beyond hope, is also beyond the self-deceits that hope induces. American life, said the tele-
vised evidence of family situation comedies and the commercials in
between them, was ranchhouses surrounded by trees, Hollywood
kitchens, smart offices, sports cars, gas station attendants welcoming
customers with a smile, kiddies who didn't brush twice a day but
would turn out just fine anyway.

He clicked off the television set, being bought on time like everything else he had. American life, said his evidence, was a shack or a
slum, a job leading nowhere in particular and certainly not inside a
paneled office, cars worn out before he owned them, gas stations
where he had to explain to his children why they could not use the
bathroom, children lucky to eat, never mind brush, twice a day
who would have to be very lucky if things were to turn out fine. This
was not the firsthand evidence of all Negroes, and each detail did not
apply universally, but the bulk of the evidence was true for most.

The middle-class white American's world of things was real to him
and he was "aggressively loyal" to the American way of life. If once,
on a Sunday drive, his children had to go and he pulled into a service
station and an attendant shook his head and he had to pull out again
bearing away his humiliation and anger, he might have begun to understand that the American way of life had an underside like the far face
of the moon. He remained insulated from experience and deaf to the
voices of experience. He did not know, could not conceive, how black
saw white as something inhuman, something blind to understanding
and deaf to cries for justice. The Negro knew it all.

Yet, what was going to become of his knowledge? For a year I had
watched the evangelism of freedom shake churches in Georgia, Florida,
Alabama, and Mississippi. The faces and the voices were like souls
themselves unfolding. Pat Watters of the Southern Regional Council
wrote:

"The mass meetings have their own special heat, a physical presence
in the South's sweating, cloud-brooding nights, and they have their own
special fervor, and their special beauty of simple people caught in something bigger than themselves, than present time, than even their
nation."

His thoughts were beautifully rendered. In the midst of their exultation, perhaps watching the tender face of a young mother singing with a
baby in her arms, or the brave, innocent eyes of a boy who would face a
white mob within the hour, I would sometimes think: How much beyond the moment does it promise? The pure Christianity filling them,

uncorrupted by the material competition that had made shambles of white Christianity, was surely going to carry the moment. The Negroes were going to get the vote, the seat in the restaurant and schoolroom, and eventually the jobs and self-assurance. At the end of the long road, perhaps fifty or one hundred years down it, would be changed from what he was into the kind of American that had held him in thrall? The Negro was just another human, or else all the preachments about equality were hollow.

In the Northern environment, with its specie of freedom, he had become everything from an amoral ghetto animal to a standard bourgeois Christian without any clearly defined morality, a black white man. Already, some of the black leadership in the South troubled an observer. Some jockeyed for position in the vanguard of the Movement, others took advantage of mass adulation for personal indulgence. Simple people, who would have followed them into hell at a word, were sometimes manipulated and lied to, because such methods of doing things served the purpose of the strategy of the leadership. We had no reason to expect that leaders from Dr. King on down should be any more than men, susceptible to temptations of flesh and spirit, fallible in judgment, though their cause was not in error. Yet, the cause that they bore nonviolently and offered to America was so transcendent, I wished that they could have been saints. The burden was too precious to entrust to mortal men. I felt it was nothing less than a last chance for American salvation, black and white.

I believe that the Negro Movement in the South gave America the chance to become the Christian nation it had purported to be from its beginning—the brotherhood of man inside a political and social structure existing for the common good. Thomas Merton, author of *The Seven Storey Mountain* and other widely read books, writes from a faith in God. The reader need not agree with that faith to agree with what he says. One need not believe in Christ to be a Christian. He tells of young Negro girl demonstrators in Birmingham placed in cells beside white prostitutes and delinquents who appeared terrified by the presence of the blacks.

> Curious that these white Southerners (people to be pitied, indeed) from their half-world of violence, petty thievery, vice and addiction, were the ones who felt themselves menaced and menaced by the clear eyes of children! The truth is that they had very good reason to fear. The action of the children was aimed at them. It was an attack not upon their property, their jobs, their social status, but upon their in-most conscience. And unless that attack could be met and deflected, these people would not be able to continue as they were.
> In all literal truth, if they "heard" the message of the Negro children, they

would cease to be the people they were. They would have to "die" to every-thing which was familiar and secure. They would have to die to their past, to their society with its prejudices and its inertia, die to its false beliefs, and go over to the side of the Negroes. For a Southern white, this would be a real death indeed.

This is the radical challenge of Negro nonviolence today. That is why it is a source of uneasiness and fear to all white men who are attached to their security. If they are forced to listen to what the Negro is trying to say, the whites may have to admit that their prosperity is rooted to some extent in in-justice and in sin. And, in consequence, this might lead to a complete re-examination of the political motives behind all of our current policies, domestic and foreign, with the possible admission that we are wrong. Such an admission might, in fact, be so disastrous that its effects would dislocate our whole economy and ruin the country. These are not things that are consciously ad-mitted, but they are confusedly present in our thoughts and fears. They ac-count for the passionate and mindless desperation with which we plunge this way and that, trying to evade the implications of our present crises.

Evasion rather than acknowledgment and expiation of guilt continued to be the dominant American reaction. I think the guilt lies buried some-where in us all who have occasionally glimpsed the wronged victim and then hurried by, averting the eyes. A few—most of them young, many of the older ones women and churchmen—dredged up the guilt. These con-science-stricken ones were unique in our society; their singular behavior created attention and made them seem more numerous than they were. Even among those who marched against prejudice or for peace in Vietnam, many seemed more motivated by hate for other Americans than by love for mankind.

Yet the American mass felt no call to crusade. Apologists articulated their feeling that there was nothing wrong with American institutions, only with the way they were misused. This seemed to say that the American character was corrupt. Then we were truly lost, for the in-stitutions have provided noble guidelines for that character for nearly two centuries; still we less and less resembled the Jeffersonian image of the American man that once thrilled humanitarians throughout the world. James Baldwin recounts a Harlem saying, "I can't believe what you say because I see what you do." One could blame institutions, character, the legacy of slavery; what we had done was *not* to create a beautiful society.

Our miseries were come thickly upon us. We were barred from em-bracing the reformation offered by the Movement, not in a cell of scruffy delinquents and sorry whores, but in a labyrinthine confinement of mod-ern complexities that seemed to turn nonviolence into a dead end for national survival and twisted Christian virtues into false trails that led back to our vices. (Lester Maddox' cook trying to turn away Negroes by waving Matthew 20:15 at them like a cross flaunted in the face of the devil. . . . "Is it not lawful for me to do what I will with mine own?") No cord of words was to lead us out of the labyrinth. Over the years, the politicians, the hucksters, the slick editorialists had taken all the good words away.

Side by side, cell by cell, we regarded each other. Surfeited white in one, denied black in the other, innocence tried to tell a morality play through the bars and sophistication unable to grasp it. "Pity this busy monster manunkind," wrote e. e. cummings, and pity seemed the proper emotion for us—a possible epitaph. Father Merton says that "a complete reform of the social system which permits and breeds such injustices" is required if the white man is to understand his sin, repent, and atone. He thinks further that the American reorganization must be carried out "under the inspiration of the Negro whose providential time has now arrived, and who has received from God enough light, ardor and spiritual strength to free the white man in freeing himself from the white man." The character of the American Negro has been flawed along with the white man's. To be inspired by those small bands of Southern Negroes, humble and proud as the first Christians, is one thing. The majority bore little spiritual relation to them and increasingly mock their forebearance and faith, believing the white man unsalvageable, feeling his taint in themselves.

As some leaders of the Movement sought to extend their scope to include alliances with labor or to question the morality of Vietnam, they were sharply challenged even by those who considered themselves supporters of racial progress. That progress was supposed to be something compartmentalized, unconnected to the other aspects of our society. Few Negroes were even beginning to call for public appraisal of the basic institutions of American life, in which an Alabama Negro with a vote, but without a decent job or hope for one, was gaining a specious freedom. Yet, the opportunity to make America ask itself a bigger question than how it feels about Negroes was being bypassed in the Movement's revolutionary rush for tangible objectives. To ask that question inevitably would mean translating moral concepts into a challenge to our political forms and laying bare those words like "democracy" and "equal justice" to see what they meant. Could not, should not, the richest government in the world provide jobs for its citizens by building factories where there was nothing but need? The question was old and abrasive. To those eternal landlords of America, warily watching the eternally dispossessed, the effort smacked of Socialism—or worse.

Hallowed Free Enterprise was not going to be a victim of Negro Emancipation or any other divisionary doctrine.

My personal gloom at the end of 1964 is apparent in these pages. Since this is a personal record of public events, let me explain the pessimistic tone. I had returned to the United States from Mexico to witness what promised to be a new American era in the making, and to share in dramatic days. Even with those considerable expectations, I found much more than I had bargained for. Past conclusions about what we were as a people soon proved inadequate. These impressions had been drawn from woefully insufficient evidence and accepted from ignorance. The more I touched the sources of America, the greater grew the dimensions of our failure. Easy apologies and facile remedies were insults to generations of Negro sacrifice—a con man's response in a time that needed new pioneers. Yet, these apologies and remedies were being offered on all sides. I don't mean to dismiss certain legislative advances that showed some awareness and concern. My conviction remains that as a nation we were missing a chance for rebirth. Rebirth may be impossible, an ideal individuals and nations put before themselves as a talisman against inevitable decay but never a real possibility on this earth. Certainly, we could be worse. We may become somewhat better.

Once one has walked with Negroes down Saint Augustine's midnight streets, or watched white hearts open to black children at a Freedom House or see black hearts receive the white, nothing in this life short of the living brotherhood of man will ever be good for one again. I feel we are destined never to live with this goodness. Too much gloom? The reaction may come from too much glory. There will never be another year in my life like 1964. The Movement in the South has helped millions of Negroes toward better lives. The Movement has been nothing less than salvation for thousands of whites. Some, such as I, with lives half over, suddenly rose up through oceans of self, drawn irresistibly by the power of black example defying gravities of ignorance and prejudice, to break through to the clearest light, the sweetest air of humanity we had ever known. The surge that carried us weakened and fell back, because a moment of truth in Saint Augustine is only a moment. The seas of everyday existence close. Our frailties weight us. Now we cannot tolerate the murky and suffocating environment below. We know that environment for the deception it is. Above is reality—the clean light, that sweet air.

We try to rise.

The Wrap-up

WE TRY
TO RISE

We try to rise.

Those words, reread across the distance of the last ten years, arouse melancholy emotions. They recall a time when, although evidence indicated that America was incapable of accepting the salvation offered by the Movement, a spiritual energy from the Movement persisted in many of us who had been close to it. This energy powered the will to continue believing in moral, even romantic, solutions to our racial dilemma. We would reveal inequities and preach the beauty of brotherhood clearly enough, hard enough, long enough, and America would truly "overcome someday."

No more. The past decade has killed that dream along with some of the finest dreamers. The dream was sniped down on a motel balcony in Memphis, riddled in Orangeburg, South Carolina, and Jackson State and Kent State and Attica. Even the memory of the dream has almost been obliterated by administrations' bombing morality to bits abroad and suffocating it at home. We have been through a murderous time and tender emotions; noble illusions are buried in the decade's rubble. What remains is bitterly earned knowledge about the nature of racism in this country: how it is ingrained in our economic and educational systems, how it is used by politicians in their Northern and Southern strategies, how it poisons the wells of our democratic existence.

Democratic existence—the phrase still comes easily enough to my mind. But 350 years of American history have rubbed the phrase's meaning thin for many blacks, who do not think as I do. Still, we must make do with what we are. Black or white, each generation has to find its own

247

passage through time, and so does each individual. We judge current realities on our own terms, drawing on our heritage of knowledge and
hopefully refining it, as we create our own history. How well or badly
this history of generations and individuals is set down is largely a function
of journalism. Journalism, in turn, influences the actions of the society
and nation-at-large to affect the course of our contemporary histories.

I may overestimate the 1964-74 decade, particularly the earlier years,
because of my close involvement with those years as a journalist. That
closeness bred a contempt for American journalism, which I saw failing
to commit itself to a description of race both truthful and inspired. Race,
in my view, remains the single most important aspect of American
life—the aspect, which in its narrowly national or broadly international
sense, will either pull us as a nation down into a mean ending or enable us to begin a reformation. I acknowledge that a moon hanging
over the Slave Market in Saint Augustine on a certain night in 1964
casts a reflection in my blood that is brighter, more indelible than any
video images of astronauts making moon landings. Persons and events
from the near-past haunt this squalid present—good men and women
destroyed, crimes unpunished, the worst surviving the best.

I have two clippings on my desk. The older, yellowing one from May 8,
1971, concerns Ben Chaney, younger brother of murdered civil rights
worker James Chaney. I had seen him first in Meridian the day after
James disappeared. He was only eleven then, but his mute, dry-eyed
grief was old beyond any counting of years. I saw him again that Christmastime and he was still full of silence as his mother told me the story
of how he had gone to the dry cleaner recently to pick up her sweater and
the owner had said, "Ain't that for the mother of the big-shot nigger what
got shot an' died a natural death?" The men responsible for his brother's
death were serving from three- to ten-year terms. Now, according
to the clipping, Ben would be serving life for murdering a white man in
Florida during a robbery and killing rampage across Southern states. He
had been a boy trying to balance on a single roller skate the last time I
saw him.

The other clipping comes from a Sunday *New York Times* travel section from February, 1974. The piece describes a fun souvenir shop run by
Lester Maddox in Underground Atlanta, an ersatz section of the city that
peddles nostalgia. The article admires Maddox' salesmanship, the ease
with which he disarms potentially hostile customers as he sells the plastic
axe handles that helped to make him famous. The story ignores the
significance of the axe handles: they are reminders of the day when
real axe handles were weapons of intimidation to keep "niggers" in

line. Maddox is the same man, you may remember, who offered customers in his Pickrick Restaurant "Kiss of Death . . . a graphic illustration of beautiful white maidenhood clasped in the arms of an African savage."

James Chaney is dead fighting segregation and Ben Chaney is locked in a cell for life with his private demons and *The New York Times* is lionizing segregationist hero Lester Maddox. I don't expect the *Times* to remember the Chaneys. But doesn't the *Times* remember what Maddox stood for when, incredibly, he became governor of Georgia? Does the paper forget that he refused to fly the Capitol flag at half mast the day of Martin Luther King's funeral? Would the *Times* run a similarly favorable story about a gift shop run by Rev. Carl McIntyre, whose philosophy is offensive to Catholics and Jews? Or has a journalistic erosion of racial concern begun that permits the *Times* travel section to run the Maddox story, while its vaunted Op Ed page can no longer find space for black themes beyond an occasional sentimental reminiscence about happy black childhoods on Southern farms or Harlem streets?

The erosion, at the *Times* and elsewhere, is real. The ghettoes each day get larger, deteriorate faster; the other signs of modern post-Reconstruction that the eye can see and statistics corroborate are real also. Journalism has decided that certain gains are sufficient. Once pouncing on Daniel Moynihan's snide memo to President Nixon urging "benign neglect" of blacks, now journalism practices what he preached.

When I refer to journalism I mean white American journalism, because the source of most news in this country is overwhelmingly white. Can you remember the last (or first) time you heard a black reporter ask a question at a White House press conference? In Washington recently, an avowedly hard-nosed, liberal magazine called *New Times* appeared. Not one name in its list of writers was black. As I write, I also have before me a book called *Eye on the World,* produced by CBS. The book features Walter Cronkite and offers "a kind of overview of the opening of the decade of the seventies." On the back cover are photographs of thirty-five CBS correspondents whose reports are quoted in the book. No blacks, no Latins are among the men who covered "the major news events at decade's dawn." CBS and the other networks do have a sprinkling, a dash of black correspondents. Executive control of network news is all white; as is control of the Public Broadcast System and every major newspaper and magazine (with the exception of *Jet, Ebony* and the *Amsterdam News*) in this country.

I have seen the effect of this white control over the years in my work with all elements of the media. The effect ranges from today's erosion of concern to past superficiality and arrogant assumptions that White

Father Knows Best on racial issues. That a white conspiracy exists in the media to deliberately misrepresent black conditions and thwart black aspirations has been charged. No conspiracy exists; none is needed. All that is needed is a prevailing personal attitude epitomized by a question that NBC commentator Frank Blair once asked me during an interview. I had written an article for *Reporter Magazine* on the slow pace of Southern desegregation. Blair, a veteran, amiable on-the-air man, was bothered by my insistence that the government should speed up enforcement of public accommodations integration.

"I'm originally from the South myself," he said, "and I understand how Negroes were wrongly treated for years. But don't you think that people's feelings have to be considered when you're forcing something new like this?"

Blair said "people's feelings" in all innocence. "People" naturally meant white people. The vast majority of journalists and their superiors in the media hierarchy think instinctively as Blair did. Their view of American reality is determined by their commonality: They are well-educated men (with a few female counterparts) from white middle-to upper-class backgrounds who have become accustomed to very good incomes and who have developed a self-important belief in their capacity to act as arbiters of social justice. Unfortunately, none of these antecedents and achievements prepare them to comprehend the black American experience. This deficiency does not deter most of them from assuming that they can comprehend and interpret and set priorities for that experience.

Despite its common denominator of white middle- to upper-classness, journalism is not a monolith. I agree with Jesse Jackson when he calls the National Association of Broadcasters "the epitome of institutionalized racism in this country." But working for the station owners who comprise NAB are individual journalists who try—as individual newspapermen and magazine writers try—to understand what they cannot intuitively feel when covering racial developments. They are not racially guilt-ridden "masochists" as a former vice president, given to moralizing in public and taking bribes in private, would have us believe. They are men and women concerned about *all* "people's feelings." They may enjoy some success so long as their commitment coincides with the interests of the media hierarchy. Interest ran high in the early sixties, when much of white America enjoyed being shocked and angered by tales of Southern goons brutalizing black men, women, and children, and did not feel threatened by Dr. King's nonviolence. Those were the days when journalism, universally inert during most of the fifties, suddenly developed a reputation for liberalism—whatever that most imprecise of American words may mean at the moment. What it meant to me at various moments since 1964 is suggested in the following accounts of personal and professional experience covering the story of race in America.

Soon after leaving ABC in mid-1964, I joined CBS as a stringer. A stringer is a part-time hand who fills in on odd reporting jobs when the network's regional correspondent is otherwise occupied. I got the job through CBS radio news director Lee Hannah, with whom I had once worked at New York radio station WNEW. Most news jobs are obtained this way at the networks—contacts between one white man and another. I'm not suggesting that this practice is limited to the networks. Friends in business do favors for friends the world over, and the best-qualified person doesn't always get the job. Given our racial divisiveness, the color in those thirty-five CBS photos becomes easier to understand. Naturally, professional qualifications are a factor in hiring. Qualifications are often in the eye of the beholder/hirer, and credentials required may vary wildly from individual to individual, depending—among other things—on race. The networks, understandably, like to project their newsmen as models of expertise, and some correspondents do develop formidable knowledge over the years. When I was hired to open ABC's Mexico City bureau, no one even asked me if I knew anything about Latin America. This oversight was fortunate for me since I knew next to nothing, but had a fair acquaintance with Spanish. While I was there, the NBC correspondent stationed in Brazil and assigned to cover the entire continent of South America spoke neither Spanish nor Portuguese.

The stringer job went well, until the day that Lester Maddox put on his bicycling performance described in the "Summertime" chapter. The regular CBS crew, headed by correspondent Nelson Benton, was covering the story. Benton was a former Navy pilot and his distaste for the Movement had always been apparent to me. I knew that he resented certain stories I had been covering in Mississippi for the radio side. These stories concerned continuing efforts to secure black voting rights by SNCC in small towns such as Magnolia. Journalism was finished with the Mississippi story by the end of the 1964 summer. The fact that, despite passage of the 1964 Civil Rights Act, the state remained locked in the grip of racism did not matter. Journalism's attention was wandering elsewhere, and to continue beating what it had decided was a dead horse was not good form.

A member of Benton's film crew approached and said:

"I just want to give you a friendly tip. The word is around that you're a member of SNCC and you're handling press relations for them in Atlantic City at the convention. Your ass is in trouble because somebody we both know is going to blow the whistle on you in New York."

A SNCC member had informally asked me to do their press in Atlantic City. The request was so informal that I never heard from him again. A few minutes after the soundman's warning, I ran into Benton, who said he had something serious to discuss with me. What was all this about my working for SNCC and why had I appeared on that black political show on Mississippi television? Didn't I understand that I was compromising my professional neutrality and damaging the position of other correspondents?

I explained that I had absolutely no affiliation with SNCC or any other civil rights group. If I ever did help them at the convention, I'd naturally stop working for CBS. As far as the black political program was concerned, David Susskind had supposedly agreed to be the moderator. When he cancelled at the last minute, I filled in. Was there something compromising about a newsman moderating a political program? Benton agreed that there wasn't and said that my explanations were good enough for him.

They certainly were. Three days later, Lee Hannah told me that as a result of Benton's charges I could no longer work for CBS. Protests went unavailing. This issue, he said, was just too hot to handle. Although the phrase wasn't in vogue then, I had been accused and judged guilty of advocacy journalism.

I tell this story now in some detail, not to paint myself as a martyr, but to give a sense of network racial double standards. A taint was attached to associating with "them." Although in other areas of newsgathering, fraternizing with news sources was a standard procedure, which did not imply that partisanship would be carried over into reportage. Certain reporters habitually hobnobbed with liberal or conservative politicians, then wrote stories about issues in which these politicians had vested interests. John Chancellor currently is the anchorman on NBC's nightly television news show. He formerly was director of the United States Information Agency. That is, he was a paid propagandist for a government agency which, among other things, presented a laundered version of American racial realities to foreign publics. Chancellor's objectivity goes unquestioned. Would there be any questions asked, do you suppose, had he been press officer for the Civil Rights Commission?

Journalistic objectivity is a myth carefully nourished by journalism.

Some stories *are* more susceptible to an objective approach than others. The tone of virtually any story can be altered by things that the journalist adds or omits. Consider the commonplace example of an inner city tenement fire. A report could stress the work of the firemen, the plight of the homeless victims, the condition of the building, or society's failure to provide safe housing for all its citizens, or the story could be judged expendable by an editor and not be covered at all. Stories about blacks—unless they were rapists or entertainers—historically went uncovered in this country. This kind of advocacy of a racist status quo, by neglecting to report the existence of those disdained by the majority, went universally unremarked. Only when the Movement created controversy that could not be ignored, did journalism begin paying belated attention to minorities. And in the process began acquiring a reputation for liberal advocacy.

The fact that many bemoaning a lack of journalistic objectivity today were among the worst practitioners of biased reporting in the past makes the advocacy-objectivity debate especially ironic. *Time* magazine in the sixties was a rasp against the sensibilities of blacks fed up with white versions of how and how fast freedom should come, against the sensibilities of blacks and whites united in their opposition to the Vietnam War. I have a clipping of a typical *Time* story of mid-sixties vintage which appeared when the Georgia House of Representatives refused to seat Julian Bond because he approved a SNCC statement condemning the war and supporting draft resisters. The article described Bond's $83-a-week SNCC salary and said he had "decided to take a fling at politics." We may wonder why an objective publication would describe a man's decision to run for political office as a fling. Since Bond remains in the Georgia Legislature ten years later, the word in retrospect seems, at least, inoperative. In the paragraph following that attempt to trivialize Bond's political ambitions, these sentences appear:

"A few days before the legislature convened, SNCC Chairman John Lewis issued a typically intemperate statement. He condemned the U.S.'s 'aggressive policy in violation of international law' and voiced his support of draft dodgers."

The most revealing words, to me, in this sample of hatchetry are "typically intemperate." If the *Guinness Book of Records* had a page for most-beaten, most-arrested black leaders in the sixties, the name of John Lewis would lead all the rest. Yet he remained the most temperate of men, sometimes to the despair of those who feared the narcotic effect of temperance on stirring black consciousness. The following is that portion of the Lewis statement concerning the draft:

> We are in sympathy with, and support, the men in this country who are unwilling to respond to a military draft which would compel them to contribute their lives to United States aggression in Vietnam in the name of the "freedom" we find so false in this country.
>
> We recoil with horror at the inconsistency of a supposedly "free" society where responsibility to freedom is equated with the responsibility to lend oneself to military aggression. We take note of the fact that sixteen percent of the draftees from this country are Negroes called on to stifle the liberation of Vietnam, to preserve a "democracy" which does not exist for them at home.
>
> We ask, where is the draft for the freedom fight in the United States?
>
> We, therefore, encourage those Americans who prefer to use their energy in building democratic forms within this country. We believe that work in the civil rights movement and with other human relations organizations is a valid alternative to the draft . . .

Time, of course, preferred to characterize it as intemperate rather than print a word of it. Didn't *Time* choose Martin Luther King as its Man of the Year in 1963? Wasn't that proof that it cared about racial progress in America? The answer is that *Time* cared about racial progress on its terms and had no problem honoring King, who was a nationally hot, popular item, and whose Ghandian style of freedom-seeking met with the magazine's approval. The Man of the Year story quoted Eisenhower's former Labor Secretary, James P. Mitchell, whom it identified as "a friend of the Negro." Mitchell warned that "militancy could quite easily antagonize important people who are now prepared or preparing to do something. What Negroes have to remember is something they tend to forget: That they are a minority, and that they can only achieve what they want with the support of the majority." The statement was a strange warning to people seeking equal legal rights under the Constitution. Especially coming from "a friend." *Time* was comfortable with Mitchell's position, and three years later when Dr. King began militant attacks on the Vietnam war and the nation's economic system, *Time* began to savage him in print.

The advocacy-objectivity issue came into sharp focus for me during the summer of 1966 with the Meredith March and its by-product of Black Power. By then, the 1964 and 1965 Civil Rights Acts were on the books and substantial progress was being made in areas like public accommodations and voting rights. Massive economic, educational, and housing problems remained unsolved for most blacks. The ghettoes' air was charged with impotent anger. Journalism remained outside, reflecting white America's self-satisfied conclusion that a racial renaissance was just about completed when, in fact, it had barely begun.

I was living in New York when James Meredith took his mysterious stroll down Highway 51 in north-central Mississippi and was wounded from ambush. A day after the march began, I came down without an assignment or money. Free-lance civil rights assignments have never been plentiful over the years, and the magazines that were open for stories presented their own difficulties. Inevitably, the best ones, the ones that were consistently liberal and were aware of what was going on, were small ones such as *The Nation.* The big ones (in those days), like *Life* or *The Saturday Evening Post,* reached millions of readers but were obtuse in their editorial understanding and superficial in their handling of civil rights stories. If one wrote for *The Nation,* one reached a handful of readers who were like-minded; one was talking to oneself. If one wrote for *The Post* or *Life,* one reached a lot more people, but at the price of tempering one's tone and tailoring the content for white middle Americans—who were responsible for much of the trouble one was writing about.

The Nation could not afford to provide a writer's travel and living expenses. The most editor Carey McWilliams ever could pay me for a story was $125. The slick *Reporter* could supply a living wage, but for all its liberal reputation I found it less than liberal in many ways, with editors who never left Madison Avenue but thought they had the Southern (and Northern) racial situations down cold. Once, I had to write a letter-to-the-editor of *Reporter* to protest the alteration of a story I'd written about Selma, which made it appear that "militant" blacks had forced "moderates" to knuckle under. That assertion was not the case at all but *Reporter* editors—and they were not alone—loved to highlight supposed black militant-moderate controversy.

Anyway, I was lucky that my friend, *Time* correspondent Arlie Schardt, let me share his motel room—and cold beer—for the ten hot, dry days on the road. Arlie refuted all that I have been writing about white journalists. A white Midwesterner, he was racially aware, dedicated to probing the substance behind the form of race "progress." Night after night he would file long, perceptive stories, which his New York editors mainly disregarded as they packaged the march to fit their current taste. That taste favored a low black profile and no rocking the boat. The situation was a clear demonstration of Spiro Agnew's charge that the Eastern Establishment press had too much power and was guilty of doctoring the news, although I'm certain Schardt was not precisely the kind of example that Agnew had in mind. Arlie was able to flee *Time* eventually, finding a more compatible home with the American Civil Liberties Union.

The march we shared was the Last Hurrah of the Movement, an existential happening that drew a line through American history, separating old and new time. I wrote in *New South*, a magazine of the Southern Regional Council:

> The marchers did not always know where they were going. But they knew where they were.
>
> On the highways bounded by cotton fields shimmering in the murderous Delta heat, in somnolent towns and awakening cities, and under the tents at night, the marchers knew they were in the middle of racist reality—Negroes physically segregated in schools, restaurants and courtrooms, economically throttled by rural peonage and urban discrimination, spiritually demeaned by the preachments and practice of white supremacy. It was bitter knowledge made more bitter because most white Americans not marching seemed unable to grasp it, to comprehend the lesson in social and political geography presented each day along the Mississippi highways.
>
> The majority of Americans from the White House out to the white surburbias of the mind were tired of marchers, of protest, of being reminded that laws were not necessarily realities . . . They had done all that could be expected of good white people and now they preferred to believe the beautiful, that only a little patience was needed to get through the "transition period."

What about the marchers themselves, what had brought them into a Mississippi smarting under another "invasion" and still dangerous?

> . . . no one can make statements in the name of all the marchers because they are a mixed bag. SCLC, SNCC, CORE, NAACP, Delta Ministry, Mississippi Freedom Democratic Party and free-lance demonstrators of every persuasion. There is Mrs. Barbara Kaye, wife of an Englewood, New Jersey, symphonic composer, and one of the original Jackson Freedom Riders. Mrs. Kaye, who brought her beautiful fourteen-year-old daughter Jennie along, sometimes lets her hair grow out presently is cutting it African again in her private protest at the "apathetic white and Black drift in civil rights." Plodding doggedly along nearby in an old lady's old-fashioned sunbonnet, is a seventy-one-year-old white woman from Douglasville, Georgia, whose parents were sharecroppers and who has plowed her own moral field at considerable personal cost. Dispensing salt tablets is Miss Helene Richardson, a doe-eyed young Negro girl from Belzoni, Mississippi, who left a tenant farm to become a registered nurse and is working the Delta with the Medical Committee on Human Rights. A Negro bus driver from Brooklyn, Vincent Young, is walking his vacation away and carrying a sign, "No Viet Cong Ever Called Me Nigger." There are beards and cleanshaves, sloppy-thinkers and acute ones, bitter Black people from Mississippi and Chicago wanting revenge, and others still seeking Dr. King's "beloved community."

The following is the story sent by UPI to more than a thousand newspapers and to hundreds of TV stations in every part of the country:

> This march has become part movement, part circus. Among the 350-odd marchers . . . are about fifty white youths who wear T-shirts and denims, sandals and weird cowboy hats adorned with Freedom buttons. One is an avowed Marxist. Another is a one-legged redhead who forsook the United States and lives in exile in Mexico.

There is one marcher who starts each day at the head of the column, then drops out when the news cameras are turned off.

Another white man approached a reporter to talk about "the coming sexual revolution" which he said would be centered around homosexuality.

"This is a great assembly of kooks," said a Mississippi highway patrolman. Most newsmen agreed.

Now I'm no paragon as a reporter. I've made factual and judgmental errors that still burn when I think of them but the UPI story was no error. The piece was intended deliberately to discredit the march in the eyes of millions of Americans, who only knew what they read in the newspapers or saw on TV. I wrote in the *New South* article:

Perhaps most newsmen in the truck rented by the wire services and TV networks that rolled at the head of the march did agree with UPI's expert appraiser of human behavior. I once saw them shoot from the truck like flushed quail when two marchers almost came to blows. Dissension was a sought-after theme. But mile after uneventful mile they sat there in the truck looking out at the shacks where the essence of the march was made flesh in the lives of Negroes whose median income was $600 a year, whose atrophied political instincts were still held in check despite the Voting Rights Act by threat of dispossession from the land, firing from jobs or other retaliations. And those who marched in their behalf, according to this great newsgathering agency, were kooks?

The astigmatic press could overlook fieldhand trucks loaded with Negro choppers heading for their $3 day-in-the-sun, serfs in a cotton industry receiving a billion a year in federal subsidies. It would not bother to investigate the Poverty Program. Most of the press could see dissensions and miss needs, point up confusion and stare straight through realities of a Deep South that was changing grudgingly and only when pressure grew too great to bear, pressure sometimes instigated by the federal government but most often by understaffed and overextended civil rights groups.

A new black time was beginning on the march. I believe Martin Luther King's nonviolent way—mostly dependent on white material and moral supprt—helped mightily to power the Movement, awaken black consciousness, and strike off psychic shackles. That a purely black energy, self-image, and style must be tapped to insure that the metamorphasis from serf to citizen would be completed was becoming clear to many blacks. Not just one way could fulfill this goal but many ways— some planned tactically, others the inspiration of the moment.

When the march stopped in the segregationist stronghold of Grenada, Michigan State University professor Robert Greene, as he addressed a crowd of marchers and black townspeople assembled in the square, stood by a bust of Confederate President Jefferson Davis. Whites stood back around the perimeters; many had come to spot black workers who would be fired the next day for participating. Suddenly, unbelievably, Greene was slapping the cold metal face of Davis and saying:

"This joker . . . we want brother Jeff Davis to know that the South he represented will never rise again."

Black cheers released emotion damned up for 350 years. A white reporter said to me: "The colored are really trying the patience of this town."

Then in Greenwood, SNCC's Stokely Carmichael made his famous Black Power declaration. The speech was not off-the-cuff. The night before, a white SNCC worker had advised me to be ready to hear something big the next day.

"We're asking Negroes not to go to Vietnam and fight but to stay in Greenwood and fight here," Carmichael cried. "If they put one of us in jail, we're not going to pay a bond to get him out. We're going up there and get him out ourselves. . . . We need Black Power! What do we want?"

When the crowd—some of them previously rehearsed—roared back, "Black Power!," a shibboleth was born. The slogan was inchoate, would be variously and sometimes carelessly interpreted by militant blacks. and over the years would be refined into political, artistic, and educational programs that are still evolving. After the shouting died that night, I talked quietly with Carmichael, and he said:

"When I talk about going to the courthouse, it's an allusion. Negroes understand me. But whites get nervous when we don't keep talking about brotherly love. They need reassurance. But we're not about to divert our energies to give it to them. . . . This nation has only responded to demands in civil rights legislation. Whites never give anything. . . . You can only talk to them on the basis of political power and you have to become more militant—in Mississippi and all over—because whites get more militant as we thrust into areas of real control they don't like to think about."

Scarcely revolutionary, I thought. Journalism reacted to Black Power as if someone had yelled, "The Martians are coming!" Newspapers, radio and television suddenly had a lot of space and time to devote to race. "Liberal" columnists like Pete Hamill—who once wrote that Dr. King looked like an "aging middleweight"—reported: "Stokely has become for some Negroes in this country what Stepin Fetchit used to be for whites: He is an entertainer." Then Vice President Humphrey lectured: "Racism is racism—and there is no room in America for racism of any color." William V. Shannon, currently a member of *The New York Times* editorial board, wrote that Carmichael "seems bent on transforming the civil rights movement into a purely Negro movement in which 'whitey' will be the new second-class citizen." Shannon, not a bad man but limited in his racial perceptions, did not speculate on why Jews initially seeking power in New York City did not invite the Irish to help manage their struggle, or why the South Boston Irish welded their power apart from the North Boston Italians. And vice versa. Instead, Shannon worried that "the furor over 'Black power' [has] almost paralyzed many politicians who are fearful that a white blacklash vote may develop against them. . . ." He singled out Dr. Thomas W. Matthew, director of the National Economic Growth and Reconstruction Organization (NEGRO), as a leader trying to "shape the separatist impulse . . . into constructive channels."*

Probably the most vehement reaction to Black Power came from Roy Wilkins of NAACP. Journalism was pleased to mass-deliver his appraisal: "It is the reverse of Mississippi, a reverse Hitler, and a reverse Ku Klux Klan." When Wilkins reversed himself a few weeks later, his reappraisal somehow got lost in the shuffle. "Once you get these people talking," he said, "you find that they all come back to the basic NAACP program. All they differ on is method and timing. They want to get it done today. We think it'll take a little longer. That's all right. That's good."

The late Robert Kennedy didn't think it was all that good. "It is the slogan," he said, "and what is associated with it that has set back the civil rights movement."

If we may return once more to the Meredith March, I would like to describe two events that set back the civil rights Movement and of which Kennedy may have been unaware, since each went largely unreported.

On June 22, marchers stopped in Philadelphia, Mississippi, the same town where Chaney, Schwerner, and Goodman had been murdered. Although thousands of hostile whites had gathered, no state police protection or federal presence was at the courthouse. As Dr. King began speaking, Deputy Sheriff Cecil Price, who had arrested the three young men, stood behind him. Price was a caricature of malevolence, tightening his jaw over a wad of tobacco, glowering, caressing a blackjack in his fat hand.

---

*Matthew was subsequently imprisoned for income-tax evasion. But President Nixon, who had been pushing Matthew as an apostle of "self-help," pardoned him. After a series of unsavory scandals surrounding a hospital Matthew ran in New York City, he was convicted on many counts of misuse of HEW funds. While these scandals were brewing, "liberal" papers like the *New York Post* ran articles extremely favorable to him. They liked his position that ghetto blacks could make it if they tried; the unvoiced implication in that position also was not disagreeable to them.

"This demonstration," Dr. King shouted over the hoots of the whites, "will go down in the history books as one of the bravest, most courageous in the history of the state. . . . Today we have seen men with hatred in their eyes, men who want to carry America back instead of forward. I believe in my heart the murderers of those three boys are around you at this moment."

"They're right behind you!" a white farm boy called, and the courthouse crowd roared approval. Deputy Price, later convicted of conspiracy in the murders, gave a signal and a man rolled a cherry bomb under Dr. King's feet. He flinched as it exploded like a pistol shot and marchers verged on panic. Dr. King proceeded calmly.

"I'm glad to have our white brothers out here. They don't understand the Movement because their minds are closed. The hate in their hearts hasn't allowed God to speak to them or to let them see we love them."

"Let me get my hands on that son of a bitch," said a giant white man in coveralls, "and I'll love *him.*"

Bottles thrown by the mob began crashing in our midst. Marchers were pummelled, stomped. How Dr. King led most of the people out and back to the safety of "Niggertown" I will never know. I do know that the demonstration is unlikely to go down in the history books because one can search the morgues and film files of journalism, and one will find only the sketchiest evidence that the incident ever took place.

One will find little about a night in Canton, Mississippi, two days later. Coming after Philadelphia, Canton was the second half of a one-two punch into that soft underbelly of the Movement, nonviolence. Many civil rights leaders from around the country were there to experience it. I believe that Canton was a small, but powerful, catalyst in transforming the Movement from a semi-religious, emotional experience into an unloving, cold-eyed struggle for survival. Canton occurred when the marchers camped on the grounds of the all-black McNeil Elementary School. The journalists who had poured from the truck to report a fist-fight were not raising the question *why* this school should be all-black fourteen years after the 1954 school desegregation decision. Neither, as it turned out, was President Johnson's Attorney General Nicholas Katzenbach.

The night itself was a kind of transcendent rebuttal to the notion that nonviolent protest, after five bloody-headed years, had any future left. Marchers had been putting up a big circus tent to camp in when the attack came. A damp El Greco twilight sopped up sound, the grass in the field moistened to a vivid green, while vast purple clouds hung overhead. Work stopped when the troopers formed file on file, as if drawn up for parade, at the end of the field. They were goggled, chunky at the hips with their shotgun shells and tear-gas canisters and gas-masks girdled around them. Then, suddenly, their shotguns came up, the canisters were fitted and they fired without warning. They came stomping in behind the gas, gun-butting and kicking the men, women, and children. They were not arresting, they were punishing.

When Mrs. Odessa Warrick, a heavy-set black woman in her late thirties, tried to rise after being stunned from the gas, a trooper kicked her back down, yelling, "Nigger, you want your freedom, here it is." Morris Mitchell, white and seventy-one years old, had brought some students to the march from an interracial Quaker school on Long Island. He tried to stop a trooper from beating a young man with a rifle butt, and the trooper said to the white-haired Mitchell, "You get back or I'll put it into you."

Although few others panicked, Carmichael lost his cool that night. He stormed up and down, shouting, "Start movin', baby. They're gonna shoot again. They're gonna shoot again . . . the people . . . get the people outa here."

CORE's Floyd McKissick said, "Keep calm, Stokely."

Dr. King said, "Stokely, let's go to the nearest house and talk. We can't accomplish anything out here on the street."

Dr. King could no longer accomplish anything, any place. The next day, the nation's chief law enforcement official, Attorney General Katzenbach, said that the "incident" had occurred because Negroes had refused to move from school grounds where they had no right to be. I talked to Dr. King and it was the only time I can remember, from a memory encompassing dozens of times I saw him hard-pressed, that he seemed physically and emotionally shaken.

"I don't know what I'm gonna do," he said. "The government has got to give me some victories if I'm gonna keep people nonviolent. I know *I'm* gonna stay nonviolent no matter what happens. But a lot of people are getting hurt and bitter, and they can't see it that way any more.

"Yes, I heard that terrible statement of Katzenbach's. He's back saying those same things he did when the accused killer of Jonathan Daniels was freed by a Lowndes County jury.* That's the price you have to pay for the jury system, he said then. Terrible. I've heard nothing from President Johnson. It's terribly frustrating and disappointing."

---

*Daniels, a white ministerial student, was shotgunned to death at high noon in Hayneville, county seat of Lowndes, as he led a racially mixed group into a general store to buy some soft drinks.

In the year and a half he had left to live, Dr. King would hear nothing from President Johnson. That silence, with its attendant message to anyone with sense enough to interpret presidential silences, meant that Dr. King was no longer a national landmark to be honored and preserved. He was just another put-down "nigger," a Paul Robeson who had had it and blew it. A war president no longer had patience with a pacifist. Johnson, suddenly obsessed with firepower, could not bother himself about the real meaning of Black Power.

"We are not interested in Black Power," said the man who once had made stirring use of the phrase, 'We shall overcome,' in a speech at Howard University. "And we are not interested in White Power. But we are interested in American democratic power with a small 'd'."

His contention was persuasive speech-making until and unless one understood that democratic power was White Power, and that Black Power was only White Power but a darker version. President Johnson— who knew better—was only going around in semantic circles.

"We are trying," he said, "to meet the poverty situation as we find it with the limited resources at our command."

Poverty *situation?* As we find it? Limited resources? Vietnam costs would run to $134 million *a week*. Ghetto blacks knew when somebody was running a game on them, and that summer of 1966 riots began flickering. Dr. King went to Chicago to form black coalitions and to try to wrest concessions from Mayor Daley, cooling things—which perhaps did not merit cooling—in the process. He emulated his Protestant namesake by tacking up a list of twelve demands on the door of city hall. He led marches into all-white Chicago suburbs, marches that were moving targets for suburban brick-throwers. He was a brave, good man living out a vision beyond its time.

The Chicago march would have been an impossible assignment for him at any time. Much of the magic was gone from his presence. I watched him walk the West Side streets, out of his Southern element, seeking to inspire black ghetto lives that lacked even the graces of Southern rural poverty—clean air and grass under childrens' feet; the absence of big-city corruptions; the measurable improvement the Movement had made over traditional, overt racial abuses. The North, which disguised its discrimination in subterfuges while people who already had the vote could eat where they chose, knew they were getting nowhere. Dr. King and I were the same age and I had always envied him for the marvelous use he had made of his life. Now, for the first time, I felt sorry for him.

"Morally, we ought to have what we say in the slogan, 'Freedom

Now,'" he somberly told a church rally. "But it all doesn't come now. That's a sad fact of life you have to live with."

The fact was that all the years of openly wrestling with the Devil in the South had not prepared him for the strength of the North's white racism and the persistence of black disillusion. Journalism talked about "backlash" as if something new were occurring. Backlash was really ingrained white Northern attitudes emerging from the woodwork as the challenge to integrate moved from the South. When Dr. King and his marchers entered all-white Chicago suburbs of boxy frame and brick houses with mini-lawns and nice cars out front, men shouted "Wallace for God!" and teen-agers chanted, "Hate, hate, hate," I wrote in *The Nation:*

> These people, depending on the section, were first- and second-generation Polish, Irish, Italians and East Europeans. They had fled their old South and West Side neighborhoods when Negroes started moving in years ago. They felt that the blacks had chased them once and vowed that they would not retreat again. The ghost of Studs Lonigan with his family moving off Prairie Avenue was among them. Poor, frustrated Studs. Had he lived, he would have been watching, bleary-eyed and pot-bellied, while his sons, perhaps a grandson, threw rocks at the marchers.
>
> The main argument of these white Chicagoans was remarkably similar to what people of the same class had said in Brooklyn and Los Angeles. We made it where we are on our own hook and now the Negroes want everything handed to them. Chicagoans were only acting out what many of their white country-men felt. Their public (or parochial) education had not prepared them to deal with anything so complex as race. Cheated of history, strangers to logic, they honestly could not see that Negro denial had been different from theirs, infinitely more rigid, and so each march was [viewed as] a coercive attempt of black to force its inadequacies on white. Was there something in the process of bourgeois success, in the grubbing fight for security, that brutalized the human response? We made it on our own hook. . . . Even if this self-glorifying appraisal were wholly true, what they had become in the process argued that it might be wise to consider some alternate way to the good middle-class life.

One Chicago white lady, quoted in *The New York Times*, supplied her own marvelous interpretation of what was going on.

"No one was prejudiced against the Northern niggers," she said. "It's the Southern ones. The Northern niggers were satisfied until that Luther King brought in his troublemakers from the South."

Eight months after his melancholy Chicago interlude, Dr. King preached one of his greatest sermons. The sermon was given April 4, 1967, the last time I saw him alive. The place was the Riverside Church, that vaulting symbol of white moral and material power. Dr. Thomas Matthew, destined to become President Nixon's most favored black felon, paraded outside, trying to attract attention away from Dr. King by selling "shares" in NEGRO for a quarter each. Inside, the vast cathedral filled with the physical and spiritual resonance of Dr. King's words:

"The war in Vietnam is but a symptom of a far deeper malady within the American spirit . . . we have been repeatedly faced with the cruel irony of watching Negro and white boys on TV screens as they kill and die together for a nation that has been unable to seat them together in the same schools . . . I could never again raise my voice against the violence in the ghettos without having first spoken clearly to the greatest purveyor of violence in the world today—my own government. . . . Somehow this madness must cease. I speak as a child of God and brother to the suffering poor of Vietnam. I speak for those whose land is being laid waste, whose homes are being destroyed, whose culture is being subverted. I speak for the poor of America who are paying the double price of smashed hopes at home, and death and corruption in Vietnam. I speak as a citizen of the world, for the world as it stands aghast at the path we have taken."

I wish there was space to reproduce the entire sermon. Possibly the reader is unaware that it was preached. Network television did not carry it. *The New York Times* gave it half a dozen inside paragraphs, although it promptly editorially condemned Dr. King's "fusing of two public problems that are distinct and separate" and lectured him on his duties as a civil rights leader. Barry Goldwater said, "This could border a bit on treason." A *Times* reader, agreeing with its editorial, drew a self-portrait that captured the image of a growing number of Americans, from its obligatory righteous opening to the choice of words in its close.

> I consider that my support of the Urban League and membership in the NAACP, to say nothing of my contributions to various liberal causes, entitle me to consider myself a white person of goodwill as that term was used by Dr. Martin Luther King in the *Times* of April 5.
>
> Far from being willing personally to boycott the Vietnam war, however, or even to have my son claim status as a conscientious objector, I assert that it is necessary to support the war in Vietnam.
>
> Dr. King's simplistic assertion that our government is the 'greatest purveyor of violence in the world today,' and his analogy between the use of new weapons by our forces in Vietnam and the use of strange medicines and tortures by Hitler's murderers in the concentration camps of Nazi Germany raise grave doubts in my mind as to his ability to think clearly.
>
> Dr. King and his ilk do not speak for me and mine.

Why a Nobel Peace Prize winner, member of a race in a ten percent minority whose sons were taking sixteen percent of Vietnam casualties, should be proscribed by *The New York Times* from speaking out against that war, again raises disturbing questions about this exemplar of American journalism. I single out the *Times* so often not because I think its policy deliberately attempts to impede black progress. After all, columnists Tom Wicker and Anthony Lewis are two writers who, over the years, have deepened their understanding of a race and whose enlightened reporting often contradicts the editorials on the page facing them. For whatever validity my writing possesses, the *Times Magazine* only once censored any of my contributions ranging from Harlem politics to rampant blue-collar discrimination in the construction industry. But the *Times,* white to the core in its management, remains an Anglo-Saxon autocrat doling out racial news. One day the newspaper may be insightful, the next cavalier or patronizing. The *Times* apparently does not feel the need for a significant black presence in its management that would be sufficiently in tune with black society to counter white decisions, such as the Dr. King editorial, which presume to know how blacks should behave in war and peace.

One grotesque result of Dr. King's Riverside Church sermon was President Johnson's attempt to certify Whitney Young as *the* American Negro leader. The White House doors, now firmly closed on Dr. King, opened wide for Young. Young was the man who had said of Malcolm X: "Let the press put him in proper context and cover him just as they do James Hoffa." He was the man who spent a few days in South Vietnam and made headlines back in the States by reporting that black troop morale was high because in addition to such things as patriotism, they "have become intrigued with the people here and their cause." He was the man who, when I asked him whether it was dangerous that only he could get the president's ear when liberal black intellectuals, Black Power spokesmen, or Dr. King could not, replied: "I don't think the president normally consults with people who are not constructive, whose attacks on him are vile, vicious, crude, and vulgar. The news media shows him the other side. He knows our motives are honest even when we disagree."

As a reward for his loyalty to the Johnson administration, Young saw donations to his Urban League increase, while Dr. King's SCLC was becoming impoverished. In an unprecedented action, the administration supplied the Urban League with a list containing names and addresses of all black servicemen eligible for discharge. The ostensible reason was to enable the League to provide job counseling for the black veterans. The move also, of course, exposed the veterans to Whitney Young's racial and political philosophies. As far as I can determine, never before in history had Defense Department records been distributed to a private group. Had they gone to SCLC or—perish the thought—CORE, what do you imagine the reaction of journalism would have been? When the records went to Young, not a peep was heard.

By the summer of 1967, whatever Dr. King or Young or the president said did not matter in the ghettoes. They went their way. They exploded. Riot is hell, no matter the provocation. Riot, and particularly minority riot, is at once too much and not enough. Riot draws blood without hope of mortal thrust. Rioters burn down their own houses, leaving untouched the houses where the source of its persecution dwells. *Life* magazine took out a full-page advertisement in the *Times* entitled, "Quench Riots—and Look Beyond." The advertisement began by dutifully conceding past racial injustice, and approving the goal of full Negro participation in American life.

"Before the 1967 riots began this goal was valid: Indeed, it was imperative and urgent. The nation has spent billions on it and was prepared to spend as many more billions as could be absorbed by feasible programs. [But] the validity of the Negro demand for justice, dignity, and equality does not in the slightest degree excuse or palliate the 1967 riots."

I do not know what billions *Life* had in mind. *Life* went on to describe Dick Gregory as "an entertainer who has turned to the headier delights of alfresco demagoguery" because, when asked what Negroes wanted, he replied: "Nothing. How in the hell are you going to make a list of four hundred years of them misusing you?" The advertisement went on to say:

"The vast majority of Negroes today have access—belated but real— to the escalator of American progress. They are not rioting but they are in danger of being trapped in a no-man's land between the irresponsibles of their own race and the predominantly white society at whose hands they have suffered grievous injustices. It is important that the Negro community make clear its dissociation from the Newark and Detroit rioters."

Life had never been noted for its sense of racial direction. The magazine's ad writers, in their most imaginative moments, could not conjure up the view of riot held by Addison Gayle, Jr., in *Liberator* magazine:

> Almost to the man, the rioters in Watts, in Harlem, in Bedford-Stuyvesant knew that rebellion would end in injury, death or jail. [But they] would know freedom and thus manhood for one short moment, for the brief span of time between the rioting night and daylight calm. There in the darkness, broken only by the flares of red, revolving lights from police vehicles and the flaming, meteor-like tail of smoke from the Molotov cocktail, in the still, hushed night

interrupted by screams of terror, of curses, of jubilation, of tears, some few
Black men who had never before known freedom and who after tonight would
perhaps never know freedom again, were enraptured by a maddening panoramic
frenzy bordering on mania. After long years of internment, the ghost of Nat
Turner was revived and men, drunk with frustration, fought their way into
that dream state of freedom so peculiar to the dispossessed of the earth.

I must admit that my knowledge of the riots is all second-hand. I
spent that summer in the South again, on assignment from the Southern
Regional Council to write about black and white poverty "from the coal
mines of Kentucky to the cotton fields of Alabama." The experience
was both depressing and infuriating. In state after state, the pattern of
the vaunted Poverty Program was the same: The illusion of federal
concern, the reality of the poor treated like outcasts in their own land.
In eastern Kentucky, jobless white mountain men—many crippled ex-
miners cheated out of pensions by their union—were enrolled in a work/
training program called Happy Pappies. Many dedicated local adminis-
trators tried to make the program work. The tools were ludicrous. Men
who might not see two thousand cash dollars in a year wasted long
hours studying how to fill out income tax forms or watched hillbilly
movies. In Beaufort County, South Carolina, where some of the worst
black poverty exists, young blacks were put to work beautifying the
road to the local country club. This program was run by a white former
Air Force colonel who told me with relish how a black clerical worker
had slashed her boyfriend during a quarrel. Above his desk was a sign
reading:

What, Get a Job?
And Have to Quit the Poverty Program?

While Northern ghettoes, some then aflame, filled each year with
blacks leaving the rural South, I saw the Agriculture Department deliberately condoning racist practices that forced poor black farmers off
the land. Many went North to welfare and family dissolution, their
roles in the Great Society fixed. Of course, the blame cannot be laid
on Johnson or any particular president. Poverty—institutionalized,
generational poverty—is built into and maintained by our economic and
political system. Some would have much, many must have little. Thirty
years of continual wartime spending helped to create a staggering
artificial prosperity. The sheer flow of dollars filtering down reduced
the total number of poor whites over those years. While sizable numbers of blacks also made it into the middle class from poverty, the total
number of black poor increased. Against this statistical background and
with the knowledge of the people that our society had reduced to in-

animate statistics, Martin Luther King planned his Poor People's Campaign—an assault, not merely on racism, but on Americanism as it was being practiced.

On April 4, 1968, I heard over the radio that he had been murdered in Memphis. Everyone in America is supposed to know exactly where they were, what they were doing, how they felt when President Kennedy was assassinated. I suppose that this is largely true. How true it is for Dr. King's death I don't know. I do know that the emotional impact of the news that Dr. King was dead did damage that has never and can never be repaired to my own capacity for hope about this country. I just that afternoon had finished a long piece for *The New York Times Magazine* called, "Which Side Are You On, Boys?" which was supposed to examine all the black points of view from Wilkins to Mau Mau chief Jomo Kenyatta. Why a white writer should get such an assignment to cover purely black turf is one of those involved questions that would require a chapter by itself to answer adequately. In the course of the assignment, I did talk to a wide variety of black activists: McKissick of CORE; Harlem's straight-shooting Bill Epton, pursuing his impossible dream of black-white labor coalitions; Rev. Wyatt Tee Walker, turned Governor Rockefeller's urban affairs assistant, complete with a press release describing him as "a living legend where civil rights is mentioned"; Herman Ferguson, a New York City schoolteacher charged with plotting to kill Whitney Young; and Young himself. One common denominator ran through all these men—with the exception of Walker— a desire to put down Dr. King. King had done more than any black since Marcus Garvey to galvanize black Americans to action. Now he was dead. After all those years with all those risks taken in half-mad places like Birmingham and Selma and Saint Augustine, he was dead one afternoon at some place called the Lorraine Motel in the grubby city of Memphis.

I got a reservation on the last plane from New York to Memphis, that night. I think my wife borrowed money for the ticket. I knew there was no assignment, no purpose in going but to be there. I was half-drunk with wine and grief, waiting at the American Airlines Terminal at John F. Kennedy Airport, scribbling in a notebook that it had been the same kind of day as the one when Kennedy was killed "grey, rainy, foreboding . . . literature's 'pathetic fallacy' realized." A band of television newsmen awaiting the same flight inspired some other entries:

"'The tragedy of it,' says one, 'is that I flew out of Memphis just last night. . . .' There is further banter. . . . 'I was out walking my dog.'

. . . 'We were at a great party.' . . . 'All the CBS guys are over in that corner' . . . not a word of grief or involvement . . . this was a nation emotionally dead . . . they were living in a mental Deer Park."

To characterize all Americans on the basis of that squalid sample would be surely overemotional, underthought and unfair. That night, I didn't care about fairness. At the Memphis Airport, I ran into Rev. C. T. Vivian. He invited me to go along with him and Rev. Ralph Abernathy and other SCLC leaders to the funeral home where they would choose a coffin. I remember now, six years later, how sustained I was just being in that car that night. I was coming apart emotionally, but these men who had loved him at least as much as I, were held together by their faith, welded together by the spiritual warmth passing among them. For a nonbeliever, the situation was not enough to convert me to a belief in their Christianity, but was enough to make me wish that whatever they had could be mine.

It was one or two in the morning and the streets of black Memphis were empty and quiet. Storefronts bore slight and scattered signs of rioting that white city officials had exaggerated into virtual insurrection, as they called in the all-white National Guard. The row houses, crabbed and poor, were dark, silent. About two blocks from the funeral home, the car turned a corner and we saw two National Guard tanks a block away, their bulk grinding over the still streets, looming in the dark like some lethal presence on a nightmare dreamscape.

C. T. said, "They bring in tanks after *they've* done the violence, when Doc is at peace and his people are sorrowing. Good God."

The director of the A. L. Lewis Funeral Home was aroused sleepily from bed and greeted us in his nightdress, a handsome bathrobe with satin lapels. Nighttime work clothes, I suppose, for a man in a particularly bourgeois business. He was composed as a man on intimate business terms with death should be, a middle-class man accustomed to gaining by losing sleep over others' tragedies. Mr. Lewis plainly was not overawed by the rank of the dead man in his charge. Dead was dead, needed disposing of, saint or sinner. He went to the point without being abrupt.

"Now you'll want a coffin that will show up well in the photos," he said.

Well, of course he was right. I don't think anybody had thought about it exactly in that way until that moment. Ranks on ranks of coffins were in his display room, empty, waiting for something to be popped into them. Martin Luther King. A hit-and-run victim. Some veteran Elk, gunned down by age. The choice was made, a casket with ruffles pinched in like a pie crust border, the wood an appropriate mahogany from Africa. Mr. Lewis asked if we wanted to see "him." The Reverend Abernathy, Vivian and others went into the inspection room, but I thought that white would be out of place at that moment. I remained by the casket that would show up well in the photos.

I finally did see him days later when the casket was about to be closed for the last time. In a building at Morehouse College, Dr. King's fraternity was to hold a last service just before the final campus rites and burial. Somehow, my friend Arlie Schardt and I were allowed into the fraternity service. People were very kind, nothing racially exclusionary was in their grief. He had taught many of us about courage, how one had to commit one's body for a belief, and there he lay with all that courage shot cold. Goodbyes to the dead are futile; there is nothing to say goodbye to. I said goodbye anyway to the best human being I had ever known.

The Atlantic Monthly asked me to write something about his death. I sent them a piece that began:

> Walking in the cortège behind the mule cart bearing his body along Atlanta's Hunter Street, you would think that all your tears had been expended. Then you would be overtaken by a sudden rush of emotion at a recollection of him, or the expression on a face in the procession that was also remembering. His death seemed doubly cruel when the mourners reached Morehouse College campus, ripe with Spring, blooming white dogwood and redbud on the lawns where he had walked as a student, that he had loved and could no longer see. Whitman joined the procession then, writing out of time, for him:
>
> > When lilacs last in the door-yard bloom'd
> > And the great star early droop'd in the
> > western sky in the night,
> > I mourn'd, and yet shall mourn with ever
> > returning Spring.
>
> Grief is the proof of love, and the grief felt that day at the death of Martin Luther King, and in the days and weeks that followed proved that the bullet that took him shattered a vessel of love unique in American history.

The editors returned the piece with the comment that it was not "eloquent" enough. Well, I'm not insisting on my own eloquence. The eloquence of his life was what I was trying to put down, the plain essence of his humanity:

> He was a prophetic racial leader, a great preacher, and a social visionary. But the essence of all that he was derived from his capacity to love and his ability to inspire other men to love. On so many nights in small and threatened Southern Negro churches that seemed like arks of light on seas of elemental darkness, he would preach a basic message:
>
> "We will come to that day when all God's children will be able to live together as brothers. You know, the white man needs the Negro to get rid of his

guilt and the Negro needs the white man to get rid of his fear. And we both need to love each other. So I say, Keep on keepin' on, and we're gonna make it. Don't you get weary, children, don't you get weary."

Then, very often, a congregation that next morning would be embarking on a perilous demonstration would sing:

"I love everybody,
I love everybody,
I love everybody in my heart,
People say they doubt it,
Still I can't do without it,
I love everybody in my heart."

The voices, particularly those bright with youth, pierced the consciousness and conscience of white listeners. They were an affirmation of faith in a kind of love alien to our experience. Dr. King, tapping his foot to the rhythm, his enigmatic eyes searching the rows of worshipful black faces, would nod in agreement with the words he had heard sung a thousand times. He could not live without it. His philosophy was that simple and that profound.

I don't think it was the presence or absence of eloquence that bothered *The Atlantic* editors so much as a description of Dr. King's final days when, abandoned by former white allies in government and ousted because of his call for continuing civil disobedience to protest Vietnam and desultory Poverty Program efforts, he withdrew into the South again.

. . . he tried to recruit a nonviolent poor people's army to march on Washington to ask for peace and justice. But this time the target was not a slop-bellied sheriff or a devious registrar. This time it was . . . the federal government, the national system, the entire complex of men and mores that had produced the rich-poor, black-white anomaly called the American democracy. It was, perhaps, a coincidence that he was killed as he was about to come to grips with the system. The tragedy suggests at least a fateful accident of timing. But it was no accident that he was exposed to death in Memphis. It was an inevitable happening in a nation profligate with its human resources, a nation that could turn away from one of its best men and leave him to survive as best he could. Inevitably he was drawn to a Southern city where the least of men in the social scale—black garbage workers—needed the kind of support only he could provide. No one else, said the national experience, gave a damn.

Institutions such as *The Atlantic* were pleased to enshrine men like Dr. King in their private pantheons. They were not prepared to track the slayers of his dream if the trail turned too close to home, too close to long-cherished assumptions about the inherently good *nature* of our country and its institutions, which was not to be confused with certain unpleasant but uncharacteristic *actions*. The actions were characteristic, the nature bearing an evil flaw. At least, that's how I felt after Dr. King's death. I still feel that way now that his presence no longer dominates the racial scene. The intervening years, for all their transient signs of progress, have not changed the essential design of things. Perhaps that conclusion would be more convincing had not a black security guard noticed some Scotch tape on a lock on a door in the Watergate building. The eventual effect of that discovery was to halt, for the time being at least, a headlong advance toward repression of black and white civil rights—which had the approval of an overwhelming majority of Americans. If that tape had gone unnoticed, the quality of the country's nature might be more apparent.

One man's view is only that and given the instability of our time, no man's predictions carry much weight. I myself wouldn't try to predict what will happen tomorrow. Sometimes, a run of hopeful developments comes into existence. Just when I am on the verge of wondering whether all the pessimistic portents of the past may have somehow been wrong, a new assault on our racial sensibilities or an old one revived snaps me back to reality. What I feel in my soul is that America will never be safe or sane or beautiful or free until the day comes when a statue honoring Chaney, Schwerner, and Goodman is raised in front of the Neshoba County courthouse. I don't think that day is ever going to come.